THE COMPLETE CRITICAL GUIDE TO
D. H. LAWRENCE

How did Lawrence become one of modernism's most dominant and highly controversial authors?

Why is criticism of his work still animated today?

So many questions surround the key figures in the English literary canon, but most books focus on one aspect of an author's life or work, or limit themselves to a single critical approach. *The Complete Critical Guide to D.H. Lawrence* is part of a unique series of comprehensive, user-friendly introductions which:

- offer basic information on an author's life, contexts and works
- outline the major critical issues surrounding the author's works, from the time they were written to the present
- leave judgements up to you, by explaining the full range of often very different critical views and interpretations
- offer guides to further reading in each area discussed.

This series has a broad focus but one very clear aim: to equip you with *all* the knowledge you need to make your own new readings of crucial literary texts.

'*The Complete Critical Guide to D.H. Lawrence* is a lucid and remarkably comprehensive survey of Lawrence's life and work and of the extensive criticism devoted to his writings. Covering the poems, novels, short fiction, plays and ancillary prose writings, and outlining most of the major critical works and positions in respect of them, Fiona Becket's *Guide* will be an invaluable resource for all students of Lawrence, lay or professional.'

Peter Widdowson, *University of Gloucestershire*

Fiona Becket lectures in twentieth-century English literature at the University of Leeds. She is the author of *D.H. Lawrence: The Thinker as Poet* (1997).

THE COMPLETE CRITICAL GUIDE TO
ENGLISH LITERATURE
Series Editors
RICHARD BRADFORD AND JAN JEDRZEJEWSKI

Also available in this series:

The Complete Critical Guide to Samuel Beckett
David Pattie

The Complete Critical Guide to Robert Browning
Stefan Hawlin

The Complete Critical Guide to Geoffrey Chaucer
Gillian Rudd

The Complete Critical Guide to Ben Jonson
James Loxley

The Complete Critical Guide to John Milton
Richard Bradford

The Complete Critical Guide to Alexander Pope
Paul Baines

Forthcoming:

The Complete Critical Guide to Charles Dickens
The Complete Critical Guide to William Wordsworth

Visit the website of the *Complete Critical Guide to English Literature*
for further information and an updated list of titles
www.literature.routledge.com/criticalguides

THE COMPLETE CRITICAL GUIDE TO
D. H. LAWRENCE

Fiona Becket

London and New York

. First published 2002
by Routledge
11 New Fetter Lane, London EC4P 4EE

Simultaneously published in the USA and Canada
by Routledge
29 West 35th Street, New York, NY 10001

Routledge is an imprint of the Taylor & Francis Group

© 2002 Fiona Becket

Typeset in Schneidler by
HWA Text and Data Management, Tunbridge Wells
Printed and bound in Great Britain by
TJ International Ltd, Padstow, Cornwall

British Library Cataloguing in Publication Data
A catalogue record for this book is available from the British Library

Library of Congress Cataloging in Publication Data
Becket, Fiona, 1962–
The complete critical guide to D.H. Lawrence / Fiona Becket.
p. cm. — (The complete critical guide to English literature)
Includes bibliographical references (p.) and index.
1. Lawrence, D. H. (David Herbert), 1885–1930—Handbooks,
manuals, etc. I. Title. II. Series.

PR6023.A93 Z56645 2002
823´.912—dc21   2001048827

ISBN 0–415–20251–5 (hbk)
ISBN 0–415–20252–3 (pbk)

For J. S.

CONTENTS

CONTENTS

SERIES EDITORS' PREFACE

The Complete Critical Guide to English Literature is a ground-breaking collection of one-volume introductions to the work of the major writers in the English literary canon. Each volume in the series offers the reader a comprehensive account of the featured author's life, of his or her writing and of the ways in which his or her works have been interpreted by literary critics. The series is both explanatory and stimulating; it reflects the achievements of state-of-the-art literary-historical research and yet manages to be intellectually accessible for the reader who may be encountering a canonical author's work for the first time. It will be useful for students and teachers of literature at all levels, as well as for the general reader. Each book can be read through, or consulted in a companion-style fashion.

The aim of *The Complete Critical Guide to English Literature* is to adopt an approach that is as factual, objective and non-partisan as possible, in order to provide the 'full picture' for readers and allow them to form their own judgements. At the same time, however, the books engage the reader in a discussion of the most demanding questions involved in each author's life and work. Did Pope's physical condition affect his treatment of matters of gender and sexuality? Does a feminist reading of *Middlemarch* enlighten us regarding the book's presentation of nineteenth-century British society? Do we deconstruct Beckett's work, or does he do so himself? Contributors to this series address such crucial questions, offer potential solutions and recommend further reading for independent study. In doing so, they equip the reader for an informed and confident examination of the life and work of key canonical figures and of the critical controversies surrounding them.

The aims of the series are reflected in the structure of the books. Part I, 'Life and Contexts', offers a compact biography of the featured author against the background of his or her epoch. In Part II, 'Work', the focus is on the author's most important works, discussed from a non-partisan, literary-historical perspective; the section provides an account of the works, reflecting a consensus of critical opinion on them, and indicating, where appropriate, areas of controversy. These and other issues are taken up again in Part III, 'Criticism', which offers an account of the critical responses generated by the author's work. Contemporaneous reviews and debates are considered, along with opinions inspired by more recent theoretical approaches, such as New Criticism, feminism, Marxism, psychoanalytic criticism, deconstruction and New Historicism.

The volumes in this series will together constitute a comprehensive reference work, offering an up-to-date, user-friendly and reliable account of the heritage of English literature from the Middle Ages to the twentieth century. We hope that *The Complete Critical Guide to English Literature* will become for its readers, academic and non-academic alike, an indispensable source of information and inspiration.

RICHARD BRADFORD
JAN JEDRZEJEWSKI

ACKNOWLEDGEMENTS

For their help and support I would like to thank Richard Bradford and Jan Jedrzejewski, who devised this *Guide* series, and Liz Thompson at Routledge for her enthusiasm and commitment to the project. Special thanks to Jon Salway.

ABBREVIATIONS AND REFERENCING

Unless otherwise stated, reference is to the Cambridge edition of the works of D.H. Lawrence. The Penguin Books edition (Penguin Twentieth-Century Classics) reproduces the Cambridge text, including pagination, and may be more generally available.

WORKS OF D.H. LAWRENCE

A	*Aaron's Rod*
Apocalypse	*Apocalypse and the Writings on Revelation*
BB	*The Boy in the Bush* (with M.L. Skinner)
CP	*The Complete Poems of D.H. Lawrence* (1977) ed. V. de Sola Pinto and W. Roberts, Harmondsworth: Penguin Books
CSN	*The Complete Short Novels* (1988) ed. K. Sagar and M. Partridge, Harmondsworth: Penguin Books
EME	*England My England and Other Stories*
F&P	*'Fantasia of the Unconscious'* and *'Psychoanalysis and the Unconscious'* (1986) Harmondsworth: Penguin Books
F	*'The Fox' 'The Captain's Doll' 'The Ladybird'*
K	*Kangaroo*
LCL	*Lady Chatterley's Lover*
LCL I	*The First Lady Chatterley* (1973) Harmondsworth: Penguin Books
LCL II	*John Thomas and Lady Jane* (1973) Harmondsworth: Penguin Books
LG	*The Lost Girl*
MN	*Mr Noon*
Phoenix	*Phoenix: The Posthumous Papers of D.H. Lawrence* (1936) ed. E.D. McDonald, New York: Viking Press
Phoenix II	*Phoenix II: Uncollected, Unpublished and Other Prose Works by D.H. Lawrence* (1968) ed. W. Roberts and H.T. Moore, London: Heinemann
Plays	*The Plays*
PS	*The Plumed Serpent*
R	*The Rainbow*
RDP	*Reflections of the Death of a Porcupine and Other Essays*

SCAL	*Studies in Classic American Literature* (1977) Harmondsworth: Penguin Books
SEP	*Sketches of Etruscan Places and Other Italian Essays*
SL	*Sons and Lovers*
SM	*The Symbolic Meaning: The Uncollected Versions of 'Studies in Classic American Literature'* (1962) ed. A. Arnold, Arundel: Centaur Press
SS	*Sea and Sardinia*
STH	*Study of Thomas Hardy and Other Essays*
STM	*St Mawr and Other Stories*
T	*The Trespasser*
TI	*Twilight in Italy and Other Essays*
W	*Women in Love*
WP	*The White Peacock*
WWRA	*The Woman Who Rode Away and Other Stories*

LETTERS OF D.H. LAWRENCE

Letters I	*The Letters of D.H. Lawrence*, Volume I (1979) ed. J.T. Boulton, Cambridge: Cambridge University Press
Letters II	*The Letters of D.H. Lawrence*, Volume II (1982) ed. G.J. Zytaruk and J.T. Boulton, Cambridge: Cambridge University Press
Letters III	*The Letters of D.H. Lawrence*, Volume III (1984) ed. J.T. Boulton and A. Robertson, Cambridge: Cambridge University Press
Letters IV	*The Letters of D.H. Lawrence*, Volume IV (1987) ed. W. Roberts, J.T. Boulton and E. Mansfield, Cambridge: Cambridge University Press
Letters V	*The Letters of D.H. Lawrence*, Volume V (1989) ed. J.T. Boulton and L. Vasey, Cambridge: Cambridge University Press
Letters VI	*The Letters of D.H. Lawrence*, Volume VI (1991) ed. J.T. Boulton, M.H. Boulton and G.M. Lacy, Cambridge: Cambridge University Press
Letters VII	*The Letters of D.H. Lawrence,* Volume VII (1993) ed. K. Sagar and J.T. Boulton, Cambridge: Cambridge University Press

For all other references the Harvard system is used. Full details of items cited in the text can be found in the Bibliography.

Cross-referencing is a feature of this series. Cross-references to relevant page numbers appear in bold type and square brackets **[28]**.

INTRODUCTION

This book examines the literary career of D.H. Lawrence (1885–1930), one of the most prolific of the English writers to dominate the high period of literary modernism even whilst he appeared to inhabit its margins, an intellectual who was deeply suspicious of the mental life, and an important critic of his culture. His legacy is a vast corpus of work in practically every major literary genre, he also painted. Lawrence was one of England's most controversial literary figures: censors balked at his representations of the sexual lives of men and women and, in the period of the Great War (1914–18), at what they perceived to be anti-patriotic sentiments in his work. Few readers remain indifferent to Lawrence's writing, and the seventy-two years since his death have produced a range of critical responses from admiration to vilification.

Part I of this book, Life and Contexts, provides a synopsis of the main events in Lawrence's life and the broad contexts which informed his thought and writing. In Part II, Works, details are given of the novels, novellas, short stories, plays, poetry and discursive, or non-fiction, writing. In Part III, Criticism, clear guidance is given on some main directions in Lawrence studies from the responses of his contemporaries to the present. Special attention is given to the influence of the Cambridge critic F.R. Leavis, and then to more recent reassessments of the work and its general significance. With this aim, the section identifies a number of clearly defined areas: Lawrence and psycho-analytic criticism; Lawrence and society; Lawrence and feminist criticism; Lawrence and questions of language.

The Complete Critical Guide to D.H. Lawrence thus provides a synopsis of Lawrence's life and contexts, a detailed introduction to his *oeuvre*, and an up-to-date account of the principal directions in Lawrence criticism. Read through, it is a comprehensive introduction to Lawrence's work and preoccupations; alternatively, cross-references between the sections make it possible to pursue a particular line of enquiry within the book, supported by an extensive bibliography.

PART I

LIFE AND CONTEXTS

Born on 11 September 1885 in Eastwood, Nottinghamshire, into a working-class family, David Herbert Lawrence was the fourth child of Arthur and Lydia Lawrence (née Beardsall). He was educated at Nottingham High School and University College, Nottingham where he studied to become a school-teacher. On qualifying, he became a class teacher for several years but resigned due to illness. He supported himself thereafter by writing. In 1912 he met and fell in love with Frieda Weekley, a free-thinking German woman with a very different social background from Lawrence, for whom she left her husband and young family. They married following her divorce in 1914. Leaving England in 1919, the Lawrences spent much of their lives travelling, settling for varying periods in continental Europe, Australia and the Americas. From his earliest years to his last days Lawrence wrote, his literary importance confirmed well before his death, in Vence (France), on 2 March 1930.

In as much as Lawrence's *oeuvre* is the result of his continual examination of the relationships between the personal, the social, the political and the spiritual, it may be the case that his thought is brought into sharpest focus by some understanding of his background and experiences. He is a writer whose work has given rise to diverse critical views **[117–158]**. His writing life spawned several controversies and some of his books were suppressed by an Establishment that he frequently offended. Lawrence continually drew on his working-class, nonconformist background to shape his ideas, even when they developed – as they did – out of resistance to his social and spiritual conditioning. In seventy years of reading and re-reading his work, few critics have felt able to ignore the relation between his life and writing (a tendency which this *Guide* reproduces!). For contemporary readers, however, important areas continue to be Lawrence's relationship to a literary tradition as well as his relationship to modernist literary practice **[14]**; the ways in which his work explores issues of self and sexuality and, in particular, masculinity; his development of social and political themes; his awareness of the environment. Theorizing Lawrence, however, seldom occurs without some reference to the contexts which produced him.

Part I of this *Guide* provides an opportunity to assess the significance to an understanding of the novels, poems and plays of Lawrence's family and social background as well as his working and intellectual relationships. For example, it is often acknowledged that Lawrence drew upon details of his family and working-class culture for the novel *Sons and Lovers* (1913), for plays like *The Widowing of Mrs Holroyd* (1914) and for other highly praised pieces, notably the short story 'Odour of

Chrysanthemums' (1911), his first novel *The White Peacock* (1911) and 'Daughters of the Vicar' (1914). It is also the case that his marriage, and early experiences with women, were examined in a book of poems, *Look! We Have Come Through!* (1917), and in the unfinished novel *Mr Noon* (1934; 1984). Lawrence used novels, in particular, to work out his ideas. The development of a personal philosophy or 'metaphysic' (which was not fixed but altered subtly throughout his writing life) is consequently at the heart of the great challenge of the major novels, *The Rainbow* (1915) and *Women in Love* (1920), and gets continual examination, revision and restatement in *Aaron's Rod* (1922), *Kangaroo* (1923), *The Plumed Serpent* (1926) and *Lady Chatterley's Lover* (1928).

(a) EARLY INFLUENCES

Biographers writing about Lawrence's parents and their families emphasize the social backgrounds of both. The principal Victorian industries included steelmaking, mining and textiles. Textiles, mining and engineering accounted for a high percentage of employment in the East Midlands where the Lawrence family lived. Arthur Lawrence (1846–1924) worked all his life in the coal mines and Lawrence grew up in the mining community of Eastwood. Most young men who shared Lawrence's social and economic background were likely to find employment in, or relating to, their local industries which in Eastwood was dominated by coal. Some of Lawrence's forebears had worked in lace-making, for which Nottingham was an important centre in the nineteenth century, and his paternal grandfather was a tailor by trade who supplied the Brinsley mine with pit clothes (see 'Nottingham and the Mining Countryside' (1929) in *Phoenix*, 1936: 133). At the turn of the century the majority of working-class children left school by the time they were fourteen but Lawrence stayed on to obtain the kind of education that could make possible a different lifestyle, and in eventually qualifying as a school teacher he obtained a profession. In 'Nottingham and the Mining Countryside' (which is a nostalgic look back at his origins) Lawrence alludes to Eastwood's industrial past as it developed from a rural settlement with its modern origins in small-scale mining into the small Victorian town which Lawrence knew, with church, chapel and market-place. The most palpable social changes occurred, as in comparable communities, with the arrival of the large privately owned mining companies. When Lawrence writes about his boyhood community and its social history in this essay he idealizes the modesty of working-class life, and rails against the obvious signs of modernization such as the products of new building schemes (new housing for workers' families). Addressing details of working life, his attention is never seriously on economic hardship or social inequality, and while much of his fiction and poetry articulates anti-bourgeois sentiments, his representation of working-class values is not separable from his highly personal celebration of a 'native' identity which is more romantic than it is political.

All accounts reveal that Lawrence was closer to his mother, Lydia (1851–1910), than to his father, especially after the sudden death of one of his brothers, Ernest, in 1901. His mother's family, on the Beardsall side, are often represented by biographers as a family marked by its social aspirations, even pretensions, in severe economic decline, nostalgic for a lost status, contemptuous of their ultimate need for thrift yet proud of their prudent management in times of crisis. Lawrence is such an autobiographical writer in so many respects that these biographers have felt able to draw extensively on Walter and Gertrude Morel in *Sons and Lovers*, for example, for indications of Lawrence's parents' lives, and their uneasy marriage. Certainly, in her memoirs, Lawrence's sister Ada is quite clear that the Morels *are* the Lawrences (A. Lawrence 1931; Lawrence and Gelder 1932).

With such strong links established between life and art it is difficult to sidestep the myths that endure when commentators attend to the character of Lawrence's parents, either in detail or at the level of the thumbnail sketch. The importance of their perceived personalities is principally to explain Lawrence's domestic allegiances and sympathies, as well as his developing personality, and to highlight the auto-biographical dimension of his work. Lawrence's father is more often than not the image of the semi-literate working man who enjoyed simple pleasures. At home in Eastwood, he apparently had few ambitions to travel beyond the masculine environments of the work-place and the public house. Biographies invariably point to his easy-going attitude to life, and his documented skills as a dancer to indicate a free nature, continually at odds with his wife's more restrained behaviour which, in its temperance and moderation, is frequently emphasized to signify her growing disappointment with her lot. She is serious-minded, the auto-didact, the reader, committed user of the local library. As a girl Lydia Lawrence had a very brief experience as a pupil-teacher, and had ambitions to start a school of her own although this plan did not come to anything. Later she worked from home with her sisters as a lace-drawer for the factories in Nottingham. As a wife and mother she ran a shop from her front room, but this was a short-lived scheme.

Critic and biographer John Worthen describes Lydia Lawrence's familiarity with her son's work-in-progress, and her interest in his reception (Worthen 1991a: 141–5). By all accounts, throughout her married life she remained aspirational, and took every opportunity to improve the family's domestic situation with strategic house-moves and necessary thrift. She is seen as passionately committed to her children and keen to raise them in opposition to their father's family culture as much as possible. Family histories and family myths are in operation here, inevitably. As Worthen notes:

> [B]oth families were working class: one child had been educated to the age of 13, the other to the age of 7. But the most powerful class distinctions always operate in borderline areas; and what divided the Beardsalls from the Lawrences was ideology, myth and expectation: that made for a deep and lasting division.
>
> (Worthen 1991a: 26)

It is a challenge to reconstruct accurately a child's feeling for its parents, siblings and extended family. With regard to Lawrence, Worthen (1991a: 51–60) provides the most detailed synopsis available, drawing attention to the facts as they are documented in memoirs and letters, both of Lawrence's loathing of his father and, after his mother's death, of the slow process of revising those familiar and frequently rehearsed feelings of contempt into tenderness (*Letters* I: 316). The first volume of Nehls's *D.H. Lawrence: A Composite Biography* (1957) also provides some invaluable accounts of Lawrence's boyhood allegiances. Towards the end of his life he produced more sympathetic accounts of his father than before, and became harsher in his judgements of his mother (and mothers in general). The tendency of most commentators is to follow the lead of the narrative apparently offered in *Sons and Lovers* and to suggest an oedipal psycho-drama playing itself out in the stifling space of the family home **[43–7; 134–8]**.

It would be pointless to deny the strength of the emotional bonds that the young Lawrence forged with his mother (confirmed by the memoirs of Ada Lawrence, Jessie Chambers and others who saw him grow up), or the force of the anger that both of them directed at different times towards his father. Lydia Lawrence's sensibilities worked in her son, and perhaps made easier his move away from the pit. By the time of his mother's death Lawrence had begun to gain recognition as a writer. He had been to college and was working (not entirely happily) as a school-teacher. He had a measure of financial independence and he could earn a little extra money through publishing. Whatever he was to become, he was not working his father's stall in Brinsley Colliery and was not likely to return to his boyhood scene in any permanent way. Arguably, any level of recognition from his father concerning his achievements and aspirations might have made it easier for Lawrence to express tenderness towards a parent from whom the break had, in fact, been made quite early in their relationship. The evidence is, however, that his father's incomprehension at Lawrence's choices persisted; an incomprehension which could only increase as his son's writing life took him further away, in every sense, from Eastwood.

Lawrence is hardly unique in his youthful rejection of one parent, but he also rejected for himself a specific masculine culture when he left home to work as a teacher. Even so, in writing, he drew on what he knew. Literary critic and cultural theorist, Raymond Williams, reserves his highest praise for Lawrence's ability to write about his first community **[139–41]**. Williams has in mind much of the early writing, which has its flowering particularly in the short story 'Odour of Chrysanthemums' and in *Sons and Lovers*: 'What really comes alive is community, and when I say community I mean something which is of course personal: a man feeling with others, speaking in and with them' (Williams 1970: 172). It is the refusal to separate the 'personal' and the 'social', argues Williams, which is part of Lawrence's triumph in the representation of the relationship between mother and sons in *Sons and Lovers*. The mother's *particular* hostility towards her husband, and his kind, is directed at her husband's means of wage-earning and his attitude to his work, his social habits and, ironically, his ease with his own community of working men. None of these are to be reproduced in her sons.

Lawrence's religious and moral education was at the hands of the large Congregationalist community of Eastwood which by all accounts reproduced and reinforced his mother's values of education, self-improvement and self-discipline (Worthen 1991a: 64–8). By means of the energies of a range of preachers and lay-preachers, Sunday school and chapel day school, temperance organisations like the Band of Hope, and the moral guidance offered by groups like Christian Endeavour, Lawrence acquired a set of moral codes and, more crucially, a *language* that informed the development of his personality and his personal philosophy. This tradition stimulated Lawrence's sense of community and Englishness (although he becomes increasingly sceptical about what 'England' comes to represent). The imagery which he learned in chapel persists in much of his writing, particularly where his emphasis is rebirth and resurrection and, in the later work, where regeneration is linked in interesting and poetic ways with apocalypse. Although at the age of sixteen Lawrence was beginning, as might be expected, to question certain orthodoxies, he remained indebted to the religious teaching he received as a youth. In his essay 'Hymns in a Man's Life' (1928), he acknowledges the 'direct' knowledge of the Bible which this teaching gave him. He also discusses the values which distinguished Congregationalism from, in his words, the 'snobbish hierarchies of class' which characterized the Church of England and, presumably at the other end of the scale, the 'personal emotionalism' of the Methodists (*Phoenix II*, 600).

The boy Lawrence was by all accounts hungry for knowledge and his predeliction for reading and nature study, combined with his formal schooling, gave him a sound foundation. His youth seems to have been characterized by bookishness, and an intense interest in the arts. His first school was a Board School but he continued his education by winning a scholarship to Nottingham High School at the age of twelve. He left in 1901 for a short spell as a clerk in a medical supplies business, a period of unhappiness which coincided with the death of Ernest Lawrence, and serious illness for Lawrence. The following year he went into education as a pupil-teacher in the British School in Eastwood, also training in near-by Ilkeston. Following common practice he completed his training at University College, Nottingham (1906–08). After that he could work as a certificated assistant teacher, and found a post at Davidson Road School, Croydon, Surrey. Lawrence draws on his experience as a teacher in the description of Ursula Brangwen's introduction to paid employment in *The Rainbow* **[49–56]**.

(b) WOMEN, RELATIONSHIPS AND MARRIAGE

Prior to 1912, Lawrence had a series of relationships with women which had implications for his writing. His relationship with Jessie Chambers – his first love with whom he had his first extended discussions on literature and art – found expression, to her dismay, in *Sons and Lovers*, where she is the model for Miriam Leivers. He had been visiting the Chambers family at Haggs Farm (which Lawrence describes as a second home), since his High School days, being friendly in the first instance with Jessie's brother. Both their families expected the long-term friendship with Jessie to be resolved eventually as an engagement, but by all accounts it was an awkward 'betrothal'. The tensions were considerable: despite the fact that both Lawrence and Chambers were still developing their adult personalities, Lawrence was clearly affected by the mutual dislike felt by his mother and Chambers – an antagonism which was quite evident to all who knew them. In addition, the young pair found that the qualities which contributed to a satisfying friendship did not necessarily produce a fulfilling romantic or sexual relationship. The criticisms levelled at Miriam in *Sons and Lovers* **[57–65]** may well also have been levelled at Jessie Chambers (on whom Emily in *The White Peacock* was also based). Lawrence ended their six-year engagement in 1910. In 1935, Chambers, using the pseudonym 'E.T.', published *D.H. Lawrence: A Personal Record*, in which she describes their friendship and the tensions which developed between them and, usefully, draws attention to Lawrence's early literary influences. Lawrence always acknowledged the value of Chambers' encouragement of him as a young writer. Quite apart from their shared love of literature and the arts, and their enthusiasm for debate, she began his public career. In 1909 she sent a selection of Lawrence's poems to Ford Madox Hueffer, editor of the *English Review*, a literary periodical which published established and new writers including Joseph Conrad, Henry James, Thomas Hardy and H.G. Wells. Hueffer (who published his own masterpiece *The Good Soldier* in 1915, the same year as *The Rainbow*), was always keen to identify and nourish new talent, and was central to the development of English modernism. A writer and critic as well as an influential editor (who, after 1919, was known as Ford Madox Ford) he met Lawrence and was extremely willing to support him, publishing his poetry and 'Goose Fair' in the *Review* in 1909 and 1910 and 'Odour of Chrysanthemums' and 'A Fragment of Stained Glass' in 1911 (the same year as *The White Peacock*). He also offered constructive criticism of other work. Lawrence published reviews in the *English Review* and, after 1911, regularly placed his poems in other literary magazines. As he acknowledged, it was Chambers' action which first stimulated Hueffer's interest, but at a personal level the relationship between Chambers and Lawrence failed.

The women who figure significantly in Lawrence's life up to and immediately after the break with Chambers are interesting not only because of their commitment to Lawrence but also because of their wider interests and personalities: the social as well as the personal contexts which helped to define them. With the expansion of secondary education in the second half of the nineteenth century it was possible for women to become teachers, and several of Lawrence's women friends trained and taught in schools achieving some financial independence (although women's salaries were lower than their male colleagues' pay, doing identical work). Although many women were active (as volunteers) in the social sphere and often in support of political parties and movements, nationally women's rights were restricted and in particular they were denied the vote in parliamentary elections. Fighting against these conditions, the WSPU (Women's Social and Political Union, established in 1903 by Emmeline Pankhurst) existed alongside the less militant NUWSS (National Union of Women's Suffrage Societies led by Millicent Garrett Fawcett), and both groups campaigned vigorously for increased women's rights including the vote. (This was gained in 1918 for most women over the age of 30 – a decade would pass before the voting age for women was reduced to 21). Lawrence was not especially supportive of political activity but several of his close women friends sought, like Ursula Brangwen, financial and personal independence and some worked for social change.

In 1909–10, as the relationship with Chambers came to an end, Lawrence developed his friendship with Alice Dax, also from Eastwood. A married woman, older than Lawrence, she was the principal model for Clara Dawes in *Sons and Lovers*. Dax, like her friend Blanche Jennings to whom Lawrence occasionally confided in letters, was committed, as her actions show, to social and political reform including campaigns to improve conditions for women (Worthen 1991a: 358–70; Feinstein 1993: 40–3). She was also 'literary' and commented on an early draft of *The White Peacock*, as did Helen Corke, a teacher he met in Croydon whom he tried unsuccessfully to involve in a sexual relationship. Corke, who had literary aspirations, was interested in Lawrence only as a writer and visionary but, crucially, her diaries (which described the suicide of her married lover) gave him the story for his second novel, *The Trespasser* (1912). Towards the end of 1910 in the traumatic days before his mother's death from cancer, he asked another close friend, Louisa ('Louie') Burrows, with whom he had studied at college, to become his wife. She accepted his proposal but they did not marry – Lawrence broke with her during a period of emotional upheaval in which he began to dread the idea of marriage (both to her and in principal, although this would change). Burrows, also a teacher, was an independently minded woman and, like Dax and Jennings, supported the suffrage movement. Like Chambers, she had aspirations to become a writer – she and Lawrence in fact co-wrote 'Goose Fair'. Their relationship had developed during the last illness of Lawrence's mother, and coincided with a period of great productivity for Lawrence even though he was teaching full time in Croydon, and ill. Worthen writes perceptively about the content of the stories at this time and in particular the kinds of marriages on which they concentrated, commenting that: '1911 was a year in which [Lawrence] was trying to come to terms with divisions in his own nature and expectations; he had bound himself to a conventional engagement while simultaneously coming to believe that those in love naturally behaved unconventionally' (Worthen 1991a: 301). The engagement with Burrows foundered.

The days of these relationships and the emotional tensions to which they gave rise were to end abruptly, however, when in March 1912 Lawrence, who had resigned his teaching post due to ill health, fell in love with Frieda Weekley, a German woman some years his senior who was also the wife of his former college professor. Their meeting permanently changed the direction of his emotional and professional life. Content to take Lawrence as her lover, she eventually agreed to break with her husband – which included taking the tough and painful decision to leave her three young children with Weekley, who would, after much acrimony, divorce her. Her presence in his life enabled Lawrence finally to close down all the troubling relationships with other women which were at different times unfulfilled, and in many ways bound up with Eastwood and the loss of his mother. Chambers had encouraged Lawrence's aspirations, as had Burrows, Dax and Corke; Frieda Weekley knew him to all intents and purposes, however, as an accomplished writer. His youth had been oriented towards family and friends, with due attention paid to propriety and respectability. After his meeting with Frieda, the break with that Nottingham background was essentially made, with important new steps taken towards self-responsibility. In his Croydon years he had come to criticise the 'mid-Victorian' moral attitudes and sexual timidity, as he saw it, of several of his girlfriends, and he had railed against the conventions of feeling that dictated love relations between men and women. His attitudes towards sexuality and marriage were not formed by the meeting with Frieda Weekley, but perhaps they were focused by the situation which her presence created. In May 1912 he and Frieda left for Metz in Germany, where her family – the von Richthofens – lived, both of them with some difficult decisions to make. When her divorce was finalized in 1914 they married in Kensington after significant trips principally in Germany and Italy as Lawrence enjoyed the autonomy of a writing life. While he was away from England he completed *Love Poems and Others* and *Sons and Lovers* (1913).

(c) A LITERARY CAREER: LAWRENCE AND MODERNISM

The modernist period, or 'era' as it has been called, straddles in its 'high' phase at least two decades of radical change (1910–30) during which many of the social values and aesthetic practices of the 'long' nineteenth century are left behind. Historically it includes the years of the Great War (1914–18) and, in Britain, post-war changes in the laws relating to education, women and public life, employment and housing, as well as the effects of economic recession. A period of extensive social and political change, it is marked also by diverse attempts in art and literature to understand, analyse and re-present the modern; as poet and critic Ezra Pound said, the task of the artist was to 'make it new'.

Lawrence is central to our understanding of modernism although many view him in practice and temperament as a figure at a distinct remove from intellectuals and practitioners like T.S. Eliot, James Joyce, Ezra Pound and Virginia Woolf, who themselves embodied radically different approaches to their historical moment. Hence the term 'modernism' is deceptive in its suggestion of a coherent, monolithic artistic movement. Literary modernism in fact describes, or contains, a range of dissimilar and contradictory approaches to new subjects, so that we can think of it as characterized by diversity and plurality rather than consensus. Many radical positions within modernism are derived from revolutionary thinkers, chief among them Friedrich Nietzsche, Karl Marx and Sigmund Freud, iconoclasts and innovators whose work encouraged a revaluation of social, political and personal 'certainties'. Other influences, however, helped along the development of modernist aesthetics. French *Symbolisme*, for example, with which the poet Mallarmé was associated, had a significant impact on the work of, among others, W.B. Yeats, Pound, Eliot and Lawrence. Wilhelm Worringer's *Abstraction and Empathy* (1908) appealed to Lawrence because of the claims it made for abstraction and new forms of consciousness expressed in 'primitive' art. There was also a great deal of interest in myth as a mode of consciousness which preceded historical understanding (which was then viewed by the 'modernist' intellectuals with scepticism), and a fascination with social anthropology, particularly the genealogy of belief systems described in Sir James Frazer's extensive study called *The Golden Bough* (1890–1915). T.S. Eliot drew on Frazer in *The Waste Land* (1922) in references to fertility rites, the dying god and spiritual mythologies. Lawrence too knew Frazer's work. Eliot was also impressed by T.E. Hulme's 'Romanticism and Classicism' (1911), a key document which was invoked to define 'modernist' aesthetics and which similarly influenced Pound in his 'imagist' phase. With Richard Aldington, Hilda Doolittle (who published under the initials H.D.) and F.S. Flint, Pound established imagism, an anti-Romantic discrete form of modernist poetry, and he edited an imagist anthology, *Des Imagistes* in 1914.

Diverse avant-garde movements at this time produced statements, pamphlets and periodicals proclaiming the radical vision of each group. These included Filippo Marinetti's manifestos, among them 'The Founding and Manifesto of Futurism' (1909) – Lawrence was familiar with Marinetti's work, and the free verse of another Italian futurist, Paolo Buzzi (*Letters* II: 180) – as well as statements on visual arts and culture from cubists, expressionists, constructivists, vorticists and the surrealists. Key statements about literature and culture were produced by T.S. Eliot ('Tradition and the Individual Talent' [1919]), Virginia Woolf ('Modern Fiction' [1919], *A Room of One's Own* [1929]), E.M. Forster, Ford Madox Ford (Hueffer), James Joyce, H.D., Richard Aldington and many others. At the heart of literary modernism is the reformation of poetry and the novel, in particular. This resulted in an increased interest in the writer's medium alongside a preoccupation with the modern human subject.

From the time he was first published, Lawrence enjoyed the support of a number of influential figures in the literary world. Writing after his death, his friend the critic and reviewer Catherine Carswell recalls his first novel, *The White Peacock*, as a *succes d'estime* and acknowledges Ford Madox Hueffer's influence with Heinemann in getting it into print (Carswell 1932: 6). Hueffer's support of Lawrence has already been described. The youthful Lawrence, in his letters, shows his pleasure at being published in Hueffer's *English Review*, and shows too that he is not reluctant to be aligned with 'the new young school of realism' and, with a sense of his contemporary moment, the 'new spirit' in literature (*Letters* I: 139). The mature Lawrence would become, in his discursive writing (such as the late essays on the novel) and in the formal treatment of complex subjects in his most achieved fiction, one of the ablest commentators on the successes and failures of modern literature (for a detailed discussion of Lawrence's modernist contexts and his critical contribution see Bell in Fernihough 2001: 179–96).

Lawrence's novel *The Trespasser*, in draft form, found a champion in Edward Garnett, an intellectual and critic who was a reader for the London publisher Duckworth, and who became, at a crucial time in Lawrence's life, his friend and mentor. Lawrence took Garnett's advice on where to revise the text, and *The Trespasser* was published by Duckworth in 1912. Garnett remained central to Lawrence's early

career, his influence persisting throughout the period associated particularly with the publication of *Sons and Lovers*. Lawrence also made the
acquaintance of Ezra Pound when he was teaching in Croydon, through
Ford Madox Hueffer. Although they were not natural friends, Lawrence
was willing to benefit from Pound's influence which was considerable
and, indeed, Pound helped his poetry into print in a number of
significant periodicals, including *The Egoist* which promoted imagism.
The fact that Pound tired of Lawrence's writing fairly quickly is not
too surprising given, ultimately, the divergent aims of each: Pound
theorized about poetry in ways which were, and would become,
increasingly alien to Lawrence. However, Pound knew Lawrence's
poetry because of Hueffer and from *Georgian Poetry* (5 vols. 1912–22)
edited by Edward Marsh, and he reviewed *Love Poems and Others* calling
it, with reservations, 'the most important book of poems of the season'
(Draper 1970: 53). After Pound, the American poet Amy Lowell
supported Lawrence's work in her annual anthology of imagist poets.
Richard Aldington and H.D. cemented their friendship with the
Lawrences at this time. H.D.'s novel, *Bid Me to Live* (1960) is in part a
fictionalized account of her relationship with Lawrence. Aldington,
like H.D., had an editorial role on *The Egoist* – he was succeeded in that
capacity by T.S. Eliot whose ambivalent views about Lawrence's literary
value became central to the question of his reception **[119; 124–5]**.
Aldington edited *Last Poems* (1932), and his work included a biography
of Lawrence, *Portrait of a Genius But ...* (1950).

In 1913, Lawrence also began the well-documented, often stormy,
friendship with the critic and editor John Middleton Murry, and the
New Zealand writer Katherine Mansfield. Murry had published
Lawrence in a quarterly which he edited, called *Rhythm*. Mutual respect
and liking followed their first meeting although during the war years
the Murrys (he and Mansfield were married in 1918) and the Lawrences
grew apart – the relationship between Murry and Mansfield, and the
Lawrences, is explored in *Women in Love* **[56–65]**. An important critic
and influential figure in modernist literary history particularly through
his association with key modernist magazines, Murry edited the
Athenaeum between 1919 and 1921, and launched *The Adelphi* in 1923
(the year Mansfield died of tuberculosis), publishing an impressive range
of writers which included Virginia Woolf as well as Eliot. In Murry,
Lawrence hoped to have found a disciple. Their eventual estrangement
was perhaps the most bitter of many he experienced (see Kinkead-
Weekes 1996: 559–62).

At this time Lawrence also got to know people who could offer him
real practical support, such as Lady Ottoline Morrell, a wealthy literary

patron, who could always accommodate him at her Oxfordshire home, Garsington Manor. He was on friendly terms most of the time with other writers including E.M. Forster and others associated with the Bloomsbury Group – a clique of artists and intellectuals who gathered around the sisters Vanessa Bell, the artist, and Virginia Woolf, and their closest associates who included the economist John Maynard Keynes and critic and painter Roger Fry – although Lawrence was the first to admit that he was not really at home in this company. He also met poet and novelist Aldous Huxley, who remained a friend and who saw a great deal of Lawrence towards the end of his life in France. Intellectual relationships, like his brief friendship with the Cambridge philosopher and pacifist Bertrand Russell (in 1915), were significant. Although they eventually had a bitter falling-out, Russell helped Lawrence to develop his highly idiosyncratic 'philosophy' which he had rehearsed in a work-in-progress (1914) called 'Le Gai Savaire' – a title that reflected Lawrence's reading of the German philosopher, Friedrich Nietzsche – a work which became 'Study of Thomas Hardy' (1914; published, unrevised, in 1936). 'Study of Thomas Hardy' (which is more about Lawrence than Hardy, although his analyses of Hardy's works are interesting), was drafted and redrafted at the same time as *The Rainbow*, and the relationship between the two texts is evident and important **[55–6; 99–101]**.

If 1912–14 had been marked by new friendships – some, but not all, literary – the period 1914–18 was a depressing time for Lawrence who viewed the war as the last throes of a degenerate 'mechanistic' Western culture. The popular view was that the war with Germany, which was declared in August 1914 (and when Britain went to war so did its dominions and colonies), would be over quickly, and Lawrence settled down steadily to write until the time came when the end of the conflict would allow him to leave England. Some of his friends enlisted. Others – like Lawrence, eventually – were rejected for military service because they were found to be physically unfit in medical examinations. Weak lungs would not have prevented Lawrence from participating in non-military 'war work', as many men and women did, but he refused because he viewed such activity as in some way colluding with the idea of war. However, he was not a pacifist, a 'conscientious objector', someone who opposed the war on moral or other personal, principled, grounds. According to Catherine Carswell, Lawrence's preferred option was 'inaction' – he would neither participate nor protest (Carswell 1932: 23). Regarding his own projects, he and Bertrand Russell (who was a pacifist) planned to work together – a series of lectures was discussed – but disagreements quickly resulted and the scheme faltered.

Lawrence expressed the new animosity he felt towards Russell to his friend Lady Cynthia Asquith in August 1915 (*Letters* II: 378–81), a few months after a trip to see Russell, Maynard Keynes and their friends at Cambridge, which Lawrence had hated. The concerns which surfaced during this visit are often cited to reinforce views about Lawrence's homophobia, stimulated by his revulsion at the Cambridge 'men loving men': essentially Keynes and his friends Francis Birrell and Duncan Grant (*Letters* II: 320). Lawrence would work on ideas about male friendship (which had for him a philosophical as well as a personal dimension) in later writing like the abandoned 'Prologue' to *Women in Love* **[63–4]**. However, much of the correspondence of this period shows Lawrence to be highly critical of his new acquaintances and becoming insistent, even strident, about the 'dead' and 'false' culture they inhabit, as well as, paradoxically, recording in his fiction his hopes for a new germination.

1914–15 was also a tense period in Lawrence's marriage. Middleton Murry notes that:

> [t]wo things were preying on him together: one was the War, the other his struggle with his wife; the two strains seemed to be making a sick man of one who, on his return to England [after the first trip abroad with Frieda], had looked radiantly well.
>
> (Nehls 1957: 255)

The issues which arose in his new marriage were examined in Lawrence's writing. Apart from the relationship with Frieda, the personal trauma that the war presented to Lawrence (in particular the indignity of the army medicals to which he was subjected) is described in the retrospective and highly autobiographical chapter of his novel, *Kangaroo* (1923), called simply 'The Nightmare', and is documented in many of the letters of this period. In *Kangaroo* **[69–72]**, it seems that the war is obscene because of its betrayal of 'manly integrity' rather than for the loss of any broadly understood political or moral values. In part as a response to the madness of the war, Lawrence began developing his idea of a small island community – a 'colony' (*Letters* II: 259) – of like-minded people determined on 'new life'. Later he called this imagined community 'Rananim', and invented as its emblem the phoenix, common symbol of renewal. It came to nothing, but the idea shows the extent to which he was thinking about an alternative life-style, and working on a symbolic language with which to express it.

Also in 1915, Lawrence, Murry and Mansfield collaborated on a periodical called *Signature* for which Lawrence intended to write a series of philosophical pieces. It was not a successful venture commercially, folding after three of six projected issues, but it enabled Lawrence to publish parts of his long essay 'The Crown' which builds on ideas first tried in 'Study of Thomas Hardy' and which, crucially, informs much of the doctrinal content of *Women in Love* **[62–3; 101–2]**. The major event of his year, however, was the publication of *The Rainbow*, and the ensuing controversy. Almost immediately the courts ordered its destruction under the Obscene Publications Act of 1857. The sexual content of the book certainly offended conventional morality, but the war-time authorities may also have had suspicions about Lawrence's German connections through Frieda (and, if one looked closely, at 'unpatriotic' sentiments expressed in the book through the character of Ursula Brangwen) **[49–56]**. The event was unusual enough for Phillip Morrell (Ottoline's husband, and a Member of Parliament), to ask questions in the House of Commons, but Lawrence seemed not to have the energy for significant resistance (Kinkead-Weekes 1996: 285– 96). Many of his comments in the letters of this troubling period are valedictory – he spoke of fleeing to America which he perceived as more liberal, and where an expurgated version of *The Rainbow* was published, but was prevented by the war from sailing – and he persists in his version of a collapsing civilization, of a decaying England and a world ending. London, the heart of empire, is 'in a black rain ... and a tube full of spectral, decayed people'(*Letters* II: 434). It was symptomatic of this culture of ghostly automata that it should reject his book of life. Although he had accepted editors' revisions and straightforward cuts of his work, he could not be optimistic for his second 'Brangwen' novel – still in progress – after the treatment of *The Rainbow*, and perhaps the thought that he had nothing more to lose gives that novel, *Women in Love*, its biting critical edge. Unable to go to America, the Lawrences moved, at the end of December 1915, to Cornwall. Settling for a time at Zennor, Lawrence, impoverished, worked on *Women in Love* – which he knew would not find a publisher in Britain – as well as a number of other pieces including poetry and short stories.

So this was a difficult period professionally and personally for Lawrence. His marriage contained tensions and had become charac- terized by struggle and resistance, often witnessed and discussed by their friends. In his reminiscences, Murry describes how he and Mansfield moved to Cornwall as the Lawrences' neighbours, at Lawrence's urging, although both had serious reservations, where they had previously enthused, about living so close. This was largely because of Lawrence's erratic moods and judgements on the motives and behaviour of his friends (Nehls 1957: 370–81; 385–7), but also reflected an unease at the open rows which periodically occurred in the Lawrences' marriage. Their friendship was strained, and Murry and Mansfield eventually retreated from the South-West.

Despite the evident tensions, Lawrence's letters record a genuine enthusiasm for the rural life available to him in Cornwall (he befriended and assisted a local farmer, William Henry Hocking, and there is speculation whether he, so different from the over-conscious Cambridge sophisticates, and Lawrence, were briefly lovers [Mark Kinkead-Weekes 1996: 377–80]). However, the Lawrences' period of residency was brought to an abrupt end in October 1917 by a formal notice to leave issued by the military authorities. In fact, they had been under surveillance, with differing degrees of intensity, for some time. Lawrence's letters were sometimes intercepted and opened, his house was searched, but he still declared himself shocked at the expulsion and ignorant of its causes. The Lawrences returned to London, renewing some old contacts, and then to a number of addresses which included a brief return to the Midlands before the end of the war made possible the first stage in a long, self-imposed, exile. In 1919 he left for Italy, a country he had first visited in 1912 and to which he would consistently return. The result of his first visit, *Twilight in Italy*, and his poems *Amores* (which were very early pieces), were published in 1916. *Sea and Sardinia* would be published in 1921, and *Sketches of Etruscan Places [Etruscan Places]*, posthumously in 1932 **[111–14]**.

Significant shifts had occurred in Lawrence's personal philosophy between the publication of *Sons and Lovers* in 1913 and this move to Italy with *Women in Love* on the horizon – it would be published in America in 1920. *Look! We Have Come Through!* (1917) and *New Poems* (1918) constituted a major poetic achievement **[82]** and *The Prussian Officer and Other Stories* (1914) was a significant collection **[91]**. He had also worked on exploratory essays like 'Study of Thomas Hardy', 'The Crown', related meditations like 'The Reality of Peace' (1917), and he was reading, and writing about, American literature in preparation for what became *Studies in Classic American Literature* (1923) **[104–8]**. He had used his writing to explore his own sexuality and had begun to develop a personal philosophy based on 'male' and 'female' oppositions and dualities. By the time he came to write *Aaron's Rod* (1922), he was thinking about masculinity and individuality which would absorb him in his later work, not least, in the novels *Kangaroo* (1923), *The Plumed Serpent* (1926) and *Lady Chatterley's Lover* (1928). Crucially, he had also started to examine the radical possibilities of the novel form, with views that would find expression in the essays of the 1920s on genre **[108–10]**.

(d) LEAVING ENGLAND: ITALY, CEYLON, AUSTRALIA

By 1919 Lawrence had written, if not published, much of the serious work which was to make his reputation as an important English writer. Between 1919 and 1922 he lived mainly in Italy including Taormina, Sicily, where he re-read the novels and short stories of the nineteenth-century Sicilian writer Giovanni Verga, whose most prominent English translator Lawrence was to become (see Hyde 1981). He also lived in Capri and Florence, the scene of a brief extra-marital relationship with Rosalind Baynes [Kinkead-Weekes 1996: 601–6]). More importantly, this is a period which shows him trying to gain some control over the publication of his work in America as well as England – indeed his sights are set on America for most of this period as the place where he felt he could consolidate a large audience. J.B. Pinker, Lawrence's literary agent in the important years since 1914, gave up that role in 1920, and Robert Mountsier, an American journalist whom Lawrence had come to know in Cornwall, agreed to act as his agent in America at this time, something which he did until 1923. This was a productive period for Lawrence with the publication of *Women in Love* as well as, in England, *The Lost Girl*, and his play *Touch and Go* (both 1920). He was also in a position to work on *Aaron's Rod* and *Mr Noon* as well as the major novellas, *The Captain's Doll* (1923), *The Fox* (1920; 1922) and *The Ladybird* (1923), and short stories. *Sea and Sardinia* took shape, as did a further volume of poetry, *Birds, Beasts and Flowers* (1923). *Psychoanalysis and the Unconscious* was published in 1921. In this short book Lawrence attempts to define his notion of unconscious functioning in contrast to Freud's ideas of 'the' unconscious. (Psychoanalysis, a mode of psychological enquiry originated by Freud, theorized the psycho-sexual development of the individual as a child, and then as an adult, in relation to the family. Lawrence, who counted analysts among his closest friends, disputed Freud's terms.) Much of his earlier discursive writing deals with 'instinctive' functioning, so it is not surprising that Lawrence at last decides to refute, in a book, other ideas on the unconscious. The *Psychoanalysis* project left Lawrence with enough enthusiasm to consider a sequel, which became *Fantasia of the Unconscious* (1922). Neither of these books attracted the broad acclaim he felt they deserved, but an understanding of their themes is useful in reading the fiction of this time **[102–4]**. This is not the sum of the projects on which he worked in this busy period – which include a history text-book called *Movements in European History* (1921) – but it shows him committed, not least, to further imaginative explorations of his developing 'metaphysic', his personal philosophy.

Lawrence's acquaintances now included, in Florence, Norman Douglas – a novelist and travel writer who had worked with Hueffer on the *English Review* – and his companions, Maurice Magnus and Reggie Turner. With these, Lawrence had experiences which would find their way into *Aaron's Rod*, and all three men can be recognised in the 'Italian' part of the book. In his lengthy introduction to *Memoirs of the Foreign Legion* (by Maurice Magnus, 1924), Lawrence describes his stay in Italy from 1919. The introduction is completely autobiographical, which is part of its value, but he also expresses his views on a kind of manly integrity which is, crucially, unheroic. Magnus, the writer of the 'parent' text, is both product and symptom of the 'vicious spirit' of the war years (upon which Lawrence can now reflect), but his importance to Lawrence lies in the more redemptive aspects of his self-knowledge. In Magnus, 'the lonely terrified courage of the isolated spirit' is set positively against the masculine spirit of 'modern militarism' (*Phoenix II*: 359).

1922 was a key year for literary modernism. It saw the publication of a range of significant texts, among them James Joyce's novel *Ulysses*, about which Lawrence was disparaging, and T.S. Eliot's poem *The Waste Land*, both works literary landmarks. In this year the Lawrences left Italy, and Europe, for a series of extremely long voyages. This was the high period of the commercial shipping lines, establishing a global network of destinations which aided the traveller and the migrant: many of Lawrence's characters, like their creator, are *en route*. Lawrence journeyed to Ceylon (now Sri Lanka), Australia, America (where he would settle for a time) and Mexico, where his experiences were to have a considerable effect on his writing. He had immediately behind him the controversies which still surrounded the publication of *Women in Love* – the threat of law suits from individuals who recognized themselves in his characters, and the threat of censorship. This was the publication year of *Aaron's Rod*, begun in 1917 and which Lawrence called, on completion, the last of his 'serious English novels' (*Letters* IV: 92). It was also the year of *England My England and Other Stories*, and the second version of *The Fox*. It is worth noting John Middleton Murry's positive reviews of *Aaron's Rod* (after his hostility in print to *Women in Love*). He called it 'the most important thing that has happened to English literature since the war ... Mr Lawrence's theme is the self-sufficiency of the human soul' (Draper 1970: 177–80). Murry also reviewed *Fantasia of the Unconscious* positively, believing it to be revolutionary. These reviews helped to improve the damaged relationship between the two men after Cornwall.

During the journey to Ceylon, Lawrence concentrated on his translations of Giovanni Verga: his versions of *Mastro-Don Gesualdo* and *Little Novels of Sicily* were published in 1923 and 1925 respectively. Arrived at their destination, the Lawrences stayed just outside Kandy with painters Earl and Achsah Brewster whom they had met in 1921 (the Brewsters co-edited *D.H. Lawrence: reminiscences and correspondence* [1934]). The visit was in part to introduce Lawrence to Buddhism, which interested the Brewsters (as did psychoanalysis [*Letters* IV: 279], about which Lawrence had by now written), but Lawrence was not engaged at all by his brief contact with Buddhist culture: 'I shrewdly suspect that high-flownness of Buddhism altogether exists mostly on paper: and that its denial of the soul makes it always rather barren, even if philosophically etc more perfect' (*Letters* IV: 218). In fact, Lawrence's feelings of alienation on this visit were extreme. To Mabel Dodge Sterne (later Mabel Dodge Luhan, a wealthy supporter of the arts who was waiting for him in America) he wrote that the forest in Ceylon was 'metallic' and he deplored the animal noises with their 'machine' quality. To her, he also writes of 'the undertaste of blood and sweat in the nauseous tropical fruits; the nasty faces and yellow robes of the Buddhist monks, the little vulgar dens of the temples' (*Letters* IV: 225). To Robert Mountsier he said: 'the magnetism is all negative, everything seems magnetically to be repelling one' (*Letters* IV: 227). Especially evident in these views, Lawrence's chief mode of expression is unequivocally that of the appalled visitor from the heart of Empire. The Lawrences stayed in Ceylon for just over a month and then left for Western Australia, arriving in Fremantle and moving on to Perth. Here he met M.L. Skinner, a writer in whom he developed a professional interest. With her permission he would re-write her novel, 'The House of Ellis', published under both their names as *The Boy in the Bush* (1924) **[69]**. The greater part of his stay in Australia, however, was apart from new friends, in Sydney and Thirroul, south of Botany Bay.

Lawrence's principal 'Australian' novel is *Kangaroo* **[69–72]**, a political fiction which deals with the aspirations of the charismatic Benjamin Cooley, nicknamed 'Kangaroo', and his disciples who call themselves the 'Diggers'. The narrative deals in part with another exploration of male friendship (after *Women in Love* and *Aaron's Rod*), this time the 'mateship' offered to Richard Lovat Somers (an English writer on tour), by some of the followers of Kangaroo, but more particularly the love of Kangaroo himself, in need of a lieutenant who is also a

23

visionary. It is usually asserted that the substance of *Kangaroo* is totally imaginative although Robert Darroch, in *D.H. Lawrence in Australia* (1981), argues the reverse. An interesting contrast emerges in the letters of this time in the language which Lawrence chooses to describe Ceylon and Australia respectively, in the context of observations which highlight his distrust of the visual, *seeing*, as a mode of *knowing* (his short story 'The Blind Man' **[95]** develops this idea). To Robert Mountsier he wrote of Ceylon, which he disliked, 'From a *cinematograph* point of view it can be fascinating: the dark, tangled jungle, the terrific sun ...' (*Letters* IV: 227, emphasis added). On the other hand, of his new country, with which he was enthralled, he said, 'But nobody has *seen* Australia yet: can't be done. It isn't *visible*' (*Letters* IV: 273, latter emphasis added).

(e) AMERICA

The trip to Australia was, without doubt, immensely productive. With *Kangaroo* drafted he continued his travels, heading for America via New Zealand and the South Seas. The Lawrences arrived in San Francisco and, almost immediately, made for the American South-West. Lawrence had been invited to Taos (New Mexico) by Mabel Dodge Sterne who was rich, admired his writing and believed that, because of his principles, he could provide a voice for the dispossessed Native American population in the preservation of whose cultures she was interested – she influenced Lawrence to oppose the Bursum Land Bill, which restricted Indian land rights (see 'Certain Americans and an Englishman' [1922]). Despite his initial reluctance to be indebted to this woman who so obviously had fixed ideas about his destiny, Lawrence obeyed her call. Sterne, whom Lawrence castigated as 'egotistical' – they quarrelled often because he did not wish to be dependent on her – published her reminiscence of their often tense friendship in *Lorenzo in Taos* (1932). By all accounts, Sterne was used to the company of distinguished individuals – the American poet and novelist, Gertrude Stein, wrote a 'portrait' of her – and she was in a position to introduce Lawrence to other artists and writers as well as to try and involve him in her interests. In a letter to his mother-in-law Lawrence revealed his wariness of Sterne, however, calling her 'another culture-bearer' with 'a terrible will to power – *woman* power, you know' (*Letters* IV: 351, emphasis added). Whatever reservations he may have had about her, he enjoyed a certain celebrity status while he was in America – he turned down the opportunity to do a lecture tour, but his publisher Thomas Seltzer kept him visible.

Sterne accommodated the Lawrences and was able, with her companion Tony Luhan, to take them to various Native American events, particularly dances, descriptions of which found their way into Lawrence's Mexico and New Mexico writing. Newly arrived, however, Lawrence had to set his own impressions of Native American culture against representations of Native Americans familiar to him from nineteenth-century and contemporary popular American fiction, and he endlessly 'theorized' America and Americans. He was quick to denounce the capitalist imperative ('America is the biggest *bully* the world has yet seen. Power is proud. But bullying is democratic and mean' [*Letters* IV: 352]), and to bring his unique mode of 'psychologising' to bear on this new territory:

> Everything in America goes by *will*. A great negative *will* seems to be turned against all spontaneous life – there seems to be no *feeling* at all – no genuine bowels of compassion and sympathy; all this gripped, iron, *benevolent* will, which in the end is diabolic. How can one write about it, save analytically.
>
> (*Letters* IV: 310).

This was written prior to the last significant revisions to his '(psycho)analytical' book, *Studies in Classic American Literature* **[104]**.

Lawrence's principal base in New Mexico was at Taos although towards the end of 1922 he moved to a nearby ranch at the foot of the Rocky Mountains, mostly to put a little distance between himself and the demanding Mabel Dodge Sterne. Some new friends, two Danish artists, Kai Götzsche and Knud Merrild joined them. Lawrence had hopes that Merrild, would do some book designs for him, principally *Birds, Beasts and Flowers* – Merrild wrote an account of their friendship in *A Poet and Two Painters* (1938). Merrild and Götzsche had links with a community of Taos artists, which must have appealed to Lawrence who was also a painter. In America the Lawrences also met the poet Witter Bynner (who described their friendship in *Journey with Genius* [1951]), and Willard Johnson. Both men appear in *The Plumed Serpent* as Owen and Villiers having accompanied the Lawrences on their first trip to Mexico in 1923. Götzsche – responsible for a portrait of Lawrence – went with him on his second trip in the same year.

Indeed, Lawrence made significant journeys between 1923 and 1925 to Mexico. On his first journey he saw many of the pre-Columbian sites of interest and spent two months at Chapala writing 'Quetzalcoatl', the first version of *The Plumed Serpent*. This and later trips took him to the ruins at Teotihuacán, many other historical sites and Mexico City. Between 1924 and 1927 he published *St Mawr* (1925), *The Princess* (1925) **[87]**, the stories which were revised for *The Woman Who Rode Away and Other Stories* (1928) **[96]**, and wrote essays about his American encounters, including 'Pan in America'. He also began formally articulating his aspirations for the novel form. That it needed radical reconstruction is implied by the initial title of 'Surgery for the Novel – Or a Bomb' ('The Future of the Novel'), which incorporated his dislike of the self-conscious, self-reflexive writing of some of his contemporaries, in particular James Joyce – he read Joyce's *Ulysses* in 1922 in New Mexico. Other important essays on the novel written at this time developed his theme of the sad state of modern fiction **[108–10]**.

At the end of 1923 Lawrence briefly returned to England. Frieda had gone ahead alone in part to see her family and Lawrence's letters of this time show a real reluctance to revisit his home ground. Unexpectedly, once in London, he arranged a formal dinner party at the exclusive Café Royal for some old friends which included Catherine Carswell, 'Kot', the translator S.S. Koteliansky, Murry, the artists Mark Gertler and Dorothy Brett. Carswell (1932) describes how in the course of a bizarre, rather 'theatrical', evening Lawrence invited each of them to return to New Mexico with him, reviving his long-held desire for a commune of like-minded, creative individuals. In the strange atmosphere of the party, Carswell writes, they assented, but only Dorothy Brett, who was something of a disciple, finally accompanied the Lawrences back to New Mexico (Brett, with whom Lawrence later had a brief affair, published *Lawrence and Brett: A Friendship* [1933]). At this time Mabel Dodge Sterne (now Mabel Dodge Luhan), gave a run-down ranch (which Lawrence called 'Kiowa') to Frieda Lawrence, for which she received the manuscript of *Sons and Lovers*. Lawrence combined periods renovating the house and its environs with excursions into 'Hopi Country' to see native dances and to visit reservations.

1924 and 1925 were extremely productive years for Lawrence. Even though he was suffering greatly from tuberculosis which weakened and nearly killed him, he yet somehow found the energy to travel and write. His 'American' experience was largely confined to the cultures and the landscapes of the South-West, and it was these places that he now felt to be familiar, if curiously *'unheimlich'*. While he revised *The Plumed Serpent*, he worked on the essays which became *Mornings in Mexico* (1927), and he wrote *David* (1926), a play (not about Mexico), which was staged in London. By the time he left America in the autumn of 1925 – the climate finally proving bad for his health – he had completed his significant essays on art and the novel and put together *Reflections on the Death of a Porcupine and Other Essays*.

26

(f) THE RETURN TO EUROPE

The last five years of Lawrence's life were spent in Europe, at first mainly in Spotorno, Northern Italy, and then near Florence. While the Lawrences had 'bases', they continued to move around, sometimes because Lawrence's ill-health required a change. The American experience was over for him and the relationship with Mabel Dodge Sterne, who had made it possible, more or less at an end. The period in Italy after the move from America produced *The Virgin and the Gipsy* (1930) which is thematically a precursor of *Lady Chatterley's Lover,* his last novel set in the English Midlands about an adulterous affair which challenges divisions of social class and expectation. Settled just outside Florence, and having made his final trip to England, Lawrence concentrated on the Chatterley novel, writing three versions **[75–9]**. Although it was not Lawrence's only project at this time, it occupied his attention significantly, and shows the influence of his last visit 'home' (described in 'Return to Bestwood' [1968] and two autobiographical sketches), as well as the direction of his developing thought on 'phallic consciousness'. Much of the 'vitalist' philosophy in *Lady Chatterley's Lover* is rehearsed in *Sketches of Etruscan Places,* a travel book which describes Lawrence's response to the remains of the 'sensual' Etruscan civilization (ancient sites between Florence and Rome) which he visited on a tour of tombs with his friend Earl Brewster (of his Ceylon trip) **[113]**. About this time Lawrence also renewed his friendship with the Huxleys, seeing much of them in his last months.

Another friend, Giuseppe Orioli, a bookseller in Florence, was willing to print *Lady Chatterley's Lover* privately. Lawrence knew that mainstream publishers would not touch the book because of the descriptions of sex it contained and the subsequent risk to the publisher of prosecution – as with *The Rainbow* he would again fall foul of the censorship laws and in England, as in America, only an 'authorized abridged', that is to say an expurgated, edition appeared in 1932. So even this last period in Europe was not free from controversy. Indeed, while he was busy organizing the distribution of *Lady Chatterley's Lover* (copies sent to Britain were seized by the police), he learned that his book of poems, *Pansies* (1929), had been confiscated on its way to the publisher because of fears concerning its content **[85]**. In the same year (the year he completed *The Escaped Cock*) Lawrence was again judged to have offended against standards of public decency when thirteen of his paintings from a show at the Warren Gallery, London, were seized with the further possibility that they might be burned by the authorities

27

(*Letters* VII: 369). Resigned to such treatment, from Bandol near the Mediterranean, where he retreated in the hope that the sea might raise his ailing spirits (he also wrote *Nettles*, *Apocalypse* and *Last Poems*), Lawrence noted to Witter Bynner that:

> it's Europe that has made me so ill. One gets so innerly angry with the dull sort of hopelessness and deadness there is over here. Anyhow, in New Mexico the sun and the air are alive, let man be what he may. But here they've killed the very sun, the very air.
>
> (*Letters* VII: 574)

He was not alone in suffering from the regulations relating to censorship: as Lawrence was aware, Joyce's *Ulysses* was seized by the authorities because of the outrage to public morality it was alleged to offer; Radclyffe Hall's novel about love between women, *The Well of Loneliness* (1928), was also banned, and literary history offers many other examples of the law at this time policing an adult readership.

Lawrence's words to Witter Bynner are a reminder not only of his wrath, sadness and immediate 'metaphysical' preoccupations, but also of his worsening state of health, and, after a short period in a sanitorium in Vence, Lawrence died. His last long work is *Apocalypse* (1931) which developed from an introduction written for Frederick Carter's book, *The Dragon of the Apocalypse*. Carter, a painter with esoteric interests, had been in contact with Lawrence in 1923 and his book offered the opportunity of a new project. In *Apocalypse*, Lawrence rethinks his views of *Revelations*, and continues the metaphoric language of rebirth and the emergence of something fine, phoenix-like, out of the destruction of his degenerate civilization. The final part of *Apocalypse* is a hymn to integration, and provides a fitting funeral oration for its writer in its emphasis on rebirth, regeneration and, in a strange way, community; a concept which Lawrence took on a long and complex journey in the course of his writing life:

> So that my individualism is really an illusion. I am a part of the great whole, and I can never escape. But I *can* deny my connections, break them, and become a fragment. Then I am wretched.
>
> What we want is to destroy our false, inorganic connections, especially those related to money, and re-establish the living organic connections, with the cosmos, the sun and earth, with mankind and nation and family. Start with the sun, and the rest will slowly, slowly happen.
>
> (*Apocalypse* 149)

That Lawrence was a man of strong views frequently expressed energetically cannot be denied, and the stamp his personality left on his many relationships is recorded in volumes of letters and a range of memoirs. His interest in and desire for friendship, contact, did not mean that he surrounded himself with admirers and hangers-on. On the contrary, he journeyed with few companions – Frieda Lawrence most constant among them. Catherine Carswell, who greatly admired Lawrence, said of him that he was 'without human dreariness'. David Garnett (son of Edward), commented on his 'agreeable' nature, and Richard Aldington noted from the start that he was an 'individualist'. After his death, E.M. Forster called him 'the greatest imaginative novelist of our generation', but his literary peers were not always so generous in their assessments, resistant perhaps, to the radical counter-voice to their practice that his work represented. Many of his friends and acquaintances, like Bertrand Russell, noted 'the energy and passion of his feelings' although, as with Russell (and Murry), this sometimes made for rapid and often irreconcilable, fallings-out. At low points, particularly during the years of the Great War, he is described as angry and intolerant of his situation. He was, at this time, quick to see slights and, with the suppression of *The Rainbow* almost immediately after its publication, not surprisingly defensive. Few were surprised, at this stage in his life, to see him reject England. However, it is clear from the records that he knew the value of friendship which transcended local disagreements, and his marriage, with its unorthodox beginnings and despite periods of conflict, infidelity and coolness, lasted. Biographical studies reveal the strains, but 'marriage' was an area of experience which Lawrence early on made central to his theorizing about male-female relationships and, clearly, valued.

Feeding his curiosity, Lawrence continually subjected his encounters, and his environment, to rigorous examination. A controversial figure, he was not approached during his life-time by serious offers to write his biography, and was never in a position – in the unlikely event that he had wished it – to authorize anyone to write his life. Following his death, as we have seen, a number of former friends took on that task, often writing in opposition to each other. In the period leading up to the Second World War, Lawrence's critical reputation was low: his comments on leadership (for instance in the 'political' novels of the 1920s) encouraged some commentators to think of him as a proto-fascist, and T.S. Eliot's reservations about his perceived values and their expression in his writing were highly influential (as were Murry's 'authoritative' statements). The re-assessment of his work principally by the critic F.R. Leavis, who read Lawrence as producing a good effect morally and spiritually, altered the situation by the introduction of a strong counter-voice to these others. Particularly in the 1950s, in the wake of New Criticism, his reputation revived, although in the 1970s his values were again under scrutiny **[117–58]**. He has become one of those writers where a great deal of biographical detail supports the almost innumerable critical studies. So it is that the 'Lawrence industry' has a dual focus, biographical and critical and, more often than not, the two domains dovetail.

FURTHER READING

Lawrence's life and relationships have been represented in a vast number of memoirs and reminiscences. At least ten volumes were produced shortly after his death by friends who were champions, defenders and critics of Lawrence, to whom the description of 'genius' nevertheless invariably stuck. The volumes by Aldington, Brett, the Brewsters, Bynner, Carswell, E.T., Corke, Ada Lawrence, Frieda Lawrence (*Not I, But the Wind*) Luhan, Merrild, Murry and Neville (see Bibliography), need to be read in parallel in order to construct the man. Aldous Huxley, perhaps most usefully, produced an edition of Lawrence's letters (Huxley 1932) accompanied by a serious and influential introduction which in part sought to defend Lawrence against the self-protective slant sometimes adopted in his accounts by John Middleton Murry, who was respected and had an audience. Readers also have access to Moore's *Collected Letters of D.H. Lawrence* (1962) which printed a greater number of letters than Huxley but which was still partial in its coverage. Since Moore, mainstream publishers like Penguin Books have issued editions of selected letters. *The Cambridge Edition of the Letters of D.H. Lawrence* (Boulton *et al.* 1979–93) in seven volumes, makes the complete letters available in a coherent format. It also provides useful biographical and historical background including chronologies pertaining to the correspondence in each volume. For quicker reference it has spawned a shorter volume, *The Selected Letters of D.H. Lawrence* (Boulton 1997).

A further invaluable source of biographical information which reprints excerpts from many accounts, as well as introducing a great deal of new material from the full range of Lawrence's acquaintances, is the *Composite Biography* (Nehls 1957) in three volumes. Accounts of the life of Lawrence as it impacted on the work have also come from the pens of critics and include studies by Moore (1951; 1974), a contentious biography by Delavenay (1972) which takes Lawrence up to 1919, Delany (1979) which deals with the effect of the war on Lawrence, and Burgess (1985). Currently, however, it is difficult to imagine a more detailed and comprehensive biography than the three-volume *Cambridge Biography* (Worthen 1991, Kinkead-Weekes 1996, Ellis 1998). With its emphasis on authenticated detail, it has clarified numerous issues relating to Lawrence's personal and professional relationships, as well as the composition and publishing history of all the texts in his *oeuvre*. Aside from this, short autobiographical pieces are available in *Phoenix: The Posthumous Papers of D.H. Lawrence* (McDonald, ed. 1936), and *Phoenix II: Uncollected, Unpublished and Other Prose Works by D.H. Lawrence* (Roberts and Moore, eds 1968).

WORK

This section provides a general introduction to Lawrence's writing. Lawrence was prolific and it is not possible here, or desirable, to give equal weighting to everything he produced. The sub-sections that follow are necessarily synoptic. They draw attention to his work in a range of genres. The commentary focuses on specific works in order to indicate Lawrence's main preoccupations, and examines the development of certain constant themes. Attention will be given to texts with an acknowledged cultural importance, but which seldom give rise to critical consensus. Part II also begins to identify specific critical issues and concerns. The intention here is not to provide new interpretations but to rehearse the relationship between Lawrence's ideas and contexts and his texts. When it is relevant, reference is made to Part I where the personal and social background to composition and publication is signalled, and to Part III where the critical debates inspired by the work are introduced.

The major novels, some of which attracted controversy when they were first published, and some of which were available at first only in expurgated versions (that is to say, not with the text that Lawrence intended) will be represented in this section. These include: *The Rainbow* (1915) which was suppressed by court-order in Britain, *Women in Love* (1920) and *Lady Chatterley's Lover* (1928). The other novels are also discussed individually. Although they traditionally figure less prominently in surveys of Lawrence's work than the novels of the war years or his final novel, they contribute something crucial to a broad understanding of the *oeuvre*. *The Trespasser* (1912), *The Lost Girl* (1920) and the unfinished *Mr Noon* (Part I, 1934; Part II, 1984) are important examples in this respect, alongside texts that are currently attracting more diverse critical attention than has been the case; for instance, Lawrence's 'Mexican' novel, *The Plumed Serpent* (1926). Artistic collaborations between Lawrence and others which produced significant work are also acknowledged, principally *The Boy in the Bush* (1924) written with the Australian writer M.L. Skinner. There is some concentration on the novellas, and the short stories will be represented, with specific reference to 'The Prussian Officer' (1914), 'England, My England' (1915) and 'The Woman Who Rode Away' (1925), each of which heads up a collection of short fiction, and which, among others, represent significant landmarks in Lawrence's artistic development.

Discussion of Lawrence's poems will similarly focus on familiar collections such as *Look! We Have Come Through!* (1917), in which he celebrated his marriage, and later works such as *Birds, Beasts and Flowers* (1923), and *Pansies* (1929) which represent different aspects of his personal philosophy, itself continually under revision. The early plays will be represented by texts which share thematic concerns with the prose, notably *The Daughter-in-Law* (1913; 1965) and *The Widowing of Mrs Holroyd* (1914). The latter relates in essentials to 'Odour of Chrysanthemums' (1911), regarded by many as one of Lawrence's most effective short stories.

There is some coverage in Part II of Lawrence's non-fiction, principally the essays, and the ways in which they draw attention to his main interests with special reference to his ambitions for the novel form, his engagement with America culture, psychoanalysis and literary criticism. Other concerns, his theorization of conflict, for example, and his social commentary, are highlighted with the critical focus on how and where these interests inform the work.

(a) THE EARLY WRITING

(i) Plays

A Collier's Friday Night was written in 1909 (published 1934). It anticipates Lawrence's third novel, *Sons and Lovers*, particularly in its representation of a strong mother-son bond which is heightened in the presence of the despised husband and father, a miner. The play takes place in the miner's home, minutely delineated in the stage directions. The second act introduces the mother's rivalry with her son's friend Maggie, an early version of Miriam Leivers (*Sons and Lovers*). The play, with its autobiographical elements, is of a period with the short stories 'Goose Fair' (1910) and, more significantly, 'Odour of Chrysanthemums', begun in 1909 and itself a fictional prefiguration of the play *The Widowing of Mrs Holroyd* which was written in draft form by 1910. This period also produced *The Daughter-in-Law* (reworked as fiction in 'The Last Straw' [original title 'Fanny and Annie'] in the *England, My England* collection of short stories). These texts show Lawrence drawing on his experience of home life and the life of the mining community he knew so well. The plays are naturalistic and, if nothing else, show Lawrence's skill in dialogue and the rendering of dialect speech. In the 'Midlands' plays, powerful and compelling human dramas are enacted in environments which perfectly support them, as in *Sons and Lovers*. The plays demonstrate Lawrence's responsiveness (as in the fiction) to the particular challenge of his form. The Irish dramatist, Sean O'Casey, reviewing *A Collier's Friday Night*, reminds the reader of the short-sightedness of the literary establishment in its cursory treatment of Lawrence as a playwright. He recognizes that the play is an early piece of writing but argues, 'Had Lawrence got the encouragement the play called for and deserved, England might have had a great dramatist' (*New Statesman* 28 July 1934).

While they draw on Lawrence's sense of his community these plays are primarily about the acute family tensions, and in particular the relationships between men and women, which Lawrence would continue to explore in a range of genres. Nevertheless, it was as a result of their powerful rendition of working-class life that they enjoyed a revival in 1965 at the Royal Court Theatre (Roberts 1986). After the 'Chatterley trial' in 1960 **[131]** Lawrence's cultural value was high, if not for reasons he would have anticipated, and in the 1960s the working-class themes of the plays had an audience. *The Merry-go-Round* (written in 1910) and *The Married Man* (written in 1912) did not attract the critical interest of the plays that got to the Royal Court, nor did *The Fight for Barbara* (written in 1912) which is set in Italy. *Touch and Go*, written in 1918, returned to the Midlands for its setting. Lawrence had the highest hopes for his 'Biblical' play, *David*, written in 1925, but he was disappointed by the reviews of the 1927 production.

Critical interest in Lawrence's plays has been relatively slight. When F.R. Leavis published his first influential monograph on Lawrence (1955), his interest was in Lawrence as a novelist, although he set a chapter aside for the short fiction **[126]**. Other critics followed suit, even where they disagreed with Leavis's judgements. Keith Sagar (1985) writes that Lawrence's fortunes as a dramatist were finished by 1913, and he makes a distinction between the early and the later writing for theatre which supports Sean O'Casey's response to Lawrence's work:

> The later plays were occasional, out of the mainstream of Lawrence's creative effort. The early plays were not. If [John Millington] Synge could make genuine dramatic tragedy out of the culture and speech of the Aran Islands, why could not Lawrence out of the culture and speech of the Nottinghamshire coalfields?

But as some qualification, based on the content of the most successful plays (as 'literature'), Sagar adds:

> All the plays he had yet written except the 'impromptus' had been on the same theme, the emasculating effect of an over-possessive mother on her sons. It seems that Lawrence could only tap this vein of dramatic energy and authenticity at this one point, the point where the life of that mining culture coincided with his own

rawest autobiographical concern. He could not have written many more variations on that theme. In any case, the writing of *Sons and Lovers* had enabled him to shed that particular sickness, and write FINIS under that stage of his life from which the colliery plays had drawn their life-blood.

(Sagar 1985: 61)

(ii) *The White Peacock*

In the introduction to G.H. Neville's memoir of his friend, D.H. Lawrence, the critic Carl Baron suggests that *The White Peacock* (1911) shares significantly in the main preoccupations of the more widely read, more critically acclaimed, later works: 'It seems to me that *The White Peacock* expresses pressures, needs and psychological patterning in imaginative form in direct line with his later handling of those same patternings when realities and experiences had taken the place of needs and fantasies' (Neville 1981: 2). This encouragement to see in the first novel an adumbration of the maturer writing is fair. In fact, *The White Peacock* sets the standard for Lawrence's writing to follow, absorbed as it is in questions of relationships. Lawrence told Jessie Chambers **[10]** that he intended to exploit the 'two-couples' structure learned from George Eliot which he does here, and not for the last time. Possibly, he also learned from Eliot's novel *The Mill on the Floss* (1860) that he could draw imaginatively on his Midlands location and an English provincial culture, but Eliot is not Lawrence's only precursor. Michael Black draws attention to this sense of a tradition in his study of Lawrence's early fiction:

> The literary ancestors [of George, Lettie *et al.* in *The White Peacock*] might be George Eliot's pairs of young people in *Middlemarch*, or Tolstoy's pairs in *Anna Karenina*; or one might see George Saxton as a failed version of Hardy's Gabriel Oak ... More strikingly, the strong rustic pair at the farm (George, Emily) set against an over-bred pair from a cultivated drawing room (Lettie and Cyril) may remind the reader of *Wuthering Heights* – Lettie's wilfulness and charm and her disastrous choice are very like Catherine Earnshaw's. But from the beginning Lawrence is in his own world, and what he owes to his models is a minor matter compared with what he has to say on his own.
>
> (Black 1986: 47)

It is his strategic development of this distance from the novel tradition which is interesting, and which continues throughout Lawrence's writing life.

The White Peacock is alone among Lawrence's novels to exploit a first-person narrator. Cyril Beardsall, well-educated, erudite and recognizably the Lawrence-figure in the book, operates clumsily as 'omniscient'. Cyril/'Sybil' sees everything but is largely outside the action, an insubstantial, sterile figure, close friend of the robust young farmer, George Saxton. Cyril's other significant male friendship is with the philosopher-gamekeeper, Annable. A gamekeeper will figure again, notoriously, in Lawrence's last novel, *Lady Chatterley's Lover*, and Annable ('a devil of the woods', 146), who 'trespasses' in the narrative of *The White Peacock* with his story of the love of Lady Chrystabel, is an interesting precursor of Oliver Mellors.

In the chapter called 'A Shadow in Spring', Annable's tale begins the familiar Lawrentian theme of 'devouring women' who are the destroyers of good men. He abuses a screeching peacock which he and Cyril encounter in the churchyard, arguing that the bird represents the soul of woman and that he should consequently enjoy wringing its neck (148). A woman, he announces, is 'all vanity and screech and defilement' (149). The basis of this misogyny is not long concealed from Cyril who learns how Annable's Lady Chrystabel, after a short spell of marriage, grows indifferent to what he calls 'the pride of my body' (150). Preferring images of men gleaned from poetry, popular romances and paintings, she becomes 'souly' (151), and Annable decamps, disguising himself as a servant, to become a shadowy adventurer haunting the columns of society gossip. It is in this context, too, that the attractions of the male body surface, consolidating and confirming the force of other aspects of the narrative. Cyril is bidden to feel Annable's biceps as proof of his bodily pride: 'I was startled. The hard flesh almost filled his sleeve' (150). By the end of this section an emphasis on touch has developed and an unconscious sympathy is expressed between the two men, which looks ahead to the bond suddenly forged between Rupert Birkin and Gerald Crich in the 'Gladiatorial' chapter of *Women in Love*, and which expresses itself in their spontaneous grasping of hands. This is Cyril and Annable:

> 'Ay,' said I, rising. I held out my hand from the shadow. I was startled myself by the *white sympathy* it expressed extended towards him in the moonlight. He gripped it, and cleaved to me for a moment, then he was gone.
>
> (WP 151; emphasis added)

Cyril, after this expression of 'white sympathy', walks into the woods to touch the 'budded gentleness of the trees' and to feel the caress of the 'velvet fingers' of the larches (152). He remembers Annable in the chapter called 'A Poem of Friendship', first as he watches George drying himself after a swim, and then as he is in turn dried by his friend. This episode establishes the importance of male friendships in Lawrence's writing, and is frequently taken as an example of the homoerotic which is both present and resisted in Lawrence:

> ... he took hold of me and began to rub me briskly, as if I were a child, or rather, a woman he loved *and did not fear*. I left myself quite limply in his hands, and, to get a better grip of me, he put his arm round me and pressed me against him, and the sweetness of the touch of our naked bodies one against the other was superb. It satisfied in some measure the vague, indecipherable yearning of my soul; and it was the same with him. When he had rubbed me all warm, he let me go, and we looked at each other with eyes of still laughter, and our love was perfect for a moment, more perfect than any love I have known since, either for man or woman.
>
> (WP 222–3; emphasis added)

The idea behind this passage, and others in the novel which dwell on the body masculine, is reworked notably in *Women in Love* (1920) and *Aaron's Rod* (1922), and reappears in much of the writing. The critic Tony Pinkney, however, cautions against reading this passage solely as privileging the love between men as a theme in the book, arguing that one of the utopian insights in the novel turns on the pleasure value of *labour* – the young men have worked the fields together for weeks and have formed an attachment based on their shared work which has its 'objective correlative' in this scene of George drying Cyril (Pinkney 1990: 15–16). As Pinkney suggests, in ways reminiscent of the first pages of *The Rainbow*, a continuity between the workers and the land which is worked is maintained, where the pleasure of 'labour' is not yet the 'toil' of the alienated worker. Even so, the reference to women that George might not *fear*, indicates the potential for oppositional sexual politics which underpins *The White Peacock*. Annable's story, for example, establishes a loathing of the 'over-conscious' woman who operates from an ideal (151). The destiny of Lettie, in this novel, provides an analogous model of feminine bad faith. Lettie resists the sensuous aspect of George, or the sensuous aspect of her attraction to him, choosing to privilege her social rather than her sexual self (this dichotomy is established in *The White Peacock*). By the end of the novel, she has married the bourgeois Leslie Tempest who serves social systems rather than himself, and she embraces motherhood as her vocation in a social rather than a 'vital' sense (compare *The Rainbow*'s Anna Brangwen who, in childbearing, enjoys 'her riches'). Lettie's choice is that in submitting to her social self she has chosen 'to ignore her own self' ... 'escaping ... the responsibilities of her own development' (284). It is his particular treatment of these themes, developed in considerable detail in *The White Peacock,* which establishes Lawrence's difference from his literary predecessors, and his modernity.

(iii) *The Trespasser*

Lawrence's next novel was altogether different in its content, structure and mode of language. He owed it to his meeting and friendship (1908–12) with Helen Corke when he became a school-teacher in Croydon **[12]**. *The Trespasser* (1912) is a significantly revised version of 'The Saga of Siegmund' written in 1910. It is by Lawrence's own admission a juvenile work, and he quickly tired of it. His harsh judgement on the book was that the style was too self-consciously poetic, but that even so, it '[ran] to seed in realism' (*Letters* I: 184). This authorial view need not obscure what is valuable in the book. If it occupies a minor position in the *oeuvre* it is, nevertheless, a novel which is underpinned by ideas of relevance to later work, and some excellent writing.

The Trespasser has its origins in the story of the tragic relationship between Helen Corke and her married lover who took his own life after they had shared a brief holiday in Freshwater on the Isle of Wight. Corke gave Lawrence access to her 'Freshwater Diaries' which describe the final days of the relationship, and she spoke to him at length about their emotional legacy. However, while it is the case that Lawrence draws heavily on Corke's accounts it is erroneous to regard the novel purely as a re-telling of someone else's story. Lawrence submitted the material offered by Corke to the dictates of his own creative intelligence, and wrote also in the light of his own immediate successes and failures with women **[10]**. His emerging theories of sexual and metaphysical conflict between men and women are tested as he charts the tension between Helena, in love with the musical, creative, man but not desirous of sex, and Siegmund who recognizes the intensity of her feelings and so cannot accept her repudiation of his body. The novel is unlike much of the early work in the intensity of narrative concentration on the central relationship – although descriptions of the family life of Siegmund and his wife, Beatrice, are often acknowledged to be among the best writing in the book. Although it demonstrates significant narrative control, therefore, it is a flawed work, nowhere more so than in Chapter XIII where Lawrence introduces, rather too self-consciously, the figure of Hampson, a mouthpiece for Lawrence's views on the oppressive love, for exceptional men, of women whose pursuit of love is confined to an ideal. Helena is one of Lawrence's much despised 'dreaming women' (*Sons and Lovers'* Miriam Leivers is another, so too is Lady Chrystabel). As commentators often point out, a vicious parody of Helen Corke also occurs late in his writing career in *Lady Chatterley's Lover*, in Oliver Mellors' catalogue of difficult women (LCL 200).

The narrative structure of *The Trespasser* is of interest because of the ways in which it shows Lawrence again both exploiting, and distancing himself from, a novelistic tradition. This is something he will continue to do, increasingly self-consciously, as an artist. The clue rests in Lawrence's description of his 'idyll'. It is essentially an island story, where the remoteness, the complete otherness, of the island to which the lovers retreat is reminiscent of literary romance. The narrative is crudely punctuated throughout with references to the Ring cycle operas of Richard Wagner (to make the point about a doomed relationship, Lawrence has the lovers occasionally dub themselves 'Siegfried' and 'Sieglinde', and makes continual reference to the symbolism of the operas *Tristan und Isolde* and *Die Walküre*). The island is the space where romantic love can notionally blossom, in contrast to the dreary suburbs. The return to realism occurs where the narrative deals principally (and highly skilfully) with Siegmund's unhappy family life and the ordinariness of his domestic environment. The plot of a man who walks out on his family is revisited much more confidently in *Aaron's Rod*, where the hero succeeds in making the break.

Part of *The Trespasser's* significance lies in the attempt to write a romance and to subject romantic love to an extended critique. This is not only about Lawrence's sense of literary history. It is also a result of his developing thought on male-female relations, which has its strongest representation in the depiction of Helena as in love with the idea of love, but resistant to sexual realities. She witholds herself. Siegmund is the focus for the novel's sympathetic treatment of masculine feeling (if feeling can be gendered) and the (literally) deadly results of sexual fear. Many readings of *The Trespasser* concentrate on the destruction of the man by the woman's sexual squeamishness, although, as we might expect with Lawrence, the issue is not that simple. Not for the last time in a novel Lawrence associates the misuse, or misdirection, of sex with death in his analyses of human action.

(iv) *Sons and Lovers*

Of this first phase of Lawrence's writing career – the phase that is, with a few important exceptions, clearly autobiographical – *Sons and Lovers* (1913) is the work most acknowledged to have an enduring significance. It is characterized by some extremely accomplished writing which demonstrates in Lawrence a maturity and a confidence that is superior to the overall achievement of *The White Peacock* and *The Trespasser*, even while these novels show his promise with the form. The relationships between individuals are now consistently subtly observed (the Morel's marriage; the exchanges between each parent and each child; Mrs Morel's measured interaction with her neighbours), and operate within the novel's chief themes. Lawrence makes commanding use of dialogue and dialect and arguably improves on Edwardian realism. In addition, specific episodes stand out because of the memorable power of the writing (for instance, Morel's expulsion of his pregnant wife from the house, and her subsequent reverie, in 'The early married Life of the Morels'; Mrs. Morel's trip to London to nurse William, and the return of his body to Bestwood in 'Death in the Family'). The book shows both what Lawrence had learned from the novels read in his youth, and the emergence of his particular voice and style.

Sons and Lovers begins, like many Victorian novels of the provinces, with a description of place. It evokes an English Midlands landscape marked since the seventeenth century by the production of coal and identified with the social changes wrought by the industrial revolution. In particular it highlights the influence of powerful private companies which, in sinking large mines and erecting miners' dwellings, produced the contours of the modern pit community (SL 9–10). The description which begins *Sons and Lovers* can be compared with the opening paragraphs of the autobiographical essay, 'Nottingham and the Mining Countryside' (*Phoenix*: 133–40), with its description of the worked country, where Lawrence invokes some literary models: '… the life was a curious cross between industrialism and the old agricultural England of Shakespeare and Milton and Fielding and George Eliot' (135).

The Morel family are of this community, but Mrs Morel's aspirations lead her on occasion to challenge its dominant values. The novel charts her best efforts to direct her sons away from the mine into jobs marked by, in her view, a respectability (and income) beyond the pit and pit culture. From the start her character is identified as 'superior' and antagonistic to her husband and his interests which she resists throughout her marriage. Part I of the book deals with the tensions in the family caused by the oppositionality of Mr and Mrs Morel, and shows Mrs Morel's success in winning the hearts and minds of her children, and in particular her sons, from her husband whose family status is eventually reduced to that of a minor nuisance. One of Lawrence's most mature achievements is to represent the contempt in which Morel is held by his family as a result of his periods of resistance (which include drunken violence) towards a wife he barely understands. These occur, however, alongside homely cameos which show him to be self-sufficient, attractively absorbed by his work and the comforting routines of his day and week, even as he is, finally, defeated by his wife's disaffection. Despite (or, perhaps, through) his crude attempts at regaining patriarchal control, and his representation often as marginal, a great deal of narrative sympathy is, in fact, set aside for Walter Morel who is, ultimately, scared of his highly strung, sharp-tongued wife. As in *A Collier's Friday Night* **[36]**, however, the main focus is on the bond between mother and sons, against this stranger-father; and ultimately on the rivalry for the heart of the artist-son (Paul) between the mother and the son's sweetheart.

Part II deals with the young adulthood of Paul Morel, the developing artist, up to the death of his mother. It charts his sexual relationships with women, first with Miriam Leivers and then with the more mature, married, Clara Dawes. The development of these relationships has to be seen in the light of Paul's love for his mother and his inability to have unproblematic relationships with other women while his love for her remains his principal emotional commitment. It is not surprising, given the popularity at this time of the ideas of the psychoanalyst, Sigmund Freud, that *Sons and Lovers* was immediately received and reviewed as a 'Freudian' novel. Freud's notion of the Oedipus complex was in circulation, and many readers interpreted *Sons and Lovers* as a fictional account of the idea given the vivid representation of the mother-father-son triangle at the heart of the book, with its implications for Paul Morel's emotional life while his mother lives. At the time of publication, Lawrence had to contend with reviews of the novel that developed this interpretation. (See, for instance, Alfred Kuttner, in Draper 1970: 76–80) **[134–8]**. A growing preoccupation with self-consciousness (as a 'theme' rather than a 'style') can also be seen as a tendency in this novel. Paul Morel strives for self-definition first as an artist, then as a man. In the closing lines of the book, he achieves a sense of individual self-hood, free at last from the women in his life (mother, lovers) who have, up to that point, defined him. (Similarly, James Joyce's *Bildungsroman, A Portrait of the Artist as a Young Man,*

1916, made the figure of the artist, and the development of an artistic consciousness, central to the work.)

The autobiographical elements of *Sons and Lovers* are easy to identify: as we have seen, Lawrence went through phases of genuine dislike for his father, and contempt for what were perceived to be his limitations. Lawrence loved his mother, was 'on her side', and cared deeply about what she thought of him as a man and an artist. The family lost Lawrence's vigorous elder brother to illness when he was a young man. Jessie Chambers was used badly by Lawrence towards the end of their long association. In addition, Lawrence had an affair with an older married woman, Alice Dax, and Lawrence and his sister tended their sick mother in her last days **[6–13]**. The book is not, however, purely autobiography. While Lawrence drew on what he knew best (as he did not always with *The White Peacock* and less so in *The Trespasser*), he was also stepping out into the new territory of abstract thought. The interesting questions are not concerned ultimately with autobiographical detail, but rather with Lawrence's developing reference to oppositionality – the nerve-worn relations between men and women which would also mark his later novels. This is evident in the description of the differences between the young Gertrude Coppard, later Mrs Morel, and Walter Morel when they first meet:

> He was so full of colour and animation, his voice ran so easily into comic grotesque, he was so ready and so pleasant with everybody. Her own father had a rich fund of humour, but it was satiric. This man's was different: soft and non-intellectual, warm, a kind of gambolling.
> She herself was opposite.
>
> (SL 17)

This oppositionality is ultimately disastrous. It is not the positive foundation for necessary self-sufficiency that was beginning to characterize Lawrence's thought about relationships.

Throughout their marriage, Mrs Morel attempts to offset her rapid disillusion with her husband by living through her sons in whom, in the absence of other possibilities (of education, of employment) she must find herself. Hence this summary in the chapter called 'Strife in Love':

> William had brought her his sporting trophies. She kept them still: and she did not forgive his death. Arthur was handsome, at least a good specimen, and warm and generous, and probably would do

well in the end. But Paul was going to distinguish himself. She had a great belief in him, the more because he was unaware of his own powers. There was so much to come out of him. Life for her was rich with promise. *She was to see herself fulfilled.*

(SL 222; emphasis added)

This vicarious mode of living is reserved for intelligent women in the book. Mrs Morel and Miriam Leivers are similar in the extent to which both live through Paul's achievements, which is how they become rivals. Theirs is a likeness, however, to which both are necessarily blind. Neither ends up with Paul. If they found a way to share him, then, given the language of self-dispersal and absorption in the narrative, nothing, in fact, would be left of him. The jilting of Miriam and the death of his mother are the events which give Paul 'release' (Chapter XIV). In 'Strife in Love', strife is evident between Paul and Miriam, as we might expect; between Paul and his mother principally when she perceives Miriam as a rival; and between Paul and his father where the father is rival – the latter says of mother and son, finding them in an embrace, "At your mischief again?" (252).

Several details in the narrative align Mrs Morel and Miriam. Neither is easily capable of 'revelling', as Paul calls it in 'Strife in Love' (226); both women are clever and aspirational. Of the young Gertrude we are told, 'She loved ideas, and was considered very intellectual' (17), while Paul's first intimacies with Miriam are about books and learning. Miriam is dangerously close, however, to the 'dreaming women' so despised in *The White Peacock* and *The Trespasser*; and possibly Mrs Morel's transformation into the practical manager of her family, together with her immersion in the small but crucial domestic economies (her liberty is as broad as her housekeeping money allows), preserve her from that fate. If her sons are clever, or talented, that is enough. Some of the novel's imagery, however, expresses the similarity of Miriam and Mrs Morel. At Miriam's house, Paul pulls some berries and leaves from a bowl saying that if she wore them in her hair she would resemble a witch or priestess, never a reveller. On returning home, he makes a gift to his mother of the berries and leaves (226–8). A 'priestess', subtly pagan, Miriam might draw his soul out of him (231–2). This fear of a man's loss of self in love occurs again, notably in the strife between the lovers in *Women in Love*. Elsewhere, Miriam is a muse – 'She brought forth to him his imaginations' (241). These are Paul's versions of Miriam, and on the whole they are versions of herself which she does not recognize. He might berate her for her soulfulness but when she approaches him physically – 'She put her two hands on his sides, and ran them quickly down' (227) – he recoils. As long as she loves him 'absorbedly' (227), he cannot risk himself in her hands – 'She did not seem to realise *him* in all this. He might have been an object. She never realised the male he was' (227). She becomes, in effect, a threat and he fears the effect of her touch on him: '"You switch me off somewhere, and project me out of myself. I am quite ghostish, disembodied"' (232). The point is not Miriam's feeling for Paul, but how he interprets her effect on him. 'Strife in Love' deals with, among other things, modes of knowledge. Towards the end of the chapter, for example, are descriptions of Paul's understanding about the nature of his relationship with his mother, but *how* he knows, i.e. 'instinctively' (251), is crucial. This points towards a later developed use in Lawrence of the language of the 'blood', and the shift to the body as the *locus* of the unconscious (instinctive knowledge), which characterizes much of the later writing. The theme of mothering would continue to get his attention but by the early 1920s Lawrence was publishing books in which he railed against oppressive mother-love, hinting at the negative emotional effects on men.

Just before the publication of *Sons and Lovers*, Lawrence wrote a 'Foreword' which was not, by his own admission, intended for publication (SL 465–73). It can be read today as a draft piece, in which Lawrence begins to explore some of the ideas which will surface in other, longer discursive texts [98–111]. It begins in quasi-Biblical style, exploiting the language of the Gospel of St John which furnishes Lawrence with some dual concepts – the Word and the Flesh – and with which he sets out an extremely obscure analysis of contemporary relations between men and women. He asserts the primacy of woman (470), and articulates an idea which was close to his heart at this time – the need for a creative man to have a supportive woman at his back. If the relation between man and woman is good, argues Lawrence (in the first eighteen months of his relationship with Frieda Weekley [13]), man is 're-born' of woman (472). This underlines Lawrence's ideal of 'marriage' at this time. If, on the other hand, the relation between them is flawed, there is no proper connection, and man wastes himself, while woman (seeking elsewhere for fulfilment) makes lovers of her sons. The final paragraph of the Foreword warns of the dangers of becoming a 'son-lover' – this is the part of the text which does speak to the novel's concerns – and how this blocks the son from achieving a fulfilling (creative) relation with a woman who is not his mother.

Further Reading

The plays have attracted little sustained critical attention, and the principal study is still Sylvia Sklar's *The Plays of D.H. Lawrence* (1975) – see also Sagar and Sklar in Keith Sagar (ed., 1982). Ian Clarke has written on *The Fight for Barbara* (in Preston and Hoare, eds, 1989), and recommends Raymond Williams' introduction to *Three Plays* in a Penguin Books edition of 1969. Four critical items on Lawrence's plays are collected in Jackson and Brown Jackson (eds, 1988: 203–16), and Roberts (1986) includes a chapter on *A Collier's Friday Night* at the Royal Court. John Worthen contributes a chapter on Lawrence as a dramatist in Fernihough (ed., 2001). Black (1991) has written a detailed commentary on the early fiction. Spilka (ed., 1963) includes a descriptive account of the plays by Arthur E. Waterman who concludes that, apart from *Touch and Go*, the plays are merely 'the hedgings of the other forms'. General studies of the novels, of which there are many, usually address the earliest fiction synoptically, with *Sons and Lovers* given more focused treatment than *The White Peacock* and *The Trespasser*. Kermode, for example, touches on the first novels (and, briefly, the plays) in the 'prologue' to his study (1973). Worthen gives the early fiction more extensive treatment (1991b), and Pinkney (1990) examines their relation to modernism in his first two chapters. Bell (1992) begins his study with an examination of the narrative styles and language themes in the first three novels. Leavis (1955) dealt with *The White Peacock* and *The Trespasser* as 'lesser novels' but felt that Lawrence had turned a corner with *Sons and Lovers*. Tedlock (1963) discusses the early fiction in his chapter, 'Early Patterns of Revolt', and (in Tedlock, ed., 1965), the sources and early criticism of *Sons and Lovers*. Raymond Williams shows how much is achieved in the language of the early writing, and the importance of this in *Sons and Lovers* (Williams 1970). Essays and articles on the early fiction are too numerous to be listed here. Of the first novels, *Sons and Lovers* is awarded singular book-length treatment as in Salgādo (1969), Draper (1986), Harvey (1987), Murfin (1987), Finney (1990), Black (1992) and Rylance (ed., 1996) – Rylance has also written recently on the sources and intellectual contexts of all three early novels (2001). Widdowson (ed., 1992) brings together some interesting pieces. The Freudian debates on *Sons and Lovers* emerge in Tiverton (1951), Weiss (1962) and Stoll (1968), although discussions about Lawrence, psychology and psychoanalysis go well beyond critiques of his third novel **[134–8]**.

(b) THE 'SERIOUS ENGLISH' NOVELS

(i) *The Rainbow*

The Rainbow (1915) has its genesis in the years immediately preceding the Great War. It was suppressed within two months of its publication in Britain and the publisher, Methuen, was prosecuted under the Obscene Publications Act of 1857. The novel had been printed only after considerable revision and rewriting on Lawrence's part, and went through a number of drafts, identified first as 'The Sisters'. Altered, it became 'The Wedding Ring' which, like 'The Sisters', anticipated much of the content of *Women in Love*. Finally *The Rainbow* was published despite certain reservations about Lawrence's uses of language, and 'sexual morbidities' (R 484; a judgement echoed by T.S. Eliot in *After Strange Gods*), reservations which would surface again in Lawrence criticism.

The Rainbow is Lawrence's first properly modernist novel. In a radically new language it established Lawrence's 'impersonal' aesthetic (this is what he meant when he called the novel 'a bit futuristic' [*Letters* II: 182]). In it, he re-presented character, addressing the continuity of human experience in the generations of the Brangwen family at Marsh Farm, and the movement towards individuation in the figure of Ursula Brangwen, the modern woman, who would also appear in *Women in Love* (1920). As *Women in Love*, so *The Rainbow* showed Lawrence's developing interest in unconscious functioning, although what he understood by 'unconscious' was very different from the defining concept of Freudian psychoanalysis. Although Lawrence shared with Freud an interest in the instinctive life, he repudiated what he knew of the scientist's theories. Indeed, the novels which came after *Sons and Lovers* showed the direction of Lawrence's thought about relations between men and women in ways which challenged popular 'Freudism'. These are books where sex is often linked with death, but where it is also a means of self-renewal, the idea of the re-birth of the self which lies at the heart of Lawrence's personal philosophy. Women's experience is often central in his writing, and Lawrence is open to the charge of misogyny directed at many of the male modernists, but as Marianne DeKoven remarks, 'This masculinist misogyny ... was almost universally accompanied by its dialectical twin: a fascination and strong identification with the empowered feminine' (Levenson ed., 1999: 174). It is possible to think this of Lawrence who both celebrated and railed against the feminine, but who, as shall be seen, acknowledged the centrality of a female principle at work in his own writing.

Lawrence's treatment of issues of self and sexuality came to operate increasingly in terms of a highly self-conscious primitivism (for example in *The Lost Girl*, and less successfully in *The Plumed Serpent*), prior to his description of 'phallic-consciousness' in *Lady Chatterley's Lover*. In *The Rainbow*, he undercuts the imperatives of an historical consciousness by substituting a contrasting mythic dimension which underpins characters' experiences. As we shall see, the Brangwens are presented first in an unacknowledged 'prologue' which recalls Genesis in its emphasis on the generational and the cyclical nature of existence (Lawrence exploits Biblical imagery throughout this novel). In the first pages a way of living and being is foregrounded, from which the *modern* individual is ultimately alienated. There is no 'voice' (no specific register) attached in the beginning to the timeless Brangwen figures, but the separate wills and allegiances of the men and women depicted are distinguished by the directions in which they look – the men to the land, the women beyond, although their lives accommodate both directions. The depiction of these men in the fields and the women at home is not 'realist'. It is one aspect of a mythic mode of writing which, in later work, approaches a highly specific primitivism. As Cristopher Nash notes, with reference to a German tradition, in Lawrence 'myth (like religious music and dance) is the communal expression not of a morality but of the primal, ecstatic energies of nature acting in the people, the Volk' (Nash 1980). It is perfectly clear, in reading *The Rainbow* (and later *The Plumed Serpent*), how this observation is borne out. Further, the 'prologue' in its impersonal scope and scale anticipates the importance and centrality of modernist explorations of time (historical, mythic and personal) which are central to Virginia Woolf's *Mrs Dalloway* (1925), T.S. Eliot's *The Waste Land* and Joyce's *Ulysses*, for example.

In Lawrence's 'mythical' mode, then, the mythic signifies a kind of understanding which is different from analytical, over-conscious, modern ratiocination. This is to recall a phrase, 'the mythical method', which is T.S. Eliot's, from his essay '*Ulysses*, Order, and Myth' (1923). It addresses James Joyce's 'epic', a 'high' modernist narrative in which episodes from Homer's epic *The Odyssey* provide a structure for the modern story which deals with a highly specific present, the wanderings of two (conventionally unheroic) Dubliners through their city on the day and night of 16 June 1904. Eliot – who was often critical of Lawrence **[119; 124–5]** – approves of Joyce's combination of the traditional and the contemporary, and celebrates his extremely self-conscious use of myth to order and control the chaotic banalities of the present. Lawrence and Joyce are in fact often viewed as antithetical – Lawrence disliked Joyce's 'self-conscious' mode of writing, and he did not use myth as a structuring principle in the same way – yet both are central, because of their differences, to an understanding of modernism.

So, Lawrence is not 'manipulating a continuous parallel between contemporaneity and antiquity' in order to make 'the modern world possible for art' in ways that Eliot found represented in W.B. Yeats and Joyce in particular. Instead, he institutes a personal mythopoeic (myth-making) style which draws (in *The Rainbow*) most often on Old Testament parallels when these seem to suggest models, modes or images of human consciousness. To take an instance, the death by water of Tom Brangwen (Chapter IX, 'The Marsh and the Flood'), recalls the Biblical Flood which, like the Creation, is one of Lawrence's favourite tropes. The point, however, is not the use of a Biblical or mythic parallel to *structure* a narrative about events happening in the present. The idea works poetically, by *association*: the fact is that Tom Brangwen is to all intents and purposes (psychologically) *part of the flood* (the 'wave' of experience). At the time of his death his *individuation* is not complete, as it cannot be at this point in the novel. This idea, this model, occurs as early as 1911 in a context not intended for publication, demonstrating the power of the metaphor for Lawrence: 'When we die, like rain-drops falling back again into the sea, we fall back into the big, shimmering sea of unorganised life which we call God. We are lost as individuals, yet we count in the whole' (*Letters* I: 256). This vision of impersonality persists even in the novel's 'prologue' in reference to undifferentiated life as the '*wave* which cannot halt' (R 9; emphasis added). It is a description which anticipates the intense and accumulative mode of repetition that characterizes the book's narrative language, of which the description, 'the pulse of the blood of the teats of the cows beat into the pulse of the hands of the men' (10), often serves as a kind of shorthand. Acknowledging *The Rainbow's* linguistic strangeness compared with anything he had written before, Lawrence called it 'a novel in a foreign language I don't know very well' (*Letters* I: 544). To return to the example of Tom Brangwen's drowning, and to reinforce the point about Tom's place in 'the whole', it can be said that Ursula is, in contrast, the only Brangwen in the novel who possesses, by the end, an individuated consciousness: she is not any longer, or at least not in the same way, part of 'the wave'.

The Rainbow, as I have said, is Lawrence's first modernist novel. The Brangwens have, for generations, farmed the same area of the Notts-Derby border, the part of England where Lawrence was born and grew up, but he is not evoking his background in the same spirit as he did in *Sons and Lovers*: he said of his new project, 'It is all analytical – quite unlike *Sons and Lovers*, not a bit visualised' (*Letters* I: 526). By the end of *The Rainbow*, the strong sense of mythologised 'tribal' identification which begins the 'saga' has given way, in the figure of Ursula Brangwen, to modern(ist) individuation. It is by charting Ursula's transformation as a result of her emotional experiences, and the development of her private and public personas towards a clear sense of her identity, that Lawrence finds a way of raising questions about selfhood which are so fundamental to exploratory modernist writing, but in a linguistic and philosophical mode which is highly idiosyncratic.

How does this process of raising and resolving questions of selfhood unfold? *The Rainbow* represents a continuation of Lawrence's exploration of sexual and family relationships, with the emphasis again on marriage. The novel describes the experiences of members of three generations of the Brangwen family as they grow up, establish themselves in adult relationships, and give way to the next generation. Tom Brangwen, farmer, inheritor of Marsh Farm (he it is who will die in the flood), is the focus of the first generation given specific treatment in the novel. His marriage is to an outsider, Lydia Lensky, a widowed member of Poland's displaced gentry who has a revolutionary background. Dispossessed and alone in England, she makes him the stepfather to the toddler Anna whom he brings up as his own, alongside the children from his marriage. This marriage is the first extended means in the novel by which Lawrence examines the development of feeling in contexts where the key players have no cultural common ground. It is a study in the positive and negative powers of practically wordless communication, and of stasis, and introduces Lawrence's extensive and sophisticated critique not of the *institution* of marriage, which does not interest him, but of the idea of marriage as a means of relating to the 'untranslatable' other while keeping the self apart and alive.

In the next generation, Anna's romance with, and marriage to, her cousin Will Brangwen provides the means of her break from the enclosed family community of Marsh Farm. Much of the narrative emphasis shifts to Will, an awkward, self-conscious youth now re-defining himself in his newly married context. An autodidact, he is passionately committed to the forms of early English church architecture, a willing student of Victorian revivals of Renaissance painters, and a craftsman in his own right. If Tom Brangwen is 'nature', inseparable from his native soil and community, Will Brangwen is 'culture', more alienated than Tom from his home ground. Lawrence makes him a draughtsman, a conservator of church furniture, a drawing master – an artisan who balances successful moments of unconscious creativity with hours of frustrated over-conscious labour. In some powerful episodes (the chapters 'Anna Victrix' and 'The Cathedral') Will and Anna continue Lawrence's examination of married love as necessarily oppositional (see 'Study of Thomas Hardy', chapters VI and VII), until Anna all but exits the narrative except as the continual, and willing, bearer of children. Will and Anna are the parents of Ursula and Gudrun Brangwen, the 'women in love' of this novel's sequel.

Ursula is the primary focus of *The Rainbow*'s third generation. As he had with Tom and Anna, the first father-daughter couple, Lawrence represents the closeness of the girl's relationship with her father in her infant years, and the necessary move away from his values and authority later. Perhaps representing a shift in himself towards greater sympathy for fathers, Lawrence also heightens, in *The Rainbow*, the oppressive maternalism of Anna as Ursula reaches adolescence and adulthood and begins the struggle for her own voice. Lawrence puts Ursula through a range of experiences, familial, sexual and professional, so that her responses are often formed in opposition to conventional social mores. Depictions of sexual encounters were cited as reasons for *The Rainbow*'s suppression in Britain with a particular frisson caused by 'Shame,' a chapter which charts the passage of Ursula's sexual love for her school-teacher, Winifred Inger. The language of other episodes with her lover the soldier Anton Skrebensky (including in the context of his time in South Africa against the Boers, discussions about service to nation and empire which Ursula reviles) also caused consternation and censure. Ursula's experiences, however, add up to more than the sexual. A 'new woman', she enters a university college and 'the man's world' where she works as a school-teacher, at first optimistic before a dissatisfaction with unheroic realities takes hold of her. Her destiny is shaped by the terms of Lawrence's criticism of English society at the time and, by testing certain 'roles' within it, Ursula suffers. However, it is her vision of spiritual recovery, which goes beyond the personal to embrace a collective experience, that closes the novel.

The conclusion is concerned with Ursula's breakdown and recovery after the end of her relationship with Skrebensky, and the last paragraphs of the book, with their intense poetic power, describe the regeneration of her spirit evoked by the image of the rainbow, which also stands for Lawrence's commitment to his new form of writing. The final chapter, also called 'The Rainbow', describes Ursula at home in Beldover convinced in her heart that she is pregnant with Skrebensky's child. In a striking description, which is about false consciousness, she writes a deeply penitent letter to Skrebensky in which she offers herself to him as a dutiful wife, in repudiation of her former desires for self-fulfilment. She believes this, at the time of writing, to be sincere: 'This was her true self, for ever' (R 449). Waiting for his reply, she slips out of the house intending to walk, and encounters in a rough field a group of horses. The powerfully poetic narrative makes this encounter transformative, and it lies at the heart of the chapter. The horses appear to menace Ursula. They operate as a group surging before and behind her as she labours in a panic to escape what becomes their oppressive sphere of influence. Their massive bodies, full of power, opposing her, correspond to the immense weight she feels pressing on her heart as she enters her moment of transition, which could also be called her moment of individuation: the narrative calls her 'a stone, unconscious, unchanging, unchangeable, whilst everything rolled by in transience, leaving her there'. After this, her 'final isolation' (454) is emphasized. Dazed, traumatized, she makes her way home and falls into a delirium: the child is lost (this has been about the birth of the self, not progeny). Her delirium is a necessary twilight for Ursula. More generally, it provides the space in which she repudiates the world (including family, Beldover, England) which has produced her, judging it 'unreal'. This recognition prepares the way for her rebirth, or the rebirth of a self glimpsed in the anticipatory imagery of the breaking husk and germinating seed: 'There was a space between her and the shell' (456). The old, or 'bygone', world is the husk; the new shoot is Ursula reborn. Coming round from her delirium she is judged fit enough to watch the world from her window, and her own rebirth, or 'liberation', expands to characterize a new 'cultural' germination which encompasses the colliers, women and children she sees 'walking each in the husk of an old fruition' (457). Over the hideousness of the new development of houses and estates, and the obsoleteness of the church-tower (a church also dominates the skyline of the book's 'prologue'), she sees a rainbow forming, recognizing it as a sign of the regeneration she has herself experienced, that the blighted population will also undergo: 'they would cast off their horny covering of disintegration' ... 'new, clean, naked bodies would issue to a new germination' (459). It is in this positive and visionary spirit that the novel ends. The language of this 'rebirth' is highly and powerfully metaphorical in the way it concludes Ursula's experience. But what notion of the self is Lawrence here developing?

To understand this it is necessary to go back a few years to an important letter of 5th June 1914 written by Lawrence to his editor and mentor, Edward Garnett [15; 124]. In a debate about characterization, Lawrence offers a new view of the self (and of the novel form). He announces his disinterest in 'the old-fashioned human element – which causes one to conceive a character in a certain moral scheme and make him consistent', and describes instead an emphasis on 'that which is physic – non-human, in humanity' (*Letters* II: 182). As Lawrence develops his theme in this letter, he rejects versions of the self based on 'the old stable *ego* of the character' (183). If Lawrence is, at some point, to throw out psychological realism, with what will he replace it? His statement to Garnett is a signal that his characters might not in the future (and certainly not in *The Rainbow*) be constructed according to existing orthodoxies relating either to a 'moral scheme' – social expectation – or to current theories of personality and the operations of the psyche. Verbalising his idea at length, perhaps for the first time, he suggests to his friend that, regarding the representation of personality in fiction:

> There is another *ego*, according to whose action the individual is unrecognisable, and passes through, as it were, allotropic states which it needs a deeper sense than any we've been used to exercise, to discover are states of the same single radically unchanged element. (183)

This is a statement about the *impersonal* nature of the self and from this point we are aware of the centrality of impersonal forces (most often relating to feeling, for instance, attraction and repulsion, rather than the usual commonplaces of love and hate) motivating Lawrence's characters – it is thus a statement of Lawrence's awareness of his departure from dominant modes of literary characterization. The letter is a crucial document in Lawrence studies.

At the start of the 1914–18 war, Lawrence also wrote his 'Study of Thomas Hardy', which is discussed in a later section of the present volume **[99–101]**. As we shall see, the 'Study' is less about Hardy the novelist (Lawrence admitted this, and it was not published as a work of criticism in his lifetime), than it was about Lawrence's developing philosophy, or 'metaphysic' as he was now prepared to call the novelist's 'vision'. He had begun to articulate his thought to Garnett, and to other friends, in letter form. In 1913 he had also written the important Foreword to *Sons and Lovers* **[47]**. In the 'Study of Thomas Hardy' he creates parables – extended metaphors – to describe the spirit of artistic creation. In a language of oppositions and symbols he argues that the mind is a 'male' principle, and 'flesh' a female principle, and for art to succeed as art in a 'living sense', as 'supreme art', the two must be in a state of true relation (his metaphor is 'marriage'), not imbalance. Developing alongside this thought are statements on 'true' marriage as a metaphysical partnership (an idea explored in *The Rainbow* – see Tom's speech in Chapter V, 'Wedding at the Marsh'). These ideas come together when he looks ahead to an art 'which knows the struggle between the two conflicting laws [law of man and law of woman], and knows the final reconciliation, where both are equal, two-in-one, complete' (STH 128). At this time it is quite clear that the art form most likely to be transformed by this process, and this understanding, is the novel. *The Rainbow* was revised in the light of these ideas (see Kinkead-Weekes 1968).

While metaphors of regeneration had been part of Lawrence's discursive writing since his unpublished Foreword to *Sons and Lovers*, and had sustained the philosophy that gave rise to the final version of *The Rainbow*, his next novel was to be much more relentless in its critique of a broken-down culture, instituting a forgetting of the possibilities of *The Rainbow*'s final chapter and to some extent a dismantling of 'the earth's new architecture' (R 459).

(ii) *Women in Love*

Women in Love (1920), like *The Rainbow*, developed from 'The Sisters' as Lawrence rewrote and revised. There was a time when he entertained the idea of reprinting *The Rainbow* as *Women in Love* 'Vol. I', alongside the new novel, a detail which shows the extent to which the books developed from a single project. However, these novels are not identical in their modes of thought or language. In the 'Foreword' to *Women in Love* – written in 1919, after the completion of the novel, and first printed to publicize the book in America – Lawrence identifies the novel's war-time provenance, showing it to have been four years in the writing. He says, 'it is a novel which took its final shape in the midst of the period of war, though it does not concern the war itself. I should wish the time to remain unfixed, so that the bitterness of the war may be taken for granted in the characters' (W 485). With his mind on the recent past, Lawrence also records his publishers' fears of prosecution, remembering the example of *The Rainbow*.

So *Women in Love* was first published in America in 1920 by Thomas Seltzer – a publisher who had a long association with Lawrence – as a private (limited) edition for subscribers. It was published in England the following year incorporating, on the insistence of the publisher, Martin Secker, many changes to the text only some of which Lawrence authorized. Seltzer also admitted to making changes but even so,

Lawrence was almost prosecuted for the content of *Women in Love* in America in 1921. While the novel sold, it produced other threats of prosecution, notably from people who recognized themselves in Lawrence's characters.

Women in Love continues from *The Rainbow* the story of Ursula Brangwen and introduces for extended narrative treatment her sister, Gudrun. Ursula is now a teacher at a local grammar school, living in Beldover with her parents. Gudrun, a sculptress with a growing reputation, has returned home to take a break from the metropolis. These are the 'women in love' of the title. Ursula forms a relationship with Rupert Birkin, a school inspector, the Lawrence-figure in the novel. Through him, Lawrence voices theories of education and social reform, and articulates views about redemptive relationships between men and women, and between men. Gudrun enters into a relationship with Gerald Crich, friend to Birkin, a 'Napoleon of industry' (64) whose family owns the local colliery. The first chapters of the book range between the Midlands landscapes which characterized *The Rainbow* and fashionable London. These locations give Lawrence an opportunity to depict many facets of a dying culture, although his critique extends beyond England as he takes his characters onto the Continent for the novel's deadly conclusion. Against a background of actual and symbolic landscapes he establishes the complex personal lives of his characters and the psychodramas which play out between them – with implications which extend beyond the personal and individual to the cultural.

Women in Love is a novel underpinned by violence. Where *The Rainbow* concluded with a vision of growth *Women in Love* enacts, in its language and themes, Lawrence's vision of death (of the self, of community). The reader is invited to contemplate the end of culture as a relic of history, and the psychical and spiritual breakdown in individuals which accompanies it. The trauma which splits the psyche, and which has its counterpart in the death of the world, splits it into a number of 'little' deaths: the death of the mind, the death of the body, and the death of the soul. It is a feature of *Women in Love*, and of the pattern of contradiction which underpins it, that life and death-instincts lie in such close proximity that they become uncannily interchangeable, and nowhere is this clearer than at the level of the book's language (see Ragussis 1978, Ingram 1990 and Bell 1992). Rupert Birkin, for instance, who so often preaches about the real value of life, adds, by the quantity and weight of his words, to the book's morbidity: he says to Ursula, 'I should like to be through with it – I should like to be through the death-process' (186).

Much of the book's force lies in the ways in which language is tested at the level of meaning. Quite familiar definitions are subject to surprising reversals as the speaking subjects find their positions and assumptions challenged by sceptical interlocutors. Birkin, for instance, tries to deprive the word 'love' of its usual meanings because it has come to him to seem limited and limiting. His language often conjoins sex and death as impulses with a shared basis in love-feeling. Indeed, it is the recurrence of a *lust* for violence against both the self and other which marks the book even while Birkin and Ursula, in particular, argue for modes of life which are personally and collectively fulfilling. When Hermione Roddice, initially Birkin's lover, hits out at him in the act which ends their unsatisfactory relationship (in 'Breadalby'), her murderous impulse is described as a 'voluptuous consummation'. She acts against him in a 'delirium of pleasure'. In her calculated attack on his body, in which she achieves a kind of freedom, we are told that 'A thousand lives, a thousand deaths mattered nothing now, only the fulfilment of this perfect ecstasy' (105). In this statement, crucially, Hermione's will-to-murder transcends the limits of her personal misery, and it is this extra-personal impulsiveness which is present at sub-terranean levels in all the characters. The fantasy of annihilation which Hermione enacts is reproduced in the significant relationships in the novel thereafter. It is an indication of their collective dis-ease of psyche and spirit.

Hermione's murderous climax has a counterpart in the sex between Gerald (youthful slayer of his brother) and Gudrun (whose counterpart in Norse mythology slew her husband). The attraction of these two is mediated from early on in the language of death and predation. In 'Death and Love', where Gerald arrives in Gudrun's bedroom with the mud of the graveyard clogging his boots, we are presented with the symbolic murder of Gudrun which perversely rouses her to almost maddening degrees of consciousness. In their 'love-making', the 'terrible frictional violence of death filled her, and she received it in an ecstasy of subjection, in throes of acute, violent sensation'. Bringing her his 'bitter potion of death' (344), Gerald leaves her oxymoronically '*destroyed* into *perfect* consciousness' (345, emphasis added). He finds renewal in Gudrun's 'murder', but this renewal is deathly: his post-coital sleep is like a death – he is 'mindless' and 'remote' (346) where Gudrun, in opposition, is completely physically awake, tortured by her consciousness of consciousness, by the extremity of her wakefulness.

The chapter called 'Water Party' provides another graphic instance of Gerald's association with death. With his sister and the doctor drowned in the lake, Gerald cannot resist the attraction their place of dying holds for him. Alongside their actual deaths (which gives them a value, according to Birkin, that they did not hold in life), Gerald's symbolic death is now enacted in his desire to return into the infinity of water to 'save' them, long after their chances of life have passed. In diving, he has, like a figure from myth, 'gone out of the world' (181). Hence the significance of his statement to Gudrun on his return to the surface: '"If you once die," he said, "then when it's over, it's finished. Why come to life again? There's room under that water there for thousands"' (184). With these words Gerald questions the Lawrentian insistence on renewal. His death-wish, demonstrated here by his continual return to the under(water)world, and his violent destiny (death by water/ice), are fulfilled in the chapter 'Snowed Up' where the terms of his death include 'murder' and 'sleep'. He dies under the brilliant light of the moon which illuminates forms starkly and relentlessly for him, as it had for Ursula in the chapter 'Moony' when she too sought the darkness.

The chapter entitled 'Sunday Evening' is a strange interlude in the novel, and practically forms a dissertation on death. More important than Ursula's complete indifference to the human tragedy of 'Water Party' (an indifference which is in keeping with Birkin's impersonal philosophy that a sentimental concentration on any aspect of human experience is an obscenity), are the ways in which 'death' is *positively* opposed to the experience of mechanical, quotidian, existence in the course of the chapter. It is in a description of Ursula giving herself up to a meditation on 'death-experience' that a sense is communicated of the 'awful nausea of dissolution set in within the body' (192) which goes beyond the personal: 'it was the same in all countries and all peoples' (193).

The beginning of 'Sunday Evening' (193–4) supports any reading that wishes to identify the dissociation of the (alienated, modern) individual from living (and lived) reality. Each of the encounters which give the novel its complex structure draws attention in a variety of ways to the issue of psychic disintegration that accompanies Ursula's reverie in this chapter. The onus is on the reader to regard this disintegration, this death or arrest of the self, as having the widest possible reference. When Birkin utters the following words to Ursula in 'Water Party', he has in mind not his immediate world but the conditions of contemporary Western culture: 'There is life which belongs to death, and there is life which isn't death. One is tired of the life that belongs to death – *our kind of life*' (186, emphasis added). It is one of those statements or observations in the narrative which begin in relation to the individual but which point also to a crisis in humanity. Prior to Hermione's attack on Birkin, for instance, the people gathered have been discussing social issues; in 'Moony', Birkin and Ursula fall into a disgreement about democracy; at the wedding of Laura Crich, and later in the mountains, they discuss the relevance of 'nation', and the decline of the West. Gerald, who as a social being represents imperial, regional and industrial mastery; mastery of men, women, and of a landscape, dies in a mountain wilderness. In the chapter 'Continental', the talk is of Englishness and England as 'a great actual unreality now, an aggregation into unreality' (395). At every juncture, then, the desperate conditions of their culture are debated by the traumatized individuals whose experiences structure the book.

While *Women in Love* represents an immense (and timely) cynicism with regard to concepts like 'nation', Birkin concludes the novel with a statement of desire for brotherhood, for community. This contradiction of his frequent theme of individual integrity is part of the point. From the beginning, he has been caught between a set of unreconcilable desires: he is an educator, yet he despises social principles; he desires brotherhood, yet he insists on the sanctity of the individual; he is attracted to the idea of extinction, yet insists on a 'metaphysic' of renewal with regard to the self. Throughout, he has been the most verbal of the key characters, yet often argues for silence. He tests out his hypotheses most usually on Ursula who parries and argues equally relentlessly, and frequently exposes the contradictory nature of his desires and speeches. Towards the end of 'Water Party', in touch with desire, he becomes critical of his relation to language, associating it with a kind of death: '"I was becoming quite dead-alive, nothing but a word-bag" he said in triumph, scorning his other self. Yet somewhere far off and small, the other hovered' (188). This shortlived revelation is one example of many that represent a preoccupation with language, its limitations and self-expression in *Women in Love*.

Despite their shared provenance the linguistic modes of *The Rainbow* and *Women in Love* are not identical. Both novels show Lawrence's language-sense at work operating most effectively perhaps at a barely conscious level, appropriately enough when his theme is the subterranean aspects of human functioning. While critics whose concentration is on 'verbal consciousness' (486) may not always agree in their interpretation of the text in hand, they will most usually agree to the centrality of questions of language in Lawrence **[149–55]**. In the Foreword to *Women in Love* (485–6) Lawrence makes reference to the resistant reader of his work at the level of language, or style. He had *The Rainbow* in mind as an example of the negative reception his work had already received, and he evokes it again: 'In point of style, fault is often found with the continual, slightly modified repetition' (486). His next description refers, obviously, to the sexual: 'every natural crisis in emotion or passion or understanding comes from this pulsing, *frictional* to-and-fro, which works up to a culmination' (486, emphasis added). Crucially, however, his principal topic here is *language*, not sex. Speaking metaphorically, he provides a profile, a suggestion, of the life of the language of *Women in Love*.

This instance points to a 'frictional' aesthetic – which is called elsewhere in his commentaries on his work 'the tension of opposites' (CP 348). This idea of necessary conflict to a significant degree directs his thought and its centrality needs to be noted. Naturally, it produces variations. The stylistic differences between, particularly, *The Rainbow* and *Women in Love* need to be understood as the different expressions of Lawrence's 'metaphysic', his personal philosophy which the novel form is to realize. In particular, the 'frictional' style of *Women in Love*, with its often over-conscious and highly verbal human subjects, can be set against the vast sweeps of narrative language in *The Rainbow* (where human feelings are not so intensely verbalized), and the use of rhythmic repetition foregrounded by 'the wave which cannot halt' (R 9), which signifies generation *and* the particular linguistic mode of that book (these modes of language are examined in Becket [1997]).

More specifically, *Women in Love* develops Lawrence's language theme by allowing a particular concentration on the short-comings of verbal expression, most especially where notions of the self, and self-responsibility, require articulation. Many of the dialogues between Ursula and Birkin combine this concentration on self and self-definition with representations of the shortfalls of language (see Bonds 1987; Bell 1992). *Women in Love* is a highly verbal novel and, as many critics have noted, Lawrence's most 'dialogic' fiction (for an explanation of this term, and its applications, see Bakhtin 1981; also Fleishman in Brown [ed.] 1990). It is a central text for literary critics who seek to establish in Lawrence a modernist emphasis on language while underlining his difference from his contemporaries. In the book, it is given to Birkin, who is not a poet or any kind of artist, to utter the rather awkwardly expressed sentiment that 'words make no matter, anyway' (W 250). This surfaces in the middle of an argument with Ursula on the nature of the love between them, each accusing the other of egocentricity, the conversation itself being a product of the damaging self-consciousness that each seeks to escape. This conflict, representative of their oppositionality, persists even through periods of mutually felt tranquillity which are, nevertheless, temporary. At the end of 'Moony', their positions are dichotomized and the principal area of conflict between them is defined: 'He said the individual was *more* than love, or than any relationship' ... 'She believed that love was *everything*' (265).

Numerous variations of this conflict are played out between them. Most contentious is Birkin's ideal of the impersonal 'equilibrium' between lovers that he first expresses at length to Ursula in the chapter called 'Mino'. This ideal continues to inspire her scepticism and, on occasion, derision, as she interprets his words as a demand for her subservience, even while he seems to praise her right to equality and personal freedom. Birkin, identified by some of the novel's earliest reviewers as Lawrence's mouthpiece, is often shown to be in a state of verbal confusion in these encounters. A man who hates his own metaphors (40), he continues to fall back on a highly conscious mode of metaphorical speech which usually gets him into trouble (29; 148). Frustrated with the language available to him, he argues for a condition of loving Ursula where there is 'no speech ... no terms of agreement' (146), and yet continues to force his theories into speech so that she can exploit his obvious difficulties. The parallels with Lawrence are manifest: he has been criticised for trying to force that which resists verbal expression into language, yet this is the paradox that he clearly, as an artist, enjoys.

So it is, in *Women in Love*, that any critique of personal relations developed by Lawrence depends on representations of conflict which return us inevitably to questions of language, meaning and the contexts for speech. That the novel is the appropriate forum for debates on the self, where the central issues inevitably dovetail into issues of language, is represented in the Foreword: 'This struggle for verbal consciousness should not be left out in art. ... *It is the passionate struggle into conscious being*' (486).

Critical appraisals of Lawrence's work frequently include reference to his constant and detailed revisions to show him incorporating new ideas, often not fully-formed but in process. *The Rainbow* and *Women in Love*, although they share a point of origin, have been aligned by critics with different discursive texts, most usually because of their highly individual treatment of specific themes and, as has been acknowledged, their different modes of language. Hence, the important place of 'Study of Thomas Hardy' in many critical assessments of *The Rainbow*. A series of essays constitute 'The Crown' (partially published in Lawrence's venture with Murry and Mansfield called *Signature* [1915] **[18]**; complete in *Reflections on the Death of a Porcupine and Other Essays*, 251–306). A philosophical text, it supplements, and in part revises 'Study of Thomas Hardy', and was written as Lawrence developed *Women in*

Love (see Kinkead-Weekes 1968). Lawrence was more pessimistic about his own prospects, and had a more pessimistic social vision, after the reception of *The Rainbow* and during the writing of 'The Crown'. Still emphasizing an oppositional life-death dynamic (underpinning creativity, human relations and social change), the narrative of 'The Crown' nevertheless gives great weight to 'corruption' and 'disintegration'. The 'flux' and 'horrible seethe of corruption' (RDP 295) get expression in the vision of European decline (moral, spiritual, political) in *Women in Love*. Indeed, Rupert Birkin echoes the sentiment in 'The Crown' that 'We may give ourselves utterly to destruction. Then our conscious forms are destroyed along with us, and something new must arise' (RDP 294). This is perhaps why Gudrun and Loerke survive the end of *Women in Love*; the artists who recognize in each other sadistic, destructive, non-attachment and who seem to drive themselves into impersonal and violent states (yet Ursula and Birkin, with his dreams of brotherhood, survive too).

Any assessment of the direction Lawrence's thought was taking, particularly towards the close of the Great War, also needs to take account of the gradually diminishing significance of marriage in his personal philosophy, and the language of his revised ideas on male-female relations and same-sex desire. Male friendships are central to the excised Prologue to *Women in Love* (W 489–506). Here, 'Prologue' refers to a projected first chapter of the novel eventually rejected by Lawrence. The Prologue's significance to critics lies in part in the exploration which it represents of the relationship between Rupert Birkin and Gerald Crich, and in particular Birkin's suppression of his love for Gerald and the forced shift of his sexual feelings onto women (see Cavitch 1969). It also helps to explain Hermione's feelings for Birkin in the published novel. The first paragraphs establish the importance of the 'abstract isolation' of the mountain landscape where the events of *Women in Love* are concluded. The rest of the chapter is marked by an intense, exploratory style in the service of a series of ideas which remain relevant to the published novel. The figure of Birkin is used to raise questions about the extremity of cultural and personal dissolution which signifies the historical moment. This is intimated in the passages concerned with education and, more broadly, the work of ideology: 'What should a man add himself on to? – to science, to social reform, to aestheticism, to sensationalism? The whole world's constructive activity was a fiction, a lie, to hide the great process of decomposition, which had set in' (496).

Against this broad-brush attempt at social critique, Lawrence juxtaposes Birkin's highly specific sense of his own emotional dissolution.

Much of the Prologue – in its representation of the troubled relationship between Hermione and Birkin, where hostilities operate largely but not exclusively at subconscious levels – focuses on the model of the cerebral woman out of touch with her sexual self. As Birkin examines his use of Hermione, Lawrence familiarly juxtaposes the language of sex and death explaining, in his own terms, the sexual failure, the hatred and fear of sex, which he perceives in repressive Western, and specifically at this time northern European, culture. In this context, there is an important shift in the narrative as it turns to the promise of the male body for Birkin, examining the tension between attraction and resistance which many readers have taken to be autobiographical.

The letters and the non-fiction represent a change of attitude towards love between men on Lawrence's part in the years of writing *Women in Love*. The concentration on same-sex desire in the Prologue is altered in the published novel to Birkin's final statement of belief in 'eternal union with a man' (481), a belief which has been intensified by his non-sexual encounters with Gerald ('In the Train'; 'Man to Man'; 'Gladiatorial'). Lawrence's opinions are marked by the tension between a tendency in his writing to associate homosexuality and dissolution (Dollimore 1998), and the clear pleasure which his writing takes in the male body and speculation about a higher form of love between men than between women and men (see Williams 1993). So it is that guilt at homosexual love in the Prologue is the strongest element, while heterosexual desire is singled out, no less so in the novel itself, as participating in the destruction of the self which Birkin fears so much. The beginning of the chapter 'Man to Man' (199–201), for instance, is a dissertation on overbearing womanhood which begins with a statement against coupledom as a betrayal of self-sufficiency. It is a theme to which Birkin returns in 'Moony', this time with Ursula as a cynical and interrogative auditor. What surfaces is a refusal, or inability, to settle the questions about self-sufficiency to which desire gives rise.

Typically, none of the contradictions in the novel are resolved. Given the repressions of the Prologue it can be no surprise that Loerke, the bisexual artist, is associated with corruption, with the rat and the sewer (428). His redeeming feature might be that he is also represented as isolated, complete in himself (450; 452), but this description is in harness to the more insistent descriptions of Loerke's degeneracy. To Birkin and Gerald, Loerke comes to represent the extremity of corruption that women in particular seek. To Gudrun, he represents eventually the death of her world (452) which she embraces. In them, Lawrence writes the inverse of the relationships he has described up to that point: a bisexual man and a heterosexual woman agreeing to a degree of proximity because of the absence of romantic love between them (458–9). The two artists in the book announce the near-death of the world; both are associated with corrosiveness and see the world as 'distorted, horrific' (451). These are the terms which they tacitly agree to share: their mutual recognition of the end of lived culture (in their discussions, they polarize 'art' and 'life'), and the corresponding knowledge each has of the other as profoundly detached from the social world. In its evocation of the death of the self, and the death of the world, *Women in Love*, which Lawrence considered calling 'Dies Irae' ('Day of Wrath', *Letters* II: 669), is a powerful document of British modernism.

(iii) *The Lost Girl, Mr Noon, Aaron's Rod*

The Lost Girl (1920) began as Lawrence's attempt at an English novel of provincial life written at an ironic distance from those by his contemporaries, Arnold Bennett (1867–1931, whose work includes *Anna of the Five Towns* [1902] and the Clayhanger series) and John Galsworthy (1867–1933, whose work includes the Forsyte novels). The period of composition of *The Lost Girl*, however, in the end straddled the writing of *The Rainbow* and *Women in Love*. It was put to one side in 1913 as 'The Insurrection of Miss Houghton', and not taken up for seven years when Lawrence rewrote it. The experience of writing *The Rainbow* and *Women in Love* in the interval was telling. If the beginnings of *The Lost Girl* are in what Virginia Woolf calls in 'Modern Fiction' the style of the Edwardian materialists, its revision demonstrates the effects of Lawrence working through the Brangwen books and his 'theory' of the novel, which anticipates some of his central themes to come. Unlike *The Rainbow* and *Women in Love* the tone of *The Lost Girl* is frequently satirical.

The novel describes the fortunes of Alvina Houghton, a middle-class girl born and brought up in Woodhouse, based on Lawrence's home-town of Eastwood. Tired of the limitations of her provincial life, Alvina challenges her family's expectations both in her decision to work – she becomes a maternity nurse – and in her relations with men. Her way out of Woodhouse, and England, is made possible by her marriage to Ciccio, a peasant from a village in the Abruzzi mountains, and one of the *artistes* in a touring 'Red Indian troupe' called Natcha-Kee-Tawara, who perform in the local theatre. They leave wintry England for Italy, and the simpler, harder life of the peasant farmer. History overtakes them, however, and the book ends on the eve of Ciccio's departure for the army and his promise that, on his return from the war, they will start a new life in America.

It has been noted that Alvina has a representative function in as much as she shares the dilemmas of Lawrentian women (like Kate Leslie in *The Plumed Serpent*, and the rider in 'The Woman Who Rode Away'), who are 'drawn to primitivist solutions' (Bell 1992: 137). Ciccio is laconic and uncultivated compared to the worthy but unexciting bachelors who have previously had claims on Alvina. Impersonal desire moves in him rather than romantic love or sentimental attachment, and it is this quality which makes him attractive to Alvina. The book is another step in Lawrence's examination of the sexual relations between men and women. In Ciccio, it also introduces the figure of the self-assured, non-intellectual male who gratifies his sexual needs and thereby, controversially, brings about the transformation of the 'modern' woman. John Worthen comments on this, calling the novels which precede *The Lost Girl* 'exploratory and painstaking', in contrast to this new style of writing which is 'brash, often comic, polemical and offensive' (Worthen 1991b).

This description also serves *Mr Noon*. *The Lost Girl* is marked by a more self-conscious intrusiveness on the part of the author than has been the case before, and of which the unfinished *Mr Noon* (written in 1920–1 and never revised for publication), with its satirical tone and ironical direct address to 'dear reader', provides a more extreme example. This, as critics have noted, gives Lawrence a chance to show contempt towards the fault-finding reader. Meanwhile, over-conscious (and also highly defensive) attempts at irony are an aspect of Lawrence's overt play with the novel form (which exploits his awareness of a tradition). We cannot know what Lawrence would have done with *Mr Noon* had he returned to it for purposes of revision. As it stands, the text is marked by extensive authorial intrusion which, when it remembers, makes points about what novels are and do. Regarding plot, Part I of *Mr Noon* shares the Midlands location of *The Lost Girl*, where the hero, Gilbert Noon, leads a desultory existence as a school-master engaged in a half-hearted love relationship. Part II (unfinished) is based on Lawrence's first travels with Frieda Weekley **[13]**. In this section of the book Mr Noon's elopement with Johanna provides another opportunity to examine relationships in contexts which challenge the sentimental love ideal.

Of the post-war novels, *Aaron's Rod*, in Lawrence's own estimation of it, concluded some of the business of *The Rainbow* and *Women in Love*. It does so by challenging the centrality in both those books of different forms of love relationship between men and women, giving rise to the emphasis in *Aaron's Rod* on the solitary male and the advantages of 'singleness'. This is more about actual solitude and separation than about the (more 'metaphysical') movement towards individuation which characterises *The Rainbow*. In *Aaron's Rod*, marriage is no longer seen as the defining relationship between men and women, and its limitations are spelled out in the character of Aaron Sisson as husband and father. The novel begins with Aaron's decision to leave his wife and children and his work at the colliery, and to earn his living by his flute. He does, in short, what *The Trespasser*'s Siegmund is unable to do. His encounters with a metropolitian bohemian set in London introduce him to a maverick thinker, called Rawdon Lilly, who spouts most of the over-conscious philosophy in the book. From London, Aaron travels (like Alvina Houghton and Gilbert Noon) to Italy where he becomes, briefly, the lover of a married woman (see the chapter called 'The Marchesa'), but this relationship only allows him to replay his grudges and anxieties about women. In the end the promise of genuine change is only ushered in when his flute is destroyed by a terrorist's bomb.

This book articulates Lawrence's bitterly felt rejection of marriage, which is one of the reversals marked by his writing at this time. Such a reversal probably had its roots in his personal experience, and it becomes central to his developing philosophy of the self, represented in this instance by Aaron Sisson's quest to find himself free from the obligation to feel according to an established relationship: in this respect the book, like *Mr Noon*, examines the authentication of feeling. Aaron's relationships are marked by a hostility towards the sentimental. The book is full of encounters and these form the basis for conversations about personal, social and political revolution, and in particular the tension between love and resistance, dependency and independence.

Rawdon Lilly is Lawrence's mouthpiece in *Aaron's Rod*, which is his first attempt at a political novel. The book concludes with Lilly telling Aaron about the need for a 'superior man' to lead people to a better kind of humanity. Lilly's vision of a superior leader is more messianic – he evangelizes – than about political authority. His concluding words in the novel are on the 'power-urge' which runs parallel to the 'love-urge' as the principal motivating impulse in human history. One phase of history (impelled by the 'love-urge', which has produced democracy as well as empire) is passing, to be superseded by a new phase (of war and, paradoxically, of eventual renewal), the era of the 'power-urge'. The figure of Aaron – as musician – and his flute illustrate how ideas about creative energy lie at the heart of this philosophy. When, at the end of the novel, the flute is destroyed Lilly assures Aaron that he need not worry – Aaron's rod will grow again, "'It's a reed, a water-plant – you can't kill it'" (AR 285). This is the promise of regeneration in the book. In the chapter called 'Words', Lilly defines the 'love-urge' as the harmful impulse to intervene in the destiny of others – it impels a lover, or a radical (the anarchist's bomb shows a desire to intervene). The 'love-urge' becomes a 'horror', hence the world war, and the political upheaval which Lawrence witnessed in Italy, for instance, as the Fascists grew in strength. The 'power-urge', on the other hand, describes the impersonal primordial force that Lawrence attempts to dramatize as positive in *The Plumed Serpent* – here, in *Aaron's Rod*, it is called 'self-central' (298) in opposition to any creed which depends on identification with something beyond the self (a God, a nation). In terms of sexual politics this philosophy is familiarly repressive: the 'power-urge' insists on submission in women to the impersonal authority of visionary men. *The Plumed Serpent* goes further than *Aaron's* Rod in exploring this aspect of the 'power-urge', in its fantasy of the messianic male.

Aaron's Rod is usefully read alongside the books on the unconscious, in particular *Fantasia of the Unconscious*, which argues for self-sufficiency in men who become independent of over-bearing figures enabling then to charge a high rate of emotional interest, in particular mothers and wives. So it is that the 'serious English' novels end with an injunction to be true to an 'integral unique self' – 'Your own single oneness is your destiny. Your destiny comes from within, from your own self-form' (AR 295). The 'greater soul' is male: by the end of the book, 'coupledom' has been found wanting and Lilly's words provide Aaron with a new model of masculine kinship.

Further Reading

It would be a hard task to disprove the claim that most critical writing on Lawrence's major fiction has concentrated on *The Rainbow* and *Women in Love*, and it is not practicable to describe here the many studies on these works and the other 'serious English' novels, particularly the great number of articles and essays in literary periodicals. Listed below, then, is a selection, and the reader is referred to the Bibliography. General studies of the fiction address the novels of the war period as Lawrence's most achieved and important writing. These include Leavis (1955), who was one of Lawrence's most consistent champions. Spilka (1955) and Hough (1956) go further afield than the novels, and show the influence of Leavis. The next two decades produced a number of closely argued critiques where the general trend (there are significant exceptions) is to divide work into discrete discussions of individual books. Influential studies of Lawrence's imagination, style and thought include Vivas (1960), Moynahan (1963), Ford (1965), Clarke (1969), Miko (1971), Sanders (1974), Beede Howe (1977). More recent assessments of *The Rainbow* and/or *Women in Love* – either within 'surveys', or within books which examine a particular critical concern (history, language, modernism, or sexuality) – include Miko (1971), Worthen (1979; 1991b), Ebbatson (1982), Holderness (1982), Sagar (1985), Bonds (1987), Whelan (1988), Edwards (1990), Hyde (1990), Ingram (1990), Pinkney (1990), Ross (1991), Bell (1992), Becket (1997), Williams (1993; 1997). Useful volumes of essays include Spilka (ed., 1963) with essays by Marvin Mudrick and Mark Schorer; Miko (ed., 1969) with essays by Mark Spilka, Eliseo Vivas, Julian Moynahan, George Ford and Alan Freeman. Colin C. Clarke edited the *Macmillan Casebook Series* volume on *The Rainbow* and *Women in Love* (1969). Bloom (1988) edited the *Modern Critical Interpretations* series volume on *Women in Love*. Baker (1983) is a monograph on *Aaron's Rod*. Jackson and Brown Jackson (eds, 1988) prints essays by Jack F. Stewart, Joyce Carol Oates and Lydia Blanchard; Preston and Hoare (eds, 1989) include essays by Mark Kinkead-Weekes (who also has an important essay on *The Rainbow* in Kalnins, ed., 1986), and John Worthen. More recently Brown (ed., 1990) and Widdowson (ed., 1992) draw together some interesting and authoritative material.

(c) NEW GROUND: THE NOVELS AFTER 1922

(i) *Kangaroo, The Boy in the Bush*

Lawrence wrote *Kangaroo* and *The Boy in the Bush* (with M.L. Skinner) as a result of his visit to Australia in 1922 **[23]**. *The Boy in the Bush* is a re-written version of Skinner's 'The House of Ellis' based on her brother's experiences in North-West Australia. Lawrence's novel is set in 1882 and tells the story of Jack Grant who arrives in Fremantle from Bedford, England, but is transformed by his sojourn in the Australian wilderness and his dream of establishing his own community. The novel represents a search for a new mode of living (BB 341–2).

Kangaroo is a novel in which issues of political belief are explored in relation to Lawrence's further thoughts on love, power and how they define manliness after *Aaron's Rod*. It was written at a time when Lawrence was translating the Sicilian writer, Giovanni Verga (1840–1922), whose stories (many of which were translated by Lawrence as *Mastro-Don Gesualdo* [1923], *Little Novels of Sicily* [1925] and *Cavalleria Rusticana and Other Stories* [1928]) deal with the hard life of the Sicilian peasant, a disenfranchised figure. Lawrence had also witnessed the rise of Fascism in Italy, and the effects of the struggle between competing ideologies prior to Mussolini's seizure of power in 1922. *Kangaroo* foregrounds political ambitions and contests in relation to two self-styled leaders of men who hold opposing views. The principal figure, called Benjamin Cooley (nicknamed 'Kangaroo'), is a charismatic leader of a right-wing group of disaffected war veterans ('Diggers'), and much of the book concerns his attempts to win the heart and mind of a travelling philosopher-poet, Richard Lovatt Somers. The other is a socialist called Willie Struthers who also woos Somers, offering him the chance to edit a people's newspaper and gain influence that way. A key question is how Lawrence balances a concern for the social with his interest in the individual, and also the extent to which his views are under revision – not only those on relations between men, but also in the way he addresses 'democracy' and revolutionary change. Lawrence's voyage to Australia is marked by moments of disillusion about how people live: as we have seen, in Ceylon he grew impatient with Buddhist culture (about which he was quite ignorant); crossing the South Seas, he made disparaging comments about Pacific cultures. Although impressed by the landscape, ambivalence about contemporary Australian culture also marks his relatively short stay there **[21–4]**.

As a political novel, *Kangaroo* gives expression to Lawrence's frequently articulated suspicion of idealism. The leaders of men in *Kangaroo* are distinguished publicly by their political affiliations, and privately by their views on the brotherhood of men. The attraction of Richard Lovatt Somers for Benjamin Cooley and Willie Struthers is, in the first place, that he has written essays on democracy. A conversation between Struthers and Somers reads as if Lawrence were talking to himself in preparation for one of his longer essays on social and political organisation. Struthers' assertion that 'the socialistic and communal ideal is a great ideal, which will be fulfilled when men are ready' (K 196) shifts rapidly to his paraphrasing of the main idea in Somers' writing – 'You want a new bond between men. – Well, so do I, so do we' (196) – and he argues for solidarity between working men against middle-class interests. The interview concludes with his attempt to persuade Somers to edit a twice-weekly Labour newspaper to appeal to the Australian heart (200). Somers interprets Struthers' position on brotherhood negatively as a modern version of Walt Whitman's 'Love of Comrades' (197), and his scepticism becomes central to this novel's exploration (and eventual rejection) of 'mateship' as a form of the 'blood-brotherhood' first expressed by Birkin in *Women in Love* (see K 104–7). Familiarly, the rejection of this brotherhood ideal signals Lawrence's fear of the consequences where, in a relationship, the integrity of individuality is abandoned: the relativity of human love for Lawrence is always displayed in the natural propensity of lover and beloved as individuals to react, resist and repel as well as to attract. Genuine personal and, he argues, cultural and political, disaster occurs 'when human love starts out to lock individuals together' (198).

Later in *Kangaroo* we are offered an account of Kangaroo's attraction to Somers manifested in his overbearing embrace of the poet-philosopher and a declaration of love. Kangaroo's supporters view him as Australia's saviour. Jack Callcott tells Somers that he follows Kangaroo because he hates the thought 'of being bossed and messed about by the Old Country, or by Jew capitalists and bankers, or by a lot of labour bullies, or a Soviet' (188). The question in the novel, however, is less whether Somers will subscribe to this, with Kangaroo as 'the big boss of Australia' (187), than on Somer's perception of Kangaroo's feelings for him as a 'lieutenant'. Kangaroo's declaration of love for him in fact stimulates a revulsion in Somers due to his sense of his 'particular self' being overlooked in Kangaroo's passion for a man of ideas to carry his cause further.

So far the discussion has concentrated on the feelings of men for men, and the grand designs of men's imagination and aspiration. Compared with the novels which precede it, *Kangaroo* is much less interested in sexual relationships between men and women. When this theme is raised the focus is on the Somers' marriage and that of their neighbours, the Callcotts. The state of the marriage between Harriett and Richard Lovatt Somers is established at the book's beginning. The chapter 'Harriett and Lovatt at Sea in Marriage' is a notable instance of authorial intrusion. It provides a short dissertation on modern marriage and describes the sources of conflict in the Somers' relationship, with a particular emphasis laid on the distribution of power within marriage.

Critics sometimes agree that Lawrence's writing is most interesting when it is most flawed. *Kangaroo* is flawed perhaps most obviously in its structure, but also in the ease with which it gives itself up to verbiage (at one point the narrator addresses us sardonically, 'I hope, dear reader, you like plenty of *conversation* in a novel: it makes it so much lighter and brisker' [282]). On several occasions in the narrative, Somers is subject to the diatribes of Kangaroo and Struthers. Most often, this gives the effect of Lawrence (in Somers) listening to, and sometimes rejecting, sometimes adding to, the principal tenets of many of his own essays. This is also true of *Aaron's Rod* and shows the centrality of 'the novel of ideas' to Lawrence at this time. In *Kangaroo*, this is evident in the chapter called 'Bits' where Somers goes off on a 'thought-adventure' (279) about the need to live from the 'central self'. 'Bits' addresses the social theme in Lawrence when it acknowledges the alienation of human subjects from their environment, but goes further in articulating a more elusive idea about the fragmented self – 'The people of this terrestrial sphere are all bits. Isolate one of them, and he is still only a bit. Isolate your man in the street, and he is a rudimentary fragment (281). Lawrence has returned here to the central observation of the 'Words' chapter of *Aaron's Rod* (and his articulation of the development of the self in *Fantasia of the Unconscious*), in Lilly's description to Aaron of the self 'developing bit by bit, from one single egg-cell which you were at your conception in your mother's womb, on and on to the strange and peculiar complication in unity which never stops till you die – if then' (AR 295). The development of the self here parallels the development of the body, and can be understood as the 'single oneness' (295) to which the individual must be true. The 'man in the street' in Somers' meditations has lost the capacity of identification with his 'self-form' (AR 295) and is in consequence a 'fragment', a 'bit' (of a *social* system). These observations develop alongside the analysis of Kangaroo's fitness to be a leader of men. Kangaroo's heresy, to Somers, is his desire to represent a multitude, that which is more than himself. Somers imagines him as a queen-bee, with the other bees clustering around him, which in Lawrence becomes a gross image. As long as he needs the 'hive', and wants to serve the 'hive', Kangaroo represents the superannuated 'love-urge' discussed in *Aaron's Rod*. Lawrence's preference, articulated in the last lines of 'Bits', is for a more impersonal mode of non-attachment which he attempts to place at the heart of his exploration of political and religious power and leadership in *The Plumed Serpent*.

(ii) *The Plumed Serpent*

The Plumed Serpent (1926) describes a contemporary revolution in religious form and feeling based on the imagined revival of a Meso-American Quetzalcoatl cult. Its principal focus is on a middle-aged Irishwoman, Kate Leslie, who travels to Mexico having tired of Europe. She soon loses interest in her fellow expatriates, and is drawn to a military General, Don Cipriano Viedma and a revolutionary, Don Ramón Carrasco, leaders of the revived cult of the god Quetzalcoatl (the plumed serpent). The novel charts the pattern of Kate's revulsion from, and attraction for, the language and spectacle of the cult with its emphasis on manly dignity and blood-sacrifice. Her entry into the old religion comes finally with her apotheosis into Malintzi, consort of Cipriano (also the 'living Huitzilopochtli'), whom she has married.

With Don Ramón (the 'living Quetzalcoatl') they form the first trinity of the blood, uniting 'light' with 'dark' blood which are the conditions, argues Lawrence, for cultural regeneration. Kate's transformation signifies the death of her modern self. Throughout, Cipriano has insisted that she sheds her 'European' self-assertiveness, and subjugates herself to 'the old mode of consciousness' (PS 415). This mode has a great deal to do ultimately with his sexual power over Kate.

After a long period in the cold – many readers find its treatment of what used to be called 'leadership' themes objectionable – *The Plumed Serpent* is enjoying something of a revival. The critic F.R. Leavis confessed that he found it difficult to get through and calls it 'the least complex of all Lawrence's novels', inferior in form and content to those that preceded it. He uses Lawrence's terms to criticize Lawrence: 'The evoking of the pagan renaissance strikes one as willed and mechanical' (Leavis 1955: 79). More enthusiastically, L.D. Clark, in the only book-length study of this novel, announced that 'two things save the book from the author: Lawrence's profound sympathy with the land he was writing about, and his uncanny skill at synthesizing form and setting and symbol' (Clark 1964: 13). Lawrence arrived in Mexico **[25]** at a time of political instability but his primary interest was not in contemporary events. The novel deals with the imagined revival of pre-Columbian religious consciousness led by men of high social and military status, and it is Lawrence's endeavour to invent a pre-Conquest sensibility in his characters which has proved most problematic to recent critics of the novel. Marianna Torgovnick, writing on literary and artistic primitivism, notices in Lawrence's version of 'the primitive' a reaffirmation of the power of Western models of self and other, and notes, too, how the primitive female in his writing is 'degenerate' while the primitive male is 'lordly' (Torgovnick 1990: 159–74). Certainly 'lordship' is practised on the women in the novel who are the focus for misogynistic judgements. The poor Mexican women are represented as lazy, and bestial ('Casa de las Cuentas'). Doña Carlota, Ramón's wife, 'pure European in extraction' (155) opposes the revival of the old religion viewing it as a heresy. On her death-bed, Cipriano abuses her – 'stale virgin, you spinster' (347) – for what he regards as her denial of herself to Ramón's vision, and wishes her dead. Teresa, Ramón's new wife is an object of contempt initially to Kate because of her 'harem' characteristics (397), although Kate is soon called on to revise her own idea of her sexual self. Sex between Kate and Cipriano anticipates that of Connie and Mellors (*Lady Chatterley's Lover*) in the idea of a superior man who controls woman's sexual pleasure, educating her to despise 'conscious satisfaction'. She must learn the value of 'impersonal' sex, 'different from the beak-like friction of Aphrodite of the foam' (422). The metaphor of 'beak-like' selfish women will return in *Lady Chatterley's Lover*. Cipriano ultimately insists on Kate's submission: as 'Malintzi' she has some status, as a white woman she must learn surrender.

Primarily because of its treatment of 'lordship' themes, and the idea of a revolutionary male community, critics have been drawn to compare *The Plumed Serpent* with *Kangaroo*. Male bonding in *The Plumed Serpent* is *organized* in the revivalist cult of the Men of Quetzalcoatl. The idea of charismatic leadership is explored in the figure of Benjamin Cooley in *Kangaroo*, and earlier in Rawdon Lilly (*Aaron's Rod*) who lectures Aaron Sisson on the necessity of submitting to a superior leader of men. While Lawrence keeps that idea for development here, the Quetzalcoatl revival, with its religious basis, allows him to make the theme of political idealism, and fidelity to political solutions, supplementary to the seductions of creating a church.

In a distortion of his previous emphasis on community, *The Plumed Serpent* indeed represents the considerable attractions to Lawrence of cultishness, in particular in its rituals and theatre (the cult has its own language in the 'hymns' of Quetzalcoatl). The devolution of power onto men who perceive themselves as gods is chilling. Cipriano has a fanatical interest in the physical and moral well-being of his men, putting them through a disciplined regime of drilling and dance, where the dance is the medium of a new consciousness in the dancer. And he executes men – blood-sacrifice at the altar of Quetzalcoatl in an episode which literalises Lawrence's homage to the 'life-blood'.

To what extent do the Mexico and New Mexico essays contribute to an understanding of this writing? In an essay written in 1928 called 'New Mexico' Lawrence compares his considerable experiences as a global traveller and is uneqivocal about the superiority of New Mexico and the South-West in its capacity to touch something in him which he eventually calls 'religious' (*Phoenix* 142–4). This religious connection is suggested to Lawrence, as so often, by dance. In a language which recalls descriptions in *The Plumed Serpent*, he writes of Native American dancing he had seen, 'Never shall I forget the utter absorption of the dance, so quiet, so steadily, timelessly rhythmic, and silent, with the ceaseless down-tread, always to the earth's centre, the very reverse of the upflow of Dionysiac or Christian ecstacy' (145). His praise, indeed his wonder, rapidly turns to a celebration of the male voice, 'the wonderful deep sound of men calling to the unspeakable depths' (145). Lawrence had arrived in a landscape in which he could experience the religious – in 'New Mexico' ritual supersedes sex in his theorising of primary sensual experience. The dance is consistently an event where a new consciousness is experienced in the individual or, in the later writing, by a community.

The main opposition in *The Plumed Serpent* is the extremity of the contrast between mechanistic modern 'white' consciousness (Kate, Owen, Villiers) and the Men of Quetzalcoatl. Lawrence may be in search of an alternative, a more impersonal, 'unconscious' mode of being in his evocation of a pre-Columbian culture. When he reinvents the Mexican myths, and represents them, however, he heightens their violence. 'Blood' has finally superseded 'psychology' in Lawrence's fiction.

(iii) *Lady Chatterley's Lover*

Lawrence supervised the private publication of his last novel in Florence in 1928 once it became obvious that his publishers would not take the risk. It was quickly banned in England and America. In England, when an unexpurgated version was finally published thirty years after his death, it resulted in the prosecution of Penguin Books (1960) under the Obscene Publications Act of 1959. The publisher was acquitted [27; 131]. 'Pornography and Obscenity' (1929) and 'A Propos of *Lady Chatterley's Lover*' (1930) constitute further statements about the disastrous effects of sexual fear, and the latter gives some account of the difficulties experienced in self-publishing.

Lady Chatterley's Lover returns to the Midlands, where the newly married Lady Constance ('Connie') Chatterley lives with her husband, Sir Clifford, at Wragby Hall. Months after their marriage he is confined to a wheelchair by injuries received on the battlefield and paralysed from the waist down. As the marriage stagnates, she deceives him by having an unsatisfactory affair with his friend, Michaelis, a playwright, but finds this, and her other friendships, empty. She then falls in love with Oliver Mellors, Clifford's gamekeeper, and the novel concentrates on her 're-birth' as a result of their sexual experience. A child is conceived and, scandalously, Connie abandons Clifford to the good offices of his motherly housekeeper, Mrs Bolton, while the lovers, in temporary separation until the scandal dies down, plan to build a new life together abroad. The theme of committed love between members of different social classes is not new in Lawrence, and neither is the theory of self-renewal through positive sexual experience. The novella, *The Virgin and the Gipsy* (1925; published 1930), for instance, rehearses the main themes which Lawrence develops in the earlier versions of *Lady Chatterley's Lover*, called *The First Lady Chatterley* and *John Thomas and Lady Jane*.

In an essay called 'The State of Funk' written in 1929, Lawrence states, in very simple terms, his criticism of the 'Victorian' prudishness about sex which oppressed him as a boy and young man:

> Accept the sexual, physical being of yourself, and of every other creature. Don't be afraid of it. Don't be afraid of the physical functions. Don't be afraid of the so-called obscene words. There is nothing wrong with the words. It is your fear that makes them bad, your needless fear.
>
> (*Phoenix II* 570)

These sentiments, and the assertion of 'the natural warm flow of common sympathy between man and man, man and woman' (569) underpin much of Lawrence's later writing on sex, and the essay usefully concentrates on some terms which help to clarify Lawrence's concerns, at least towards the end of his life. In particular it underlines the reasons for Mellors' persistent reference to sex using the 'common' words. 'Desire', in this essay, is a negative term (it is 'rampant', 'lurid') alongside the more positive 'sympathy' (569). 'Warm-heartedness' and 'compassionateness' resonate positively, reminiscent of 'tenderness', the single word which was the projected title of what became *Lady Chatterley's Lover*. 'Warm-heartedness' finds its way into Mellors' vocabulary as he lectures Lady Chatterley ('It's all this cold-hearted fucking that is death and idiocy' [LCL 206]), and voices Lawrence's theme that an ignorance of self in relation to sexuality contributes to cultural, as well as personal, 'dissolution'.

At first glance the principal paradox about *Lady Chatterley's Lover* is that in it Lawrence, by setting out to talk about sex, does precisely the thing he apparently most despises. In the first half of the book, he sets up a series of sterile conversations which take place between Clifford and his forward-thinking friends on men, women and sex. It is part of Lawrence's point to contrast the painful self-consciousness of these conversations with the discussions between Mellors and Connie. However, one of the risks to the novel's seriousness must surely lie in Mellors' remarks to his penis, 'John Thomas', conducted in the dialect that Lady Chatterley more often than not finds ridiculous: 'Tell lady Jane tha wants cunt. John Thomas, an' th' cunt o' lady Jane! –' (210). For some readers this extensive verbalization is awkward in part because of all Lawrence's protestations against having 'sex in the head', his phrase for describing an over-conscious concentration on sex (F&P 129: for the most extensive discussion of this see Williams 1993). To what extent does the gamekeeper, the 'natural man', have 'sex in the head' despite Lawrence's best efforts to make it otherwise, and to what extent is he the antidote to the problem? In other words, is this the book where Lawrence, against his best intentions, submits to his own version of 'sex in the head', or does the novel in fact constitute a complex critique of the 'modern' tendency, as Lawrence sees it, to reduce sex to a level where it is merely the scratching of some libidinal 'itch'? This is a complicated question which has to do, in the first instance, with the relation in Lawrence's writing between sex and language.

The focus is, in *Lady Chatterley's Lover*, on the regenerative aspects of sex (Connie, with Mellors, is 'reborn, woman'). The emphasis is still on phallic power as transformative, last explored by Lawrence in novel-form in *The Plumed Serpent*. As in that book, *Lady Chatterley's Lover* subscribes to a fantasy of female orgasm and its effects – for Lawrence, the potential of sex to revivify the self is manifested only where modern 'mental consciousness' (F&P 68) is shed (in women) for something more unconscious. The little 'deaths' of orgasm are central to the process of Connie's rebirth. A language of violence is developed – 'It might come with the thrust of a sword in her softly-opened body, and that would be death' (173) – but the brutality of *Women in Love*, for instance, where the languages of sex and death are often interchangeable, is displaced by the enactment of regeneration which dominates descriptions of sex in the later book.

Lawrence had written his essays on the novel genre by the time of *Lady Chatterley's Lover*. In Chapter 9, however, he allows himself to give the reader a small reminder of its real value:

> And here lies the vast importance of the novel, properly handled. It can inform and lead into new places the flow of our sympathetic consciousness, and it can lead our sympathy away in recoil from things gone dead. Therefore the novel, properly handled, can reveal the most secret places of life: for it is in the *passional* secret places of life, above all, that the tide of sensitive awareness needs to ebb and flow, cleansing and freshening.
>
> (LCL 101)

It is the higher form of the novel which is properly revelatory, he now argues. With 'proper handling' it deals in and with the deepest experiences of the spirit and psyche. This passage on the promise of his chosen form occurs in a context where Lawrence underlines his particular distance from a novelistic tradition. Lady Chatterley finds herself absorbed in listening to Mrs Bolton's gossip about Te017rshall, the village, and its inhabitants. Clifford, too, shows himself to have an appetite for the details of people and their lives which Mrs Bolton with relish imparts. However, '[i]t was more than gossip. It was Mrs Gaskell and George Eliot and Miss Mitford all rolled in one, with a great deal more, that these women left out' (100). Mrs Bolton's gossip, which runs to 'volumes', proves to be masturbatory according to Lawrence's lexicon: it 'excite[s] spurious sympathies', is 'mechanical' and 'deadening to the psyche' (101). It constitutes a kind of pornography, akin to that provided by popular fiction which is 'humiliating' and appeals to the public's vices (101). Gaskell, Eliot and Mitford perhaps constitute an over-conscious aesthetic. It is fascinating that Lawrence evokes, in this instance, women writers, and then prepares the ground to develop the distance between his use of the novel and their practice.

There are many other references in this novel to the status and value of the work of art which are often made obliquely through a criticism of the 'maker'. The focus is not so much on the artist figure who occasionally succeeds, unsupervised and untutored (this is, on occasion, the experience of Will Brangwen or Paul Morel), but more on a stifling self-consciousness manifested in Michaelis as dramatist or Clifford Chatterley who also writes. They are the mediocre players. Lawrence's spat with high modernism is evident in the occasional side-swipes at his eminent contemporaries: Connie's dismissal of the French writer Marcel Proust (*A la recherche du temps perdu*, 1913–27) in a tone which is reminiscent of Lawrence's discursive style, is a case in point, 'He doesn't have feelings, he only has streams of words about feelings. I'm tired of self-important mentalities' (LCL 194). These are the poles of fictional practice which Lawrence as maker must transcend: the mediocrity, or 'pornography', of popular fiction versus the 'self-important mentality' (to Lawrence, no less pornographic) of high modernism. As it is, *Lady Chatterley's Lover* bravely (some might say disastrously) plays with the seriousness of form. At the end of the novel, for example, Mellors is unexpectedly located in epistolary mode. The book ends with the text of a letter which he writes to Connie, in which Mellors alternates between a kind of folk wisdom ('A man has to fend and fettle for the best') and the emancipatory discourse which characterizes some of Lawrence's essays: 'Whereas the mass of people oughtn't even to try to think – because they *can't*. They should be alive and frisky, and acknowledge the great god Pan' (300). Finally, the sex-language debate is evoked – 'so many words, because I can't touch you' (301) – a privileging of the tangible which has dominated since the book's beginning.

Implicated in the rebirth of the self in this novel is the regeneration of England, and the engine of that regeneration is 'phallic-consciousness', evolved in Lawrence's terms out of 'blood-consciousness'(F&P 183). The impotence of Clifford Chatterley as a member of the ruling class is symbolic of the impotence of his culture. Its salvation lies in the 'natural' man. Some of the last essays, 'A Propos of *Lady Chatterley's Lover*' and 'Pornography and Obscenity', take up the arguments of the novel proposing that only revolutionary changes in attitudes to sex can make possible any kind of positive revolution in the culture.

Further Reading

Selected reading relevant to the whole body of novels has been indicated in previous 'Further reading' sections, to which can be added Humma (1990) on the later novels. Monographs dedicated to single novels are less common than critical surveys. There is relatively little published on *The Boy in the Bush* although Partlow and Moore (eds, 1980) includes an essay by Charles Rossman. For a detailed discussion of *Kangaroo* and its contexts the most extensive study is Darroch (1981). Worthen discusses its form (1979). Rick Rylance considers it in the context of Lawrence's political fiction in Brown (ed., 1990). Heywood (ed., 1987) includes an essay on allusion in *Kangaroo* by Peek. The first full-length study of *The Plumed Serpent* is Clark (1964). Torgovnick examines Lawrence's primitivist aesthetic in *The Plumed Serpent* in her comparative study (1990). Chong-wha Chung discusses dualism with reference to *The Plumed Serpent* and, briefly, *The Boy in the Bush*, alongside the other novels in Preston and Hoare (eds, 1989). L.D. Clark, in the same volume, includes *The Boy in the Bush* and *The Plumed Serpent* in his discussion of the 'pilgrimage novels'. Rossman (1985) examines the contexts for the New Mexico and Mexico writing, and Kinkead-Weekes discusses the 'decolonising imagination' in *The Plumed Serpent* and other New Mexico texts in Fernihough (ed., 2001). Some critics compare and contrast the three versions of the Lady Chatterley novel (Sanders 1974), as does Worthen (1991b). Squires (1983) and Britton (1988) are also interested in its origins. Squires and Jackson (eds, 1985) brings together a range of essays and different approaches to *Lady Chatterley's Lover*. The first extended feminist critique is from Millett (1969) with a 'reply' from MacLeod (1985). Smith (ed., 1978) includes an essay by Spilka. Book-length studies with discussions of this novel and others include Moynahan (1963), Daleski (1965), Williams (1997), Bell (1992).

(d) POETRY

To date, reference is most often made to *The Complete Poems* edited by Vivian de Sola Pinto and F. Warren Roberts, which itself refers to collections published by Heinemann as well as a range of other printed and manuscript sources. De Sola Pinto and Roberts bring together key prefaces, introductions and forewords to his volumes of poetry by Lawrence. It is not possible here to examine all of Lawrence's poetry in the kind of detail it deserves and so the focus will be on three of his books – *Look! We Have Come Through!* (1917), *Birds, Beasts and Flowers* (1923) and *Pansies* (1929) – and some prefaces. His public life began properly, as we have seen, with the publication of poems in the *English Review* edited by Ford Madox Hueffer [11]. After that, the books are *Love Poems and Others* (1913), *Amores* (1916), *Look! We Have Come Through!*, *New Poems* (1918), *Bay* (1919), *Tortoises* (1921) *Birds, Beasts and Flowers*, *Collected Poems* (1928), *Pansies*, *Nettles* (1930). *Last Poems* was published posthumously in 1932, edited by Richard Aldington [16]. Identifying Lawrence and James Joyce as the twin cardinals of modern writing Aldington risks a comparison which the contemporary reader might like to review: 'The great difference … is that Joyce's writing is founded on the conception of Being, and Lawrence's on the conception of Becoming' (CP 593).

In a preface called 'Poetry of the Present', written at the conclusion of the Great War for the American edition of *New Poems*, Lawrence praises Walt Whitman's 'sheer appreciation of the instant moment' (183). It is an interesting judgement, and it is not the last time that Whitman figures centrally in Lawrence's discursive writing (see *Studies in Classic American Literature*) [104–8]. In 'Poetry of the Present', Whitman's value to Lawrence lies in what is perceived to be his disregard of both the past and the future as the proper focus for poetry. 'Eternity', the 'forever' which is both past and to come and which is so often evoked in poetry is, argues Lawrence, merely 'an abstraction from the actual present. … The quivering nimble hour of the present, this is the quick of Time' (183). The key-word in Lawrence's poetics at this point, then, is 'present' as the only point of origin (of thought, of the self) to which we have unmediated access. Any critique of Lawrence's writing which includes an assessment of his thematisation of time, or indeed of the self, needs to take this concentration on the instant, the present, very seriously. It underpins much that is central in his 'metaphysic'.

'Poetry of the Present' has a sense of urgency about it. In it Lawrence finds many formulations for describing over and over again the richness of the instant. He is drawn rapidly into a language of mobility and impermanence. He begs to be saved from anything 'fixed, set, static' (182), asking, in terms which have an oxymoronic resonance, for 'the still, white seething, the incandescence and the coldness of the incarnate moment: the moment, the quick of all change and haste and opposition: the moment, the immediate present, the Now' (183). In comparison with many of his modernist contemporaries, this ahistorical emphasis on present-time is part of his writerly specificity. Central to his apprehension of 'the Now' is Lawrence's use of metaphor. A common image in his writing for the instant, the present moment, is the 'running flame' (182) which persists in its continuous changeability. A flame cannot be anatomised into its constituent parts; it has a free-form immediacy which makes it a good image for Lawrence to exploit as he casts the fluidity and mobility of the present into language; into new poetic forms.

Towards the end of 'Poetry of the Present' he collapses his concentration on time into his concentration on questions of the self, because his insights into the poetic treatment of the present are central to his representations of continually changing selfhood in the poetry and fiction. Perhaps because of its clarity on these questions the critic Holly Laird calls 'Poetry of the Present' 'one of Lawrence's few significant statements on poetry' (Laird 1988: 238).

Laird, in a lengthy and detailed study of the poems, emphasizes the centrality of self to his poetic project. In this context, another term becomes central. 'Life', for Lawrence, in many ways eludes definition: we recognize it in the living but cannot say what it is, except by taking refuge in metaphor. Descriptions of biological functioning offer merely classification, taxonomies which are continually subject to revision: 'If we try to fix the living tissue, as the biologists fix it with formalin, we have only a hardened bit of the past, the bygone life under our observation' (182). The life of the self, then, for Lawrence is utterly mobile – at its most available it is located in the senses, but it has no history, having something of the quality of the instant moment in its passing presentness, in its immediacy and elusiveness, in its relation to the living. In a slight conceptual shift, Lawrence, using a familiar metaphor of unchartered territory, brings time and self together as subjects for poetic treatment: 'One realm we have never conquered: the pure present. One great mystery of time is *terra incognita* to us: the instant. The most superb mystery we have hardly recognized: 'the immediate, instant self' (185). We could add, then, that his interest is in the self in time.

(i) *Look! We Have Come Through!*

Look! We Have Come Through!, in its range of styles and deployment of certain vocabularies, provides a strong sense of Lawrence's rich poetic practice, and of the developing direction of his thought. As many critics have noted, it is a volume which can be read as accomplished autobiographical reflection and poetic abstraction: perhaps it narrows the gap between them. It has its origins in a turbulent and transitional period of Lawrence's life, after the death of his mother and includes the beginning of his relationship with Frieda Weekley and their marriage **[10–13]**.

The book is contemporaneous with important discursive work like 'Study of Thomas Hardy' and *The Rainbow*, as well as the first Italian writing and a host of shorter works. The temptation is often to relate the written works to the immediate experiences of the writer (and Lawrence's personal experiences lie very close to the surface in most of the poems in *Look! We Have Come Through!*). However, a concentration on the developing 'metaphysic', aside from 'the life', is at least as interesting. Lawrence may be seen developing and revising his thought. As we might expect from works like 'Study of Thomas Hardy' and *The Rainbow*, much in *Look! We Have Come Through!* deals with the relations between men and women and Lawrence's theorization of marriage. The 'argument' to the volume is autobiographical, with its description of a man (for 'protagonist' read 'author') who leaves his native territory for stranger lands – 'terra incognita' is a metaphor Lawrence often used – with his new love, a married woman, who leaves her children for this new relationship. It is quite possible to wonder how ironic Lawrence is being in his description of the pattern of conflict and reconciliation between these two figures which is resolved only when 'they transcend into some condition of blessedness' (CP 191).

Look! We Have Come Through! is comprised of interrelated groups of texts, although critics do not always agree on the constitution of these groups. Laird (1988) and Kinkead-Weekes (1996) both discuss groupings of poems within the book. Kinkead-Weekes notes the dialogic nature of the collection, observing that 'The poems begin to read one another more complexly than each reads in itself' (Kinkead-Weekes 1996: 359). His groupings reflect this. Laird identifies the group of 'rose' poems and a 'night' sequence, as well as a sequence of elegies as Lawrence deals with failed relationships, and sequences which turn on new and married love respectively (Laird 1988). Lest anyone suspect that the volume is plainly and simply a celebration of the union of man and woman, many of the poems express reservations, identifying the myth of wholeness which surrounds affirmations of 'married' or committed love. 'Bei Hennef', for instance, sets up the principal emotional relationship, as Kinkead-Weekes notes, in interactive terms ('call'/'answer'; 'wish'/ 'fulfilment'), but ends by questioning the completeness of the relationship by drawing attention to the lovers' suffering in spite of their union (CP 203). This is resonant of the sense in *The Rainbow* of the limitations of married love, even where marriage is represented as the principal form of personal, spiritual and emotional fulfilment. By the time *Women in Love* appears, the argument is expressed in a 'starry' and 'cosmic' language which says that, particularly for Rupert Birkin, one-to-one is not enough, while Ursula is depressed by the thought of 'others' intervening in her relationship. So marriage is still an important frame of reference in *Women in Love*, but not without reservations. Reference to 'the balanced, eternal orbit' in 'Both Sides of the Medal' (236) in some measure foreshadows the language of *Women in Love* where Birkin takes refuge in a series of celestial metaphors in order to explain his position to an increasingly sceptical Ursula. Such scepticism is not so significantly a part of *Look! We Have Come Through!*. The idea of a relationship being sustained by necessary proximity, which means necessary distance (in emotional terms), resounds in the pointedly titled poem, 'Wedlock', where the survival of the self (and, therefore, the survival of the relationship) depends on the recognition that although the lovers are happily together 'you are not me' and 'I am never you' (248).

Lawrence always found himself at the mercy of timorous publishers and editors, and some of the material in *Look! We Have Come Through!* gave these cause for alarm. The assumption most usually was that he wrote principally about sex, whereas Lawrence could legitimately protest that his real subjects – language, the birth of the self where sex is a resource not an end, the present – were overlooked by publishers' readers whose immediate fears blocked their understanding. In 'Manifesto', the point is very much the self-sufficiency of the lovers: as in 'Wedlock', 'real liberty', argues the poem, is that 'we shall have each our separate being' (266). Descriptions of the body in 'Manifesto' are in the service of a philosophy of the self, and a developing philosophy of singleness which, paradoxically, does not depend on the denial of relationship with another but on the maintenance of self-identity within the relationship. Whatever 'self' is for Lawrence, it is elusive or, rather, it eludes *language*, so that many of these poems bear witness to the struggle to express a value (selfhood) which can be felt more easily than it can be described, even poetically.

'New Heaven and Earth' (256) draws on ideas present in 'Study of Thomas Hardy' which were in process in earlier work like the Foreword to *Sons and Lovers*. Lawrence deploys an old pun on 'trespassing' to describe a passing away as the old self disembarks from the old life into the new. Resurrection imagery combines with images of conflict and the familiar Lawrentian idea of the destruction of the old giving way to the birth of the new. The 'terra nova' discovered by the 'I' of the poem recalls the imagery of 'Study of Thomas Hardy' as the traveller fetches up on an unknown shore. In Part VII of the poem it is clear that the speaker has been suddenly transformed by unconsciously touching the woman who is already familiar but not 'known' to him, and this touch is the means of his deliverance from 'death' to 'life'. More powerful than sight, touch will recur in Lawrence's writing. In this poem it is, along with blindness (the triumphant speaker in the final lines of 'New Heaven and Earth' is 'sightless'), a central trope for non-cerebral knowing. It also provides a clue to the 'feeling' nature of Lawrence's language which indicates the presence always of values, barely quantifiable moments, of which language – poetic language – can give only a sign. So, in focusing on a moment when a woman is touched, Lawrence both is, and is not, writing about sex. As so often in his writing, key issues – language, self-renewal, the importance of the present moment – dovetail.

(ii) *Birds, Beasts and Flowers*

Birds, Beasts and Flowers (1923) is often cited as a transitional work. Gilbert (1972) sees it as mediating, in its principal themes, much that the critical and travel writing also contained. Laird (1988), in discussing the volume, refers to *Studies in Classic American Literature*, also 1923. In her analysis, Laird draws attention to the play with genre in *Studies*, highlighting in *Birds, Beasts and Flowers* Lawrence's preference for the fable form over the epic, and gives much of her discussion over to the structure, composition and chronology of the volume (Laird 1988: 133, 136–9). Interestingly, in terms of Lawrence's relation to his modernist peers, she introduces her discussion with a brief comparison of *Birds, Beasts and Flowers* – with its treatment of the mythic, the present and the transition from an 'old' consciousness to a 'new' (also a preoccupation of *Studies in Classic American Literature*) – and T.S. Eliot's poem *The Waste Land*. She is careful to address the differences of poetic vision, but her comments throw light on Lawrence's relation both to tradition and to literary modernism: 'Eliot's disintegrated world in which a poet-priest, Tiresias, appears at the periphery, exiled, resembles that of Lawrence. In Eliot, however, we hear a more Arnoldian reverence for tradition – and greater despair. In Lawrence, the Carlylean vein flows with passionate rage' (129).

The 'prefaces' to each section of *Birds, Beasts and Flowers* – usually thought of as prose poems because of the quality of their language, metaphoric mode and the synoptic, multi-layered thought – were prepared for the Cresset edition of the volume (1930). 'Flowers' (CP 303) introduces the mythic dimension of some of the poems in the volume, as in the Persephone myth through which is figured the passing of an old consciousness into a new. In 'Reptiles' (348), Lawrence articulates – or re-articulates – one of the most central tenets of his 'metaphysic': 'Homer was wrong in saying, "Would that strife might pass away from among gods and men!" he did not see that he was praying for the destruction of the universe; for, if his prayer were heard, all things would pass away – for in *the tension of opposites all things have their being* –' (348, emphasis added). This necessary tension gets expression in the polarities of light and dark, mind and blood, north and south, which informs much of the thought in *Birds, Beasts and Flowers*. The 'cross-wise cloven psyche' described in 'Tortoise Shell' (356) relates to the dissertation on the cross in the first essay on the writer Nathaniel Hawthorne in *Studies in Classic American Literature* (SCAL 90-1), the symbol which expresses the division in man between blood and 'blood-knowledge' and its opposite, mind ('spiritual consciousness'). This kind of correspondence suggests that Lawrence's instruction to the reader of *Studies in Classic American Literature* holds good for the reader of *Birds, Beasts and Flowers* – 'You *must* look through the surface … and see the inner diabolism of the symbolic meaning. Otherwise it is all mere childishness' (SCAL 89).

(iii) *Pansies*

'Introduction to *Pansies*' (CP 417–21) explains the structure of the volume: 'It suits the modern temper better to have its state of mind made up of apparently irrelevant thoughts that scurry in different directions, yet belong to the same nest' (417). In the 'Foreword' (423–4) he is more forthcoming about the appropriateness of poetry for these 'thoughts' (Pansies/*Pensées*) because he wishes them not to have the 'didactic element' of prose (423). Back to the 'Introduction', and in describing the genesis of the poems he typically challenges the 'natural' distinction between mind and body: each poem is a 'true thought, which comes as much from the heart and the genitals as from the head' (417). This is a quality he had spotted and admired in Whitman in *Studies in Classic American Literature* (SCAL 180). The material in the 'Introduction' about the need for the mind to accept 'obscene'words is much more relevant to *Lady Chatterley's Lover* than to *Pansies* (although *Pansies* was seized by the police) **[27]**.

It is fair to say that there is no principal organizing theme to *Pansies*, as Lawrence confirms. Some, like 'How Beastly the Bourgeois Is', 'The Oxford Voice' and 'The Middle Classes', demonstrate his anti-bourgeois stance, and underlying the point about the assumption of superiority is the old idea of a polished surface concealing a rotten interior which extends to culture and society more broadly. 'Leave Sex Alone' and 'The Mess of Love' return to the 'sex in the head' theme (discussed in *Fantasia of the Unconscious*), which is given extensive treatment in *Lady Chatterley's Lover*. 'Ego-Bound Women' is also an echo from that novel, while 'Elderly Discontented Women' continues to worry at (or about) the condition of 'modern' women. Other poems examine social systems – 'Democracy', 'Wages' – questioning the ability of social organization to keep man alive and, more often, in 'The Root of Our Evil', 'The Ignoble Procession', 'Money Madness' and 'Kill Money', for instance, baulking at the 'perverted instinct' (487) of capitalism. 'Dies Irae' and 'Dies Illa' take up themes of great phases of evolutionary change resulting in the old systems being superseded (at best) by a new consciousness. Some of the 'pansies' seem valedictory, others speak, as promised, to an instant of reflection.

Further Reading

Laird (1988) examines the representation of Lawrence's key ideas in relation to the self within the body of poetry. This study can be usefully contrasted with Gilbert (1972), Murfin (1983), Mandell (1984), Lockwood (1987) and Ingram (1990) who examine Lawrence's language and imagery, his texts and contexts, his relation to a tradition, and the development of his 'metaphysic' in the poetry. Bannerjee (1990) is useful on sources. Sagar (1985) includes chapters on *Birds, Beasts and Flowers*, and *Pansies, Nettles, Last Poems* in the context of a larger study which examines creative processes in Lawrence. Katz-Roy (1992) also considers the language of the last poems. Perloff (1985) discusses *Birds, Beasts and Flowers*. Hebe R. Mace examines the form of Lawrence's poetry in Jackson and Brown Jackson (eds, 1988). Pollnitz writes on the 'dark god' in the poetry in Kalnins (ed., 1986); R.P. Draper writes on poetic language and imagery in Heywood (ed., 1987); Tom Paulin discusses the challenge of ideological commitment versus aesthetic freedom expressed in the poetry in Preston and Hoare (eds, 1989); Helen Sword provides a survey of the main themes in Fernihough (ed., 2001). Among an earlier generation of critics, Hough (1956) takes issue with the view of Lawrence's poetry expressed in Blackmur (1954). Marshall (1970) awards the poetry book-length treatment.

(e) THE NOVELLAS

Alongside the short story, the novellas, or shorter novels, provide Lawrence with an alternative form for the further development of the 'metaphysic'. In his study of Lawrence's fiction, Frank Kermode (1973) concluded that in his writing 'Eternity inheres in the productions of time; it is achieved in the life of the individual consciousness. All Lawrence's temporal projections ... are therefore, in the last analysis, allegories of personal regeneration, rather than historical prophecies' (138–9). If Lawrence had never written novels, poetry or plays, or philosophy, the body of short fiction and novellas would constitute an organic and coherent *oeuvre*, and Kermode's words would remain as fitting. The novellas comprise *The Captain's Doll* (1923), *The Fox* (1920; 1922), *The Ladybird* (1923), *St Mawr* (1925), *The Princess* (1925), *The Escaped Cock (The Man Who Died)* (1928; 1929), and the posthumously published forerunner to *Lady Chatterley's Lover*, *The Virgin and the Gipsy* (1930).

In *The Captain's Doll*, 'personal regeneration' is glimpsed as a possibility only after the sceptical rejection of romantic love on the part of Hepburn, the captain of the title. Similarly, *The Ladybird* institutes a discussion on the word 'love', with Count Psanek echoing Birkin's dissatisfaction with the available definitions in *Women in Love*. Using the curious threesome of Basil, Daphne and the Count, Lawrence combines the mythic and the uncanny in a tale where the 'collapse' of the 'old self' of the woman results in a kind of bondage to (or possession by) the otherworldly figure of Psanek, and the promise of an eternal encounter in the underworld. A variation on the isolated threesome and uncanny attraction-revulsion is developed in *The Fox*. This story charts the relationship of two women, Banford and March, attempting self-sufficiency on an isolated small-holding. The division of labour in this 'family' reflects the traditional gendered roles, with Banford maintaining the house and March, described as resembling a 'graceful, loose-balanced young man' (CSN 136; F 8), seeing to the work out of doors. The homestead does not thrive, however, and in particular the women are bothered by the nocturnal evil of a fox. Encountering it, March finds that she cannot destroy it as a countryman might, and instead it 'possesses' her, demon-like. After this, a young man, Henry Grenfel arrives at the house ('to March he was the fox' [143; 14]), and he begins to erode the friendship between the women. By his 'posses-sion' of March, he manipulates her into agreeing to marry him and, in a deliberate tree-felling, he murders his rival, Banford. The tale ends with Grenfel and March waiting to embark for Canada. The conflict between them is described in terms of Grenfel's insistence that she gives up her independent will to live as his mate, set against her struggle to keep her self-consciousness awake.

St Mawr was begun after Lawrence's first visit to Mexico **[25]**, and after a very brief return to England. It draws on his experience of the American South-West, and what was for Lawrence a new *imaginative* territory. In *St Mawr* the focus is on a woman who finally repudiates male companionship and sex in an attempt to contact the 'sacred sex' in herself. The first time a body of Lawrence's work was most thor-oughly examined, the critic F.R. Leavis **[126]** compared *St Mawr*, which he called a 'dramatic poem', with T.S. Eliot's *The Waste Land*, very much to Lawrence's advantage:

> *St Mawr* seems to me to present a creative and technical originality more remarkable than that of *The Waste Land*, being, as that poem is not, completely achieved, a full and self-sufficient creation. It can hardly strike the admirer as anything but major.
>
> (Leavis 1955: 225)

Leavis tries to give a sense of *St Mawr*'s representative value to the 'Lawrentian' in terms of the achieved relation between fiction and philosophy, or 'metaphysic'. His is also a reminder that the narrative deals as surely with the degeneration of Western civilization as Eliot's poem. *St Mawr* starts with a modern marriage. Lou Witt – who, at the novella's conclusion will 'ride away' to a less self-destructive destiny than her counterpart in the short story, 'The Woman Who Rode Away' – is married to Rico, one of Lawrence's over-conscious males (an artist, he is cosmopolitan and brittle). This is another narrative where a woman rejects an orthodox commitment (to a man, to family), and removes herself from the 'frictional' relationships which have so far defined her, of which the language speaks: the marriage is 'a strange vibration of nerves, rather than of the blood. A nervous attachment, rather than a sexual love. A curious tension of will, rather than a sponta-neous passion ... This attachment of the will and the nerves was destructive' (CSN 279; STM 24).

We are told in the beginning that Lou, young and rich, 'had had her own way so long, that by the age of twenty-five she didn't know where she was' (276; 21). This metaphysical dislocation is redeemed in part by the presence of the stallion, called St Mawr, which she acquires for Rico. As Rico and the horse are in a continually antagonistic relation to each other, the significance of St Mawr in the narrative is principally his significance to Lou as a counter to the 'null' world she inhabits. In the figure of the stallion is invested an energy, a vigour, which is literally 'reined in'. Central to the narrative is Lou's awakening to the spirit of evil, inspired by the sight of Rico trying to control St Mawr from the saddle as the sensitive animal panics and rears, unnerved by the sight of a dead snake underfoot. She thinks later of people 'thrown backwards, and writhing with evil. And the rider, crushed, was still reining them down' (341; 78–9).

As Frank Kermode (1973) notes, the main characters in *St Mawr* have a 'doctrinal' function, something which extends to the grooms, Phoenix who is Indian, and Lewis who is Welsh, as well as to Lou's mother, Mrs Witt. The latter delivers powerful statements about the death of feeling in the modern world, statements which are bound up with her own reflections on death in a world where the living are already 'dead'. The narrative ranges between the open spaces of the American South-West and the comparative littleness and sterility of industrial, social England, as Lawrence develops his critique of modern civilization. The book draws to its close in a discursive mode which reflects on the present: 'And every civilization, when it loses its inward vision and its cleaner energy, falls into a new sort of sordidness, more vast and more stupendous than the old savage sort. An Augean stables of metallic filth' (CSN 422; 151). The book ends with Lou's affirmation of her isolation from men, and her removal to a ranch in pioneer country where personal regeneration might be possible.

Lou's destiny, which is predicated on a rejection of 'modern social life' (406; 137) arrived at through her rejection of modern sexual experience, can be contrasted with the destiny of the Christ-figure in *The Escaped Cock* (*The Man Who Died*). Among Lawrence's last works, this narrative deals with the return of Christ from the tomb, and the parallel awakening of his sexual self in an encounter with a priestess of Isis, who conceives a child. Like *Lady Chatterley's Lover*, this tale is much more about 'phallic consciousness' as the principal antidote to a crippling self-consciousness, than it is about sex. And, also as in *Lady Chatterley's Lover* (and indeed in *St Mawr*), personal rebirth is established as the necessary prefiguration to cultural rebirth (in those stories of

England and America). *The Escaped Cock* is another move into a mythic and religious, rather than an historical, mode: the 'man who died' encounters the priestess who serves 'Isis in Search', scouring the world for the fragments of the disarticulated body of Osiris: 'she must gather him together and fold her arms round the re-assembled body till it became warm again, and roused to life, and could embrace her and could fecundate her womb' (CSN 577). As usual in Lawrence, sex serves the ends of psychic, spiritual, personal and cultural regeneration. John Worthen is right when he states:

> It is the final paradox of *Lady Chatterley's Lover* and 'The Escaped Cock' that they should ... be the most religious of Lawrence's fictions: the ones in which he most consistently used sex as an example, an opportunity, a metaphor and a myth.
>
> (1991b: 119–20)

So is the idea of 'marriage' to a god more effectively achieved in *The Escaped Cock*, as a genuine expression of Lawrence's philosophy, than in the over-conscious mode of *The Plumed Serpent*, where the principal idea of rebirth and cultural regeneration is submerged under the crudely doctrinal? **[72–5]**.

The Princess (1925) is another New Mexico story, written just after *St Mawr* and contemporaneous with revisions to *The Plumed Serpent*. After her father's death, a British heiress, Dollie Urquhart ('The Princess' as her father has always called her), is at a loose end. In her late 30s, and 'virginal', she arranges a break at the Ranch del Carro Gordo with her companion, Miss Cummins, equally 'virginal'. The Princess is on a desultory search for a husband now that her father has gone. Only the Spanish-speaking Mexican mountain-guide, Romero, attracts her, and she arranges for him to take her and Miss Cummins deep into the Rocky Mountains, on a longer trek than the usual tourist jaunts. Miss Cummins is forced to turn back once her horse suffers an injury, but the Princess and Romero press on to Romero's cabin, several days' ride away. They make a simple camp as the cold closes in. Overnight, the Princess has a dream of the oppressive snow burying her, and she wakes, freezing. Allowing Romero to warm her, the narrative dramatizes her ambivalence towards his 'annihilating' sensual presence (CSN 462; STM 188). In the morning her antagonism grows, especially in the face of Romero's evident pleasure at her submission. When she articulates her dislike of sex, and repudiation of him, he throws her clothes into the icy river to strand her, and rapes her. This incarceration and abuse continues until towards the end of the week two horsemen approach the cabin, and Romero is killed in a gunfight. The point of the story lies in the Princess's 'willed' attraction to Romero which develops alongside her denial of the life of the body. The language applied to her throughout is of an otherworld figure – she is like a 'changeling', never 'at home' in company, without vivid connection to those close to her, even Miss Cummins who is, throughout, merely an employee. The Princess's fastidiousness is interpreted as a denial of life and, like Banford in *The Fox*, she is punished by the impersonal violence of the man, reflected in the impersonal contours of the 'primitive' landscape.

Further Reading

F.R. Leavis (1955) granted *The Captain's Doll* and *St Mawr* their own chapters. Other monographs on the fiction that include consideration of the novellas include Spilka (1955), Widmer (1962), Moynahan (1963), Sagar (1966; 1985), Cavitch (1969), Cowan (1970) and Ruderman (1984). Material in edited collections includes Daleski, in Gomme (ed., 1978), Blanchard (1978), Gilbert (1985), Turner (1986), Devlin (1988), McDowell (1988) and Kinkead-Weekes (2001). Conveniently collected in one volume (Jackson and Brown Jackson 1988) are essays by different critics on *The Fox* (Draper), *The Virgin and the Gipsy* (Guttenberg) and *The Escaped Cock* (Cowan). A great deal of material is published in periodicals.

(f) THE SHORT STORIES

Lawrence is one of the key short-story writers of the modernist period. The three major collections are identified respectively by their inclusion of 'The Prussian Officer' (1914), 'England, My England' (1915; 1922) and 'The Woman Who Rode Away' (1925; 1928). The stories that constitute the collections are central to an understanding of Lawrence's major preoccupations, such as his exploration of the relationships between men and women; the instinctive life; the realization of self awareness; the examination of cultural, as well as personal, dissolution and the related critique of Western civilization as misdirected in its pursuit of ideal values; the multi-directional exploration of mythic and religious themes. As 'fables' they draw attention to Lawrence's highly successful handling of the form and demonstrable authorial control. At their best each is a finely crafted text, which synoptically and directly apprehends much that is dealt with in more exploratory fashion in the novels in particular, although it would be erroneous to view the short stories as 'rehearsals' for the longer projects.

The Prussian Officer and Other Stories (1914) is Lawrence's first collection of short stories. Draper (1970) prints a contemporary review which states shrewdly: 'Here are twelve short stories from Mr D.H. Lawrence's pen – all brilliant, all superhuman, and at the same time *in*human' (81). It is a judgement which echoes Lawrence's statement to Edward Garnett that what interests him is 'that which is physic – non-human, in humanity' (*Letters* II: 182). 'The Prussian Officer' describes first the relentless bullying of an orderly by his captain, and then the effects on the young soldier, called Schöner, of his revenge taken when he murders his tormentor. While there is a sexually sadistic element to the story that many critics have noted, this does not dominate the narrative which rather explores at length the violence that each man does to *himself* in doing violence to the other. At the tale's beginning the officer is a mechanism: he functions as a soldier rather than a living man, and when he notices the capacity for living in Schöner he finds the recognition of it insufferable. Lawrence employs imagery which he may have learned from the Italian futurists **[15]** to communicate the crisis in the officer at the level of self, and the language describes an impersonal violence which recalls episodes in *The Rainbow*. When the officer strikes the cowed and startled Schöner he finds the experience is paradoxically both satisfying and self-destructive: 'Deep inside him [the officer] was the intense gratification of his passion, still working powerfully. Then there was a counteraction, a horrible breaking down of something inside him, a whole agony of reaction' (8). When the bullied Schöner can take no more, and finds relief in the unpremeditated murder of the officer, he takes flight. Dazed by the violence which he has expressed, he suffers both the death of the spirit and, finally, literal death. The other side of love, for Lawrence, is not hate, but this death of the soul in conflict with the other. After he has received a kicking from the officer, the abused Schöner, a victim, is 'inert', he submits to his own 'nullification', he is 'disintegrated' (10). Reality and unreality change places as he begins to feel his existence only in the shadows: he no longer has 'his living place in the hot, bright morning' (11). His murder of the officer – in the act itself – is a kind of release from his new condition of 'mechanical obedience' (13). As with Gerald Crich in *Women in Love*, the end of Schöner's pain is achieved in his absorption by the distant mountains which he sees as he dies: 'he wanted to leave himself and be identified with them' (20).

The narrative language dramatizes Lawrence's thesis that the death of culture (degenerate European modernity) is indistinguishable from the death of the 'living' self. The officer may be a mechanism, dead to himself, because of his place in the military establishment which works against life (and in this he shares the condition of *The Rainbow*'s Anton Skrebensky), but the story is not about 'militarism'. Revising 'The Prussian Officer' in 1914, however, Lawrence, revolted by the war, turned it into a fable about a culture in 'recoil' from itself.

Lawrence did not intend 'The Prussian Officer' to head up the collection, although few of the remaining stories in this volume have its narrative power, linguistic control and symbolic tightness. 'Odour of Chrysanthemums' (the main theme of which he reworked in his play, *The Widowing of Mrs Holroyd*) **[36]**, however, has long been considered exceptional. It is written in the mode of domestic realism in which Lawrence excels. Elizabeth Bates, a wife and mother, waits for her collier husband to return from his day in the mine. He is late. The children come home, the evening closes in, the tea threatens to ruin and so the incomplete family sit down in the shadows to eat. Elizabeth is sure her husband is in the public house. With the children in bed, she goes to make enquiries of his mates, barely suppressing her sense of indignity at having to ask where he is, to discover that no-one has seen him leave work. She returns home, having alerted others to his absence, and waits with her mother-in-law for his return. It transpires that there has been a fatal accident at the pit. The body is brought back to the house for the women to lay out as is the custom, in the parlour. Chrysanthemums have been a minor, symbolic presence in the narrative, accompanying the stages of Elizabeth's waiting. Their symbolic value to her is revealed in the answer she gives to her little girl's comment that the flowers her mother has tucked into her apron are beautiful:

> Not to me. It was chrysanthemums when I married him, and chrysanthemums when you were born, and the first time they ever brought him home drunk he'd got brown chrysanthemums in his button-hole.

> (PO 186)

In the parlour with the body is the 'cold, deathly smell of chrysanthemums' (193–4). The women together wash and clothe the body, the mother grief-stricken but Elizabeth is at some level arrested. Facing the dead, she comes to understand the difference between her conception of Bates as her husband, and father of her children, and what he 'is'. Death restores the truth to her that 'they had denied each other in life' (198). The conclusion is closer to the view in 'Study of

Thomas Hardy' that a 'balanced' relation is necessary between the sexes, than to the more personal solutions of *Sons and Lovers*, for instance. The spectacle of the dead man enables Elizabeth to understand the extent to which her marriage was a social arrangement, and as such an encounter between strangers, and that there has been no unconscious connection between them – this is the meaning of 'denial' in her meditation. Accompanying this realization is the scent of the flowers in the room. The concentration is not on an unhappy marriage as, in Lawrence's terms at this time, it was no 'marriage' at all. In the battles between husband and wife Elizabeth was fighting him, not fighting *for* herself. The point of the story lies in the distinction. It is her encounter with the dead that forces the woman to choose life in the final lines of the narrative, 'which was her immediate master' (199).

Another collection, *England, My England and Other Stories*, was first published in America in 1922 (publication in Britain was two years later). In the same year, Lawrence published *Aaron's Rod* and *Fantasia of the Unconscious* for which he had high hopes. The *New York Times* published a review of *England My England* which identified the 'sex war' as its organizing theme:

> For one reason or another, through one set of circumstances or another, there is a conflict, open or concealed, between the prota-gonists, man and woman, of nearly every tale. And in practically all of them it is the man who is the victim, the terrorized and dominated, weakly submissive, struggling or defiant.
>
> (Draper 1970: 188)

As with his other collections, most of the stories in this volume had appeared in print elsewhere, in magazines and periodicals. Half of the stories were written during the Great War, a turbulent period for Lawrence not least because of the suppression of *The Rainbow* in 1915. The others are just post-war, so that most belong to his 'Cornwall' period [19], apart from 'The Primrose Path' which preceded it. It is interesting to consider the stories written more or less alongside *Women in Love*.

'England, My England', begun in 1915, starts with a marriage and ends with the death of the protagonist in the war. The marriage between Egbert and Winifred deals with an attraction across social classes. With the arrival of children, the alienation of Egbert within the family begins (here is an echo of Will Brangwen's alienation in *The Rainbow* [EME 11]). His habitual carelessness as one of life's amateurs means that, in an accident which is partly his fault, his young daughter

is maimed and made lame. The family closes against him and, against
expectation, he finds them 'unreal' – which means that the active
emotional life he experienced as a young husband has gone.
Disastrously, he takes refuge in the suddenly more 'real' mechanism of
military life when he joins up to become a soldier. There is no spiritual
rebirth for Egbert: he is killed by a German shell. The story in part
allows Lawrence to show European culture – 'German militarism' and
'British industrialism' (28) – as degenerate and deathly, and in Egbert's
literal death is expressed the death of feeling which Lawrence extends
to his culture. The final episode – Egbert's death – shows war to be far
from heroic.

If 'England, My England' deals in part directly with the war, others
like 'The Blind Man' expoit the highly personal effects of conflict. In
that story an injured veteran, blinded in Flanders (46), learns to live at
an instinctive level which is simply less available to the sighted. 'The
Blind Man' and 'Hadrian' are both powerful fables about the transforming effects of touch over sight, and show how 'unconscious'
knowledge of others is gained through the immediacy of touch which
cannot lie. Maurice Pervin's disability, in 'The Blind Man', is revelatory
to him. Because he must 'feel' his surroundings he finds a new, immediate world opened up to him as a result of his disability, and 'wanted
no intervention of visual consciousness' (54). When he forces Bertie
Reid, his wife's cousin, to touch his sightless eyes and battle scar, Reid
cannot take the naked knowledge of the man which is suddenly
available to him. Pervin, on the other hand, rejoices in the knowledge
that he gains through touching Reid's face: '"Oh, my God," he said,
"we shall know each other now, shan't we? We shall know each other
now"' (62), but Reid, unused to such unmediated, and unasked for,
closeness, is 'broken' (63). This is a subtle story which turns on
Lawrence's suspicion of the visual, the primacy of sight in Western
understanding, and he substitutes another sense. New modes of
consciousness are explored in other contexts which turn on touch, and
proximity, as in 'The Horse-Dealer's Daughter' which examines the
terms of the new-found love between a doctor and a young woman
whom he rescues from drowning.

Other stories in this collection, like 'Tickets Please', 'Samson and
Delilah' and 'The Last Straw' are finely observed realist tales drawing
on Lawrence's knowledge of Midlands working-class life. 'Tickets
Please' charts the 'subtle antagonism' between John Thomas and Annie
who work on the tramway. John Thomas has a reputation as a 'ladies
man' of which Annie is fully aware, but she allows herself to be courted
by him and they enjoy a period of real companionship until Annie's

interest in him becomes more personal – 'she did not want a *mere* nocturnal presence' (39). Alarmed by her new interest, John Thomas, to her great surprise, jilts her. The rest of the tale deals with Annie's revenge. With Nora, and the other women who work on the trams, who have all 'walked out with' him, Annie conspires to trap their former beau in a room ('outside was the darkness and lawlessness of war-time' [40]). Taunting him to choose one of them, the forced encounter degenerates rapidly into real violence against John Thomas: 'Strange, wild creatures, they [the women] hung on him and rushed at him to bear him down' (43). Scared, but emboldened by defiance, he chooses his chief tormentor, the jilted Annie, who is deeply disturbed and angered by his audacity. In creating this feeling in her, he has 'won' the struggle between them. The 'lawlessness' of wartime, reflected in the behaviour of the women, has not defeated the 'phallic' hero, John Thomas.

The theme of the attractiveness of sensual men is continued in 'The Last Straw' which describes the return of a woman formerly in service to her home-town, where she intends to marry her first-love, a working-man. Her ambivalence about his worth to her, when she does return, is resolved only after he is accused by an angry mother – a crude country-woman – of getting her daughter, Annie, pregnant. Fanny, a 'superior' woman, decides to stay with Harry as if his sexual irresponsibility makes possible her desire for him. Harry's mother is delighted that Fanny has not dropped her son, as Fanny is a woman with a legacy of £200 and some savings. Unlike other of Lawrence's women, Fanny experiences a 'prompting' more than an awakening (see 'The Horse-Dealer's Daughter'). The story is comic, and slightly satirical.

'The Woman Who Rode Away' is the title-story in a third, and very different, collection published in 1928 which contains frequently satirical stories written over the preceding four years. Most of the stories were placed elsewhere before being included in this volume, which was not conceived organically. As in other works, many of them draw on Lawrence's acquaintances and are often critical – 'Smile', 'The Border-Line', 'Jimmy and the Desperate Woman' and 'The Last Laugh', for example, are satires written with the character of John Middleton Murry in mind; and 'Two Blue Birds' and 'The Man Who Loved Islands' satirize the novelist, Compton Mackenzie. Some, like 'Glad Ghosts', were requested for other anthologies – Lady Cynthia Asquith commissioned this story for a collection of ghost stories, but settled for 'The Rocking-Horse Winner' when the content of 'Glad Ghosts' presented problems. 'Sun' is a curious fable about a woman's sexual transformation as she takes the sun for a lover.

In 'The Woman Who Rode Away' (1925), a white woman leaves her marriage to a much older man (this is the destiny preserved for 'The Princess', Lawrence's near-contemporaneous short novel **[90]**), and her remote home in the Sierra Madre mountains, in search of the 'Chilchui' Indians and the romantic adventure that they represent. Indifferent to her family's insistence that she stay on the ranch, she rides alone into the mountains where eventually the encounter about which she has fantasized takes place. She submits to being taken by Chilchui men to a remote settlement where, over a period of months, she is stripped of her quotidian identity, drugged and prepared for sacrifice. The story ends in the seconds before her death as the priest waits for the moment when the rays of the winter sun shine through a phallic column of ice which hangs in the mouth of the sacrificial cave: 'Then the old man would strike, and strike home, accomplish the sacrifice and achieve the power' (WWRA 71).

This story has for a long time been central to debates about Lawrence's misogyny, in large part because of the voyeuristic pleasures of the text in descriptions of the woman's imprisonment and preparation for sacrifice, particularly in the face of her willingness to suffer any number of bodily humiliations: she is pawed and watched over until her dehumanization and objectification is complete. In a highly influential reading, Kate Millett, in her book *Sexual Politics*, concludes that this narrative, as pornography, glorified in the 'death-fuck' (Millett 1969: 292 **[143]**). More recently, critics have been willing to reassess 'The Women Who Rode Away' in ways which increasingly emphasize the parallels between the woman and the tribe as marginal. As Sheila Contreras puts it in a recent article:

> The white man has metaphorically *stolen* the sun from the Chilchui, who must now reclaim it through the body of a white woman, the commodity of exchange between male cultures. The symbolic rape of a white woman reverses the white man's colonial rape of the Chilchui world.
>
> (Contreras 1993–4: 99)

As in *The Plumed Serpent*, the white woman's submission is central to the tale's logic. Her whiteness, as well as her sex, matters. Mid-narrative, the white woman is contrasted with the native women in the dance: 'Her kind of womanhood, intensely personal and individual, was to be obliterated again, and the great primeval symbols were to tower once more over the fallen individual independence of woman' (60). In this way Lawrence represents his agitation at 'nervous conscious' modern women, set against the 'impersonal passion' of the others.

Further Reading

F.R. Leavis (1955) commits a chapter to 'The Tales', as does Hough (1956). The first full-length study of the short fiction is Widmer (1962) and many of his contemporaries make some reference to the short fiction in their assessments of Lawrence (Moynahan 1963, Ford 1965). More recent book-length studies on specific works include Cushman (1978) on the genesis of *The Prussian Officer* collection. Harris (1984), Thornton (1993) and Kearney (1997) are studies of the short fiction. Michael Black (1986) writes at length on the early short stories with reference to their place within Lawrence's *oeuvre*, and to the evolution of ideas, and styles, that they represent. Surveys tend to give some attention to the short stories (e.g. Worthen 1991). Mara Kalnins and Clyde de L. Ryals write on the short fiction in Jackson and Brown Jackson (eds) (1988). These titles are in addition to the innumerable articles and essays on individual stories.

(g) DISCURSIVE WRITING

Lawrence's output included a vast *corpus* of discursive writing principally, but not exclusively, in the form of essays. Like the Foreword to *Sons and Lovers* (1913) **[47]** these were not always intended for publication, although most are now in fact available. This writing represents extended debates (like 'The Crown') as well as discrete, shorter pieces. The essays represent a mode of writing in which Lawrence could state his personal philosophy in contexts supplementary to the fiction. The discursive writing, which is always exploratory, is often highly metaphorical as Lawrence animates the relation between 'thought' and 'poetry', both of which are *creative* initiatives.

(i) 'Art and the Individual'

The earliest extant whole piece of discursive writing is significantly on aesthetics and on what Lawrence terms 'Aesthetic Interest'. This essay, 'Art and the Individual', originated as a talk given to a group of his friends in Eastwood in 1908. It represents a wide-ranging introduction to the principal criteria of aesthetic judgement in which Lawrence displays his credentials as a young intellectual. The talk draws on much of the reading he has done as a student, including his reading of European literature and philosophy, and on contemporary critical material and reviews. Crucially, 'Art and the Individual' shows a feeling for language that underpins much of Lawrence's mature fiction and poetry. It does so in a brief meditation on words and the limitations of language:

> It is Art which opens to us the silences, the primordial silences which hold the secret of things, the great purposes, which are themselves silent; there are no words to speak of them with, and no thoughts to think of them in, so we struggle to touch them through art ...
>
> (STH 140)

The essay concludes that an appropriate response to culture, in the individual, is the result of self-education.

(ii) 'Study of Thomas Hardy'

It is generally acknowledged that Lawrence's 'Study of Thomas Hardy' (written in 1914 and published posthumously), communicates more about Lawrence's fledgling political and aesthetic philosophies than it does about Hardy's writing, although his comments on *The Hand of Ethelberta* (1876) and *Jude the Obscure* (1896), for example, are full of insight. Lawrence read Lascelles Abercrombie's book, *Thomas Hardy: A Critical Study* (1912), having announced 'I am going to do a little book on Hardy's people' (*Letters* II: 198). As a work of literary criticism, it was a project which he was invited to undertake and which, although he did not pursue it (as a book) into print in his lifetime, he found compelling. It should not be taken either as Lawrence's last word on Hardy or the European novel, or his last word on his philosophy of art. It is an unfinished document. As one commentator has noted, the sequence of chapters that we are most familiar with in the 'Study' is not necessarily that which Lawrence intended. Furthermore, '[w]hat we have is a set of draft chapters; some of them are drafts of the same chapter, or attempts at saying similar things, and some do not lead on from the previous chapter' (Black 1991: 148). As a work-in-progress, it ran parallel to his completion of *The Rainbow* – Daleski (1965) and Kinkead-Weekes (1968) draw attention to the importance of ideas in 'Study of Thomas Hardy' to an understanding of the 'metaphysic' of that novel **[49–56; 133]**. In common with other key examples of Lawrence's discursive writing, then, 'Study of Thomas Hardy' provides a useful sketch more than a polished literary critical endeavour. That he altered the title as the book developed to 'Le Gai Savaire', which has a Nietzschean suggestiveness, underlines the extent to which what began genuinely as a critique of Hardy's writing had become, in process, something much more personal and self-reflective. He certainly discovered things at this point about his own 'characterization' from Thomas Hardy. Hardy's fictional characters begin to figure in the third chapter of the 'Study' and almost immediately they are tested against Lawrence's model of self-preservation and self-value: 'all of them are struggling hard to come into being' (STH 20). As literary criticism, it becomes at points a comparative study of Hardy and Tolstoy which concludes with Lawrence's unmasking of novels that, even while appearing to expose the sinister mechanisms of social control in destroying free individuals like Tess Durbeyfield and Anna Karenina, sustain the dominant ideology – society triumphs.

The meditation at the heart of 'Study of Thomas Hardy', however, deals with the creative possibilities of conflict, either within the individual (the artist), or between individuals (usually between men and women). Creative conflict is described in this work as the inevitable opposition between 'male' and 'female' principles that co-exist within the individual. Religious and artistic creativity is theorized according to this model of conflict, which Lawrence elsewhere (in the context of poetry), calls 'strife' (CP 348) **[85]**. Developed alongside this exploratory meditation is a debate on human relations, men and women, and in particular the idea of an achieved balance between male and female principles (represented by the metaphor of 'Law' and 'Love'), as a means of enabling the individual self, reborn, to 'come through' (see *Look! We Have Come Through!*) **[82]**. This finds expression in the revised *The Rainbow*, where it informed (and developed from) Lawrence's meditation on marriage. 'Study of Thomas Hardy', then, is an idiosyncratic investigation of a number of themes: aesthetic, metaphysical and personal. Occasionally, Lawrence represents contemporary concerns as a means of talking about the sexes, as in the chapter entitled 'Still introductory: about Women's Suffrage, and Laws, and the War, and the Poor, with some Fancyful Moralising', but his interest is not really in social reforms.

'Study of Thomas Hardy', we must remember, comes out of the early period of World War I. Much of Lawrence's thought at this time is crystallized in his anti-war sentiments. He pathologizes conflict in many of these early statements in ways which have their echoes in the fiction. In the 'Study', he warns of 'men in whom the violence of war shall have shaken the life flow and broken or perverted the course, women who will cease to live henceforth, yet will remain existing in the land, fixed and at some lower point of fear or brutality' (STH 17). Lawrence employs martial metaphors to describe the struggle, the fight, not for the victory of king and country, but of the self. Hence, his philosophy of individual integrity can be seen to sharpen itself against the whetstone of European conflict. It is in this very particular context that 'the unknown', which is positive, and the 'void', which is negative, gain an established position in Lawrence's lexicon.

By the end of the 'Study', the birth of the self out of strife is related to phases of human consciousness – so that sometimes Lawrence is talking in global terms about culture and destiny, and sometimes about the personal and individual. Although this thought informs the writing which ran immediately parallel to 'Study of Thomas Hardy', other 'aesthetic' issues are foregrounded which are of equal significance in the writing to follow. Lawrence arrives at a confident description of artistic consciousness famously summed up in his often-quoted assertions that 'It is the novelists and dramatists who have the hardest task in reconciling their metaphysic, their theory of being and knowing, with their living sense of being'; and 'the metaphysic must always subserve the artistic purpose beyond the artist's conscious aim. Otherwise the novel becomes a treatise' (STH 91). With these words, Lawrence established his sense of the great potential, yet to be realized, of the novel form.

(iii) 'The Crown'

The 'Study of Thomas Hardy' was followed in 1915 by 'The Crown' which Lawrence attempted to publish in the form of six essays in a little magazine, started up by himself, Murry and Mansfield, called *Signature* [18]. It failed, and Lawrence only succeeded in publishing the whole text in 1925, in *Reflections on the Death of a Porcupine and Other Essays*. 'The Crown', like 'Hardy', employs dualistic imagery and, at times, becomes difficult and contradictory. Nevertheless, it introduces for extensive development many of the terms that Lawrence worked into *Women in Love*, and shows the extent of his thought on modern culture as 'disintegrative' and marked from the inside by 'corruption' [56–65]. The work as a whole embodies a difficult philosophy through which the effects of the war can be detected, accompanied by some hope of regeneration: 'We may give ourselves utterly to destruction. Then our conscious forms are destroyed along with us, and *something new must arise*' (RDP 294; emphasis added). The emphasis on the necessity of destruction is difficult to take but it is the antidote to different forms of 'nullity' posited elsewhere in the essay. 'Disintegration', 'corruption', 'reduction'and 'dissolution' are the key terms of the piece.

(iv) *Psychoanalysis and the Unconscious* and *Fantasia of the Unconscious*

It is a stated hostility in Lawrence to the popularity of Freud among his contemporaries which begins the first book, *Psychoanalysis and the Unconscious* (1921). *Fantasia of the Unconscious* (1922) is less concerned with Freud (although, with Jung, Freud is cited as an influence in the 'Foreword'), and is more obviously exploratory and metaphorical. On what, then, is Lawrence's scepticism of psychoanalysis founded? He is the first to admit that he has not read Freud. Frieda Weekley and her circle are most usually credited with introducing him to psychoanalysis: 'I never read Freud, but I have learned about him since I was in Germany' (*Letters* II: 80). Had he wished to study it, Lawrence, a linguist, could have read *Die Traumdeutung* (1900) in the original, but anyway had access to *The Interpretation of Dreams* in translation, and other texts were becoming available. Among his friends in Britain could be counted Freudian analysts, principally David Eder (they met in 1914), who translated Freud into English, and Barbara Low. Lawrence also discussed psychoanalysis with Ernest Jones who wrote on child psychology. In 1919, in Italy, Lawrence felt inspired to take up the topic: 'I am going to do various small things – on Italy and on psyco-analysis [sic] – for the periodicals' (*Letters* III: 426-7), to express 'something definite in place of the vague Freudian Unconscious' (*Letters* IV: 40). Both books, but especially *Psychoanalysis*, are intent on retrieving the idea of 'the unconscious' from the Freudians.

The reviews of *Psychoanalysis* and *Fantasia* were not universally positive, although John Middleton Murry praised Lawrence's project (Draper 1970: 184–7). It is some time since Lawrence has been taken seriously as a reader of Freud, and yet his engagement with the psychoanalytic is not too surprising. He shared Freud's interest in the instinctive life. Possibly he read into Freud's scientism a betrayal of that instinctive life. Freud, very early on in *Psychoanalysis and the Unconscious*, is dismissed as a *clinician*, at the very worst 'the psychiatric quack'. There is a suggestion of Jekyll and Hyde in 'the psychoanalytic gentleman' who moves through the previously unchartered terrain of the mind only to dwell in a subterranean 'cavern of dreams', where he finds, 'a huge slimy serpent of sex, and heaps of excrement, and a myriad repulsive little horrors spawned between sex and excrement' (F&P 203).

Where Freud developed a language for the psycho-sexual dramas of infancy, and unconscious processes, Lawrence displayed a complete intolerance of his methodology: 'Psychoanalysis, the moment it begins to demonstrate the nature of the unconscious, is assuming the role of psychology' (204).

The two books on the unconscious, then, set out to challenge what Lawrence most resented in psychoanalysis as he understood it – the absolute adherence to the Cartesian distinction of mind and body in Freud's thought (this is the *'cogito ergo sum'* of the French philosopher René Descartes [1596–1650]). In *Pansies*, it is claimed 'I am, I don't think I am' (CP 474). In anti-Cartesian mode, then, *Psychoanalysis* and *Fantasia* give the fullest expression to Lawrence's psycho-biology, a physiology of emotional feeling – a genealogy of the unconscious. Central to *Psychoanalysis*, in particular, is the confidence with which Lawrence locates non-deliberate, instinctive, 'knowledge' in the sensual *body*, continually resisting what he perceives to be the psychoanalytic concentration on *mind*. This insistence gives rise to the materialist philosophy of the ganglia and plexuses, the important sites of feeling – of 'consciousness' argues Lawrence – which are ambivalently present in the body. Knowledge of the world and of the other (not-self), is established in these centres of consciousness in the chest and abdomen, the solar plexus and the cardiac plexus. It is from such centres, and from the life-blood, Lawrence argues, that individuals act: 'blood-consciousness ... is the very source and origin of us' (183). Paradoxically (in language), this is the Lawrentian *'un*conscious'.

The phrase 'blood-consciousness' occupies a central place in Lawrence's lexicon. It has often been taken to have racial meaning, where 'blood' is given more weight than 'consciousness' in the construction. At the time of writing *Fantasia*, however, Lawrence's emphasis was on the 'life-blood' as the bodily centre of 'unconscious' feeling and functioning. Individuals act, he argues, from the blood before they act from the mind. 'Mental consciousness' is the domain of the social self, rather than the sensual self. In the chapter of *Fantasia* called 'The Lower Self' Lawrence develops his 'elemental' model. It is a chapter which resorts to his familiar language of binary oppositions: moon/sun, night/day, dark/light, blood/mind, male/female. Social functioning is understood in these terms: to wake from night into day is to travel from the blood and the darkness (the 'source' of us) into the light, but at the end of the day there is a return from 'mental consciousness and activity' to 'the darkness and elemental consciousness of the blood' (183). Unlike Freud, Lawrence's primary interest is not pathology, but he argues that a perversion (an over-development) of the 'upper consciousness', principally in women, leads to 'modern' self-consciousness and a perversion of sex (188–9). This model lies behind the characters of Kate Leslie (*The Plumed Serpent*) and the Princess (*The Princess*). In both texts, as we have seen, this emphasis on 'the darkness and elemental consciousness of the blood' (183) acquires an objectionable racial dimension.

This interest in the roots of consciousness persists in Lawrence after the books on the unconscious – this is demonstrated in the discursive writing of the American period. Later, in 1927 he favourably reviewed *The Social Basis of Consciousness* by Trigant Burrow, a psychologist who had broken away from Freud's ideas in certain particulars. Much of Burrow's work deals with social as well as individual behaviour. In the text read by Lawrence, Burrow shows what seems to the reviewer to be a pleasing concentration on group analysis (and group-consciousness) over and above the privately negotiated relationship of analyst/analysand in a one-to-one clinical context. Although elsewhere Lawrence writes at length on the integrity of the individual, he must always balance this emphasis with an idea of a sympathetic community. As usual, we learn more about Lawrence than about the book under review, and in particular about his views on communality (as opposed to 'society', which is negative). Burrow's preference for group therapy represents a creative situation which appeals at this time to Lawrence once he has cast the idea in the light of his own assumptions.

Hence, Burrow moves Lawrence to express that which lies at the foundations of many of his own statements on egocentricity versus community. In the review, he articulates his own reservations about the 'self-conscious phase of [man's] mental evolution' (*Phoenix* 378) which produces repressive social systems (ideals). Lawrence despises the idea of social expectations which mould the subject at the level of the unconscious; he objects to the idea that 'Freudism' returns 'cured' and well-adjusted people back to a society which has its orthodoxies firmly in place. The analyst, who restores the subject to 'normality', polices positively dissenting individuals. As Lawrence puts it, 'Individuals rebel: and these are the neurotics, who show some sign of health' (380).

(v) *Studies in Classic American Literature*

The essays on American literature, with their concentration on uncon-scious levels of creativity and resistance ('Never trust the artist. Trust the tale' [SCAL 8]), have been described as psychoanalytic studies of literary texts (Wright 1989). This is despite Lawrence's evident scepticism of Freudian psychoanalysis **[102]** – and it is not 'Freudian' readings that Lawrence suggests. *Studies in Classic American Literature* offers a highly idiosyncratic critique of a body of texts; poetry and fiction. It also shows Lawrence attempting to theorize a culture with which, at the time of publication, he was newly acquainted.

The essay on Benjamin Franklin is the first 'case study' that properly opens the volume and it helpfully and clearly enables Lawrence to set out his stall. Franklin's injunctions to his fellow Americans offer them the spectre, argues Lawrence, of 'the ideal self' produced by a social morality, albeit a worthy morality. Hence Lawrence's satire on the maxims of Benjamin Franklin and on his 'creed'. The cultivated and rational man defined by Franklin as the ideal is only part of the story for Lawrence, and probably the worst part: Franklin, with his social programme for the new America, 'says I am nothing but a servant of mankind'. In contrast insists Lawrence, 'I am absolutely a servant of my own Holy Ghost' (SCAL 25). The integrity of the individual to be an individual is threatened by the social programme.

Crèvecœur mirrors Franklin when he demonstrates a need to regulate and control nature. Crèvecœur's fantasy of nature, of the new American farmer and his relation to the soil, is a 'predetermined fancy' (35), argues Lawrence. Where much of Crèvecœur's writing comes from 'blood-knowledge', however, that is the 'tale' speaking over the 'artist':

> You can idealize or intellectualize. Or, on the contrary, you can let the dark soul in you see for itself. An artist usually intellectualizes on top, and his dark under-consciousness goes on contradicting him beneath. … Crèvecœur is the first example (31).

That last comment puts Franklin in his place. In both examples – Franklin and Crèvecœur – idealism is the problem and the obstruction to knowledge, but because Crèvecœur is (despite himself) an artist (30) a kind of truth emerges out of his text that he cannot repress for all his embracing of Franklin's kind of rationalism in concert with his own sentimentalism. In Crèvecœur, then, comes Lawrence's first example of the principal creed of *Studies in Classic American Literature*, that 'Art-speech is the only truth. An artist is usually a damned liar, but his art, if it be art, will tell you the truth of his day' (8). Franklin might privilege 'eternal' truths, as he also believes in the 'immortal' soul; but the artist shows truth to be relative and contingent – and in Lawrence's terms, alive.

The essays on Fenimore Cooper take a slightly different direction. They begin by stating the impossibility of 'reconciliation' between

Native, and white, Americans. In the *Leatherstocking* novels, Lawrence sees a model of 'wish-fulfilment' – his term – in the posited blood-brotherhood of Natty and Chingachgook, an ideal which, he argues, shows a real ignorance of history. It is an 'evasion of actuality', 'a sheer myth' (57). This is so because Cooper has not understood that processes which are bigger than the individual have to be worked through before old antagonisms can be transcended:

> To open out a new wide area of consciousness means to slough the old consciousness. The old consciousness has become a tight-fitting prison to us, in which we are going rotten.
> You can't have a new, easy skin before you have sloughed the old, tight skin.
>
> (SCAL 57–8)

The whistle-stop critique of the *Leatherstocking* novels shows that Lawrence now has his theme. Where Cooper's vision is big, with its new morality and the myths of the 'new world' which it seeks to create, Poe is different. All interior, Poe deals with 'the disintegration-processes of his own psyche' (70). The essay 'Edgar Allan Poe' can usefully be read alongside 'The Lower Self' chapter of *Fantasia of the Unconscious*.

Reading 'Ligeia', Lawrence offers a psychoanalysis of Poe which employs the language of *Fantasia* (SCAL 73–4). 'Ligeia', with its over-conscious 'anatomizing' style, is a tale about the perils of 'volition' in love; of the insistent human will which works against the real 'living' self. Ligeia's intensity (recalling Poe's 'earnestness'), underlines the reductiveness of the 'will-to-love' and the 'will-to-consciousness' (81), hence the emphasis in Lawrence's interpretation on the disastrous effects of her (and Poe) craving the sensations of love (77). This same 'meretricious process' (83), which characterizes Poe's style as well as his plots, dogs 'The Fall of the House of Usher' with its emphasis on the wilful identification of one lover with another, at the cost of their self-sufficiency.

If Poe palpably glorified his 'sickness' in art, Nathaniel Hawthorne enables Lawrence further to peel away the surface in order to uncover the 'symbolic meaning' (89). In his reading of *The Scarlet Letter* Lawrence expresses himself again in polarities presented first in *Fantasia*: he describes his dualism of 'blood-consciousness' and 'mind-consciousness' **[103]**, and says that in America lip-service is paid to the spontaneity of the 'blood' (as in the nature writing of Crèvecœur), but that this is meretricious in such a 'mental' culture. *The Scarlet Letter*'s Dimmesdale, for instance, despises the life of the body but, worse, when he transgresses with Hester he makes a bed-fellow of one of his 'spiritual brides' (96). His self-disgust, expressed in his scourging of his body, is a masturbatory impulse to Lawrence (96), as is his acknowledgement and acceptance that he and Hester have offended social laws. The elevation of moral purity to a creed, combined with the impulse to dismantle the foundations of this creed, is a tendency which Lawrence believes he recognizes in American culture: Hawthorne simply offers a 'parable' in illustration (89). Hester is able to work against the spiritual aspirant in Dimmesdale through sex because both believe that sex is sinful – this, argues Lawrence, is their folly. Her outward humility conceals her pleasure in victory, and in this she is a version of Ligeia. Vengeful, she works with Chillingworth, who is 'mind' not 'spirit', to bring the pure Dimmesdale down. Her daughter, Pearl, stands for modern overconscious woman, to take revenge on men in her time.

The remaining essays on novelists, Dana and Melville, focus on impersonal and inhuman forces figured most effectively in terms of the sea. In Dana's *Two Years Before the Mast* and Melville's *Typee*, *Omoo* and *Moby Dick*, Lawrence finds writing which addresses the elemental, natural forces that his work, in its way, seeks to privilege. Their books give Lawrence a chance again to attack idealism, always mentally derived, and to privilege an impersonal mode of consciousness (Melville's 'dream-self', for instance [142]). However, it is only in the reading of Whitman that Lawrence's reader is given anything like a sense of the closing of the great division between mind and body that so absorbs his attention and which eludes, he argues, the other American writers.

Whitman is a poet whom Lawrence admired from his earliest days, with some significant reservations. The essay which concludes *Studies in Classic American Literature* weaves its argument around one major theme to which other discussions are then related: the morality of the work of art. Whitman succeeds best when his art is 'moral', when sympathy 'with' does not become sympathy 'for' (we are back to the integrity of feeling). Lawrence states:

> The essential function of art is moral. Not aesthetic, not decorative, not pastime and recreation. But moral. The essential function of art is moral.
>
> But a passionate, implicit morality, not didactic. A morality which changes the blood, rather than the mind. Changes the blood first. The mind follows later, in the wake.
>
> (SCAL 180)

Of Hawthorne, Poe, Longfellow, Emerson and Melville, Lawrence says: 'they give tight mental allegiance to a morality which all their passion goes to destroy. Hence the duplicity which is the fatal flaw in them, most fatal in the most perfect American work of art, *The Scarlet Letter*.' (180). In Whitman, in contrast, Lawrence finds, from among the American writers who absorb his attention, a genuinely radical and iconoclastic thinker. He does not necessarily agree with Whitman's formulations – about 'Democracy', or the 'love of comrades' (178) to which Lawrence refers sceptically in *Kangaroo* **[70]** – but he finds in his work some acknowledgement of the value of extreme experience: Whitman writes of 'the transitions of the soul as it loses its integrity' (179). The singular achievement of Whitman in relation to his fellow writers, and an American tradition, is his work's refusal to reinforce the values of inherited ideals. Lawrence's essay appears to be highly critical of Whitman when he is perceived to be caught up on a fixed idea (mental allegiance), and only relents where poetry becomes the vehicle of radical and resistant thought. Whitman's importance also lies in his ability to see the soul (self) in terms of the 'flesh' – 'belly', 'breast', 'womb' (180). As this foregrounds Lawrence's religious and artistic impulses it is fitting that the Whitman essay concludes the book. In the American books, the old morality has given way to a new vision.

(vi) Essays on the Novel

'Art and the Individual' anticipates Lawrence's extensive writing on fiction, and in particular, the function and value of the contemporary novel. This is the case in 'The Future of the Novel' (1923; originally called 'Surgery for the Novel – Or a Bomb'), 'Morality and the Novel', 'The Novel', 'Why the Novel Matters', 'The Novel and the Feelings' (all written in 1925), alongside more tightly focused responses to particular writers, such as the essay on John Galsworthy, completed in 1927.

The first half of 'The Future of the Novel' represents Lawrence's dislike of the self-reflexive, linguistically self-conscious, experimental fictions of some of his 'high modernist' contemporaries, with Dorothy Richardson's *Pointed Roofs* (1915) and James Joyce's *Ulysses* (1922) singled out for particular criticism. However, Lawrence also finds in popular fiction an equally undesirable form of self-consciousness from that to be encountered in the 'avant-garde' writing of his contemporaries. He deals derisively with the romantic westerns of Zane Grey, and best-selling writers who, in their sensationalism, appeal actually to banal orthodoxies of feeling. He is satirical, for instance, about 'Sheik heroines with whipped posteriors, wildly adored' (STH 153). Both high modernism and popular fiction represent, for Lawrence, then, puerile and insensitive uses of the novel form which is still, he argues, in its infancy (we remember the high hopes he had for the novel in 'Study of Thomas Hardy'). It is in the course of articulating his resistance to a number of tendencies in modern fiction that he promotes the idea of an unselfconsciously 'philosophical' fiction, to which condition, we must assume, his own writing aspires:

> It seems to me it was the greatest pity in the world, when philosophy and fiction got split. ... So the novel went sloppy, and philosophy went abstract-dry. The two should come together again, *in the novel*. And we get modern kind of gospels, and modern myths, and *a new way of understanding*.
>
> (154; emphasis added)

Art and thought should dovetail in the novel for 'newness', not novelty.

Lawrence's preoccupation with questions of genre, and principally the novel form, is occasionally foregrounded in his fiction. In *Kangaroo*, in the chapter called 'Bits', a debate about the function of the novel is combined with reflections on the self: 'Now a novel is supposed to be a mere record of emotion-adventures, flounderings in feelings. We insist that a novel is, or should be, also a thought-adventure, if it is to be anything at all complete' (K 279). In *Lady Chatterley's Lover*, too, Lawrence meditates on genre, examining how 'properly handled', the novel can direct the flow of 'sympathetic consciousness', although it can also pervert this flow and 'glorify the most corrupt feelings' in the hands of a bad artist (LCL 102) **[77]**.

In 'Morality and the Novel' the responsibility of the writer of fiction, argues Lawrence, is to remain true to a sense of shifting values that constitute human feeling, rather than reinforcing myths about the dominant status, in fiction, of one value over another. Consequently, he insists:

> All emotions, including love and hate, and rage and tenderness, go to the adjusting of the oscillating, unestablished balance between two people who amount to anything. If the novelist puts his thumb in the pan, for love, tenderness, sweetness, peace, then he commits an immoral act: he *prevents* the possibility of a pure relationship, a

pure relatedness, the only thing that matters: and he makes inevitable the horrible reaction, when he lets his thumb go, towards hate and brutality, cruelty and destruction.

(STH 173)

Lawrence himself, it must be said, was not above putting his thumb in the pan (he had just finished the over-conscious and dogmatic *The Plumed Serpent*). The metaphor of balance in this passage combines with an image of strife, of opposition, central to the expression of the same idea in other contexts (the 'Reptiles' section of *Birds, Beasts and Flowers*, 'The Crown' and 'Study of Thomas Hardy'). If a novel deals effectively with 'true' and 'vivid relationships', then that novel is 'moral' (174).

Originally called 'The Modern Novel', but published as 'The Novel', this essay of 1925 continues the defence of a 'relational' aesthetic which is expressed in the earlier pieces: 'The novel is the highest form of human expression so far attained. Why? Because it is so incapable of the absolute' (179). To explain this position, Lawrence provides examples of novels that fail, on his terms, through an insistence on a number of indirectly stated general principles (absolutes) that are seen to direct characters' destinies; this is a didacticism which is sustained and reinforced by the novelist (he discussed this in *Studies in Classic American Literature* **[104]**). These principles are most often recognizable as aspects of a dominant ideology, a morality or social code – an ideal. However, as he shows in *Studies in Classic American Literature*, the artist's 'under' consciousness, in the novel, will usually work against repressive orthodoxy.

Published posthumously, 'Why the Novel Matters' and 'The Novel and the Feelings' reinforce Lawrence's sense of the importance of the novel defined less in 'literary-critical' terms and more in relation to his personal aspirations for the form: he claims, 'The novel is the book of life. In this sense, the Bible is a great confused novel . . . about man-alive' (195). Consistently, his view is that depictions of false consciousness show up in the novel better than in any other kind of writing. In 'The Novel and the Feelings', articulating this notion of false consciousness, Lawrence polarises *knowing* ('education') and *feelings* in order to identify a crisis in modernity which has forced these values apart. For the artist, this crisis becomes a matter of language. Lawrence's statement 'We have no language for the feelings' (203) is at the heart of his hopes for his own novels.

Further Reading

The most extensive commentary on the 'Study of Thomas Hardy' and related discursive writing occurs in Black (1991). This provides a useful examination in chapter by chapter analyses of the metaphors and modes of argument employed by Lawrence in the early essays. Much of the work done by Black shows continuity in Lawrence's thought at the level of language, where coherence might not be thought to exist. Ellis and Mills (1988) also concentrate on the exploratory writing and the development of Lawrence's thought. Heywood (1987) discusses the psycho-physiological writing as do, with different emphases, Ellis (1986), Hayles (1982; 1984) and Vickery (in Salgādo and Das [eds] 1988). Ebbatson and Delavenay also contribute chapters on Lawrence's thought to Heywood (ed., 1987); see also Ebbatson (1982). Schneider (1984) examines the writing which seeks to take issue with Freud; Becket (1997) examines metaphor as a mode of understanding in Lawrence's books on the unconscious. Gordon (1966) considers Lawrence as a literary critic. Ellis and de Zordo (1992) re-present several decades of responses to Lawrence's non-fiction. Hough (1956) includes a section on 'The Doctrine', a phrase taken up much later by George Zytaruk in Balbert and Marcus (eds, 1985). As always in Lawrence criticism, these book-length studies and chapters supplement a wealth of writing published in journal articles.

(h) TRAVEL WRITING

Lawrence is a writer who continually subjected his environment – in Italy, for example, or Mexico – to imaginative analysis. He had a real curiosity about cultures other than his own but his best 'travel' books are multi-layered meditations which take 'place' as a starting point and go out in many directions. From 1912 his dissatisfaction with England was expressed in extensive journeys abroad and, after 1919, he settled for long periods in Italy and America, with some experience of other continents [21–7]. Apart from many detailed essays and articles on diverse cultures, the principal travel books are *Twilight in Italy* (1916), *Sea and Sardinia* (1921), *Mornings in Mexico* (1927) and *Sketches of Etruscan Places* (1932). The present discussion will concentrate on the Italian books.

(i) *Twilight in Italy*

The heart of *Twilight in Italy* consists of seven essays about the people and community of Lake Garda ('On the Lago di Garda', TI 103–226). Most closely observed, as so often in Lawrence's fiction, is the figure of the peasant most mythologized, perhaps, in the study of the 'half-diabolic' Pan-like 'Il Duro' (TI 173–8). Many of the encounters described in *Twilight* reinforce the essential 'strangeness' which persists between the traveller and the native 'folk'. This lack of a common ground is behind the compulsion *and* the constraint in the wonderfully observed encounter, for example, between Lawrence ('I') and the old spinner woman in 'The Spinner and the Monks'. The narrator comes across her as he leaves the darkness of the village church of San Tommaso for the sunlit terraces outside, but lingers, finding her absorption in her work attractive. He sees in her presence confirmation of his distance from her reality, and her indifference to his. Later, the narrator notices two monks somewhere below, walking in their 'wintry' garden. In the twilight, they seem to him to occupy the place where day and night meet. Such encounters and visions are understood metaphorically as well as actually: they illuminate Lawrence's dualistic thought, the 'two principles' which he also articulated in 'Study of Thomas Hardy' **[99]**. The 'neutrality' of the twilight, for instance, enables the narrator to think through the different values, or properties, to him of 'day' and 'night' consciousness. These are some of the first terms in his thought which would translate into the major works of fiction. The fifth essay in the series, called 'The Dance', also anticipates details in the writing of dance as a transformative experience, particularly in *The Rainbow* and *Women in Love*, but in 'On the Lago di Garda' it is enough for Lawrence to note the unconscious dimension of experience (in instinctive action) which is at the heart of spectacle.

Earlier in the volume, in 'The Lemon Gardens', the language is similar to that of the Foreword to *Sons and Lovers* **[47]** in its emphasis on the symbolism of the flesh and the Word, and the language of principles, 'Infinites', to describe cultural and social process. Such interventions show the extent to which 'travel writing' is a modest description of the metaphysical speculation undertaken in the 'Italian' texts. These formulations describe Lawrence's philosophy of self-regeneration through vital experience, and inform his observation that the cost of over-conscious, 'modern' civilization ('the mechanising, the perfect mechanising of human life' [TI 226]) is the destruction of the 'Self', as evident here as in his 'home' culture (discussed in the Brangwen novels). So, in part, what is revealed in *Twilight in Italy* are some of the terms of

Lawrence's developing philosophy of the instinctive, intuitive, life set against his version of the 'horror' (225). His visions of Italy helped him to formulate a language in which to translate this particular experience.

(ii) *Sea and Sardinia*

Sea and Sardinia (1921) is a much more conventional travel book than either *Twilight in Italy* or *Sketches of Etruscan Places*. Lawrence left England for Italy the second time in 1919, and lived there before setting off in 1922 for America, to which he would travel by going east, via Ceylon and Australia **[21–7]**. His brief excursion in January 1921 from his home in Taormina, Sicily, to Sardinia provided a diversion from *Aaron's Rod*, which he was concluding. He travelled with Frieda Lawrence (the 'queen-bee', or 'q-b', of the narrative), and describes vividly their preparations to leave, under the shadow of Etna, and the day-to-day details of their journey, arrival, sojourn and departure. *Sea and Sardinia* demonstrates Lawrence's skilful attention to particulars which is also an aspect of his literary realism, especially in the 'Eastwood' fiction. The narrative concentrates less on predictable tourist spots and more on the minutiae of chance encounters and environments – peering through the condensation on train windows to fathom the cause of a delay, or the liberating hills and valleys of the drive to Nuoro, for example. Most often we see the land through its effect on Lawrence, the narrator as 'revived'. It is a short-lived, but personal, odyssey. Although there are passages which reflect on the condition of post-war Italy through encounters with individuals ('To Terranova and the Steamer' and 'Back'), Lawrence makes little direct reference to the political crises of liberal Italy (Mussolini's march on Rome would take place in 1922), although turning points in *Aaron's Rod* are described with reference to local conflict.

(iii) *Sketches of Etruscan Places*

In 1925, Lawrence left New Mexico for the last time **[27]** and settled for a while just outside Florence. *Sketches of Etruscan Places* (published posthumously as *Etruscan Places*) was the result of Lawrence's tour, with his friend Earl Brewster, to the Etruscan sites of Cerveteri, Tarquinia, Vulci and Volterra **[27]**. He quickly polarizes, in this writing, the will-to-power of ancient Roman culture with the spontaneity and vitality that he perceived in the iconography, art and simple architecture of the Etruscans. The book is an imaginative 'inhabiting' of the religious and domestic values of a fundamentally sensual, anti-intellectual people, closer in spirit perhaps to that which Lawrence hoped to discover in the Native American cultures of his Mexico and New Mexico writing. The contrast between the agrarian Etruscan and the militaristic Roman cultures has its contemporary counterpart in Lawrence's representation of the easy-going Tuscan peasants (in a continuation of Lawrence's rustic idealism), and the provincial fascists. On his last brief trip to London Lawrence had visited the British Museum, interested in the Etruscan artefacts. In Italy, looking at the tombs, he found himself imagining a culture which acknowledged the life of the body in ways that spoke to his immediate concerns in writing about the contrasting sterility of 'civilized' post-war England. His 'Etruscan' book is contemporaneous with the latter stages of the composition of *Lady Chatterley's Lover*, and the two volumes illuminate each other in their dissatisfaction with 'mental conscious' modernity, and the development of Lawrence's theme of 'phallic consciousness'. In *Sketches of Etruscan Places*, an animated and sensual life is expressed in the values which Lawrence ascribes to the symbolic phallus ('lingam') and arx (womb) which are represented in stone at the entrance to tombs for men and women respectively ('Cerveteri')

> And perhaps in the insistence on these two symbols, in the etruscan world, we can see the reason for the utter destruction and annihilation of the etruscan consciousness. The new world wanted to rid itself of these fatal, dominant symbols of the old world, the old physical world. The etruscan conscious was rooted, quite blithely, in these symbols, the phallus and the arx. So the whole consciousness, the whole etruscan pulse and rhythm, must be wiped out.
>
> (SEP 20)

So it is that, in his detailed discussions of the representations of men, women and animals on these tombs, Lawrence finds, perhaps because he needs to find, a 'profound belief in life' which gets a special restatement in his last writing.

Further Reading

Twilight in Italy and *Sketches of Etruscan Places* in particular are discussed together or individually in L.D. Clark (1980), Meyers (1982), Ellis and Mills (1988), De Filippis (1989 and 1992), Black (1991) and Kalnins and Donaldson (eds, 1999). Janik (1981) and Tracy (1983) discuss Lawrence's travel literature, and Hostettler (1985) considers the travel books in relation to the fiction. A great deal of related material is published in literary journals.

PART III

CRITICISM

The aim of this section is to consider a range of critical responses to the work of D.H. Lawrence. Consequently, the views of his contemporaries and early commentators (which included T.S. Eliot, E.M. Forster, Aldous Huxley, John Middleton Murry and Rebecca West, among others who are now less well remembered) will be represented and placed in context, together with the views of more recent critics. Since his death Lawrence's general significance has altered considerably – both the work and the man have sustained the extremes of positive and negative reaction. In the 1930s T.S. Eliot (a critic as well as a poet) was largely responsible for the dominant view of Lawrence as a flawed, undisciplined writer with questionable values. Critic F.R. Leavis, however, taking issue with what he came to view as Eliot's distortions, very successfully re-positioned Lawrence as a creative genius who offered a body of work and, crucially, directions for living. Highly influential in the 1950s, Leavis inspired many to re-read Lawrence. In 1960 the trial and acquittal of Penguin Books at the Old Bailey for the publication of an unexpurgated *Lady Chatterley's Lover* further sustained Lawrence's reputation as a social prophet **[27; 75]**. While counter-views were offered to this championing of Lawrence and his 'human' values, on the whole his positive profile survived until the 1970s when Kate Millett's feminist analysis of his sexual politics (1969) forced a re-think, and inspired further distinctive and wide-ranging responses. In the next two decades there followed biographical studies and ambitious editorial projects, and literature which drew in the main on feminist, Marxist and psychoanalytic scholarship: if Lawrence's perceived values were still an issue, the focus was also more strictly on textuality and, occasionally, the historical. Bearing in mind the vast body of Lawrence criticism, this section of the *Guide* offers a synopsis of its main directions. Where, in the 1950s and 1960s, the emphasis tended to be on the novels, and principally on *The Rainbow* and *Women in Love*, latterly a great deal more interest has been shown in the short fiction, poetry, plays and travel writing. Lawrence is a writer who, as we shall see, has engendered some extreme responses both during and after his lifetime, and who is certain to continue to inspire critical debate.

(a) LAWRENCE AND HIS CONTEMPORARIES

Contemporary reviews of Lawrence's work are usually interesting and informative, if not quite in ways that the reviewer might have intended.

Anyone interested in Lawrence might find it useful to examine the
character and drift of reviews that accompanied or immediately
followed the publication of, not least, the novels (Draper reprints a
broad selection of these in *D.H. Lawrence: The Critical Heritage* [1970]).
Responses to *Sons and Lovers*, for instance, acknowledged new strengths
in a young writer, now properly launched on his career, strengths which
had not been sustained in *The White Peacock* and *The Trespasser* (although
Lawrence's rejection of the psychoanalytic interpretations of *Sons and
Lovers*, typified in the response of Alfred Booth Kuttner, has already
been noted **[44]**). Lascelles Abercrombie, whose poetry had appeared
alongside Lawrence's in Edward Marsh's volume *Georgian Poetry*, noted
the poetic power of this third novel in his review for the *Manchester
Guardian* (Draper 1970: 67–8), drawing attention to the author's skills
of characterization despite manifest flaws of structure and execution.
In the *New York Times Book Review*, Louise Maunsell Field praised
Lawrence's realism and, like many, made a point of identifying Mrs
Morel as a compelling figure (Draper 1970: 73–5).

Two years later Lawrence could not have been fully prepared for
the negative reviews of *The Rainbow* which contributed to the processes
that resulted in the book's destruction in England **[19; 49]**. Among
many, Robert Lynd of the *Daily News*, and James Douglas writing in
Star (Draper 1970: 91–2; 93–5) condemned it, Douglas seeing in
Lawrence a repulsive irreverence for life and an inexplicable scepticism
towards the central moral values of the day. The main problem was
sex: to Lynd the book is 'a monotonous wilderness of phallicism' (92)
while Douglas feels distaste at the 'hard, stiff, pontifical worship of
the gross' (93) and in recommending the book's 'isolation' (94) he
recommends its suppression. Much later, in 1932, abridged editions of
an equally controversial book, *Lady Chatterley's Lover*, were reviewed
but commentators, among them V.S. Pritchett (287–8) and Henry
Hazlitt (289–92), were able to denounce both censorship in general,
and the particular treatment meted out by several hands to Lawrence's
text.

It is perhaps no surprise that Lawrence – who found for himself
that writing for newspapers could pay quite well – often took a dim
view of critics' motives and, if many of his comments are believed,
viewed critics (and most particularly reviewers) as hacks spinning a
few words in return for coin. He most usually encountered printed
criticism of his own work in reviews – in national papers within Europe
and America, and in the cutting-edge literary periodicals of the day –
although critical studies were published in his lifetime. In America, in
1924, Herbert Seligmann published *D.H. Lawrence: An American*

Interpretation. Interestingly, Lawrence maintained contact with him and trusted his judgement – Seligmann reviewed *Lady Chatterley's Lover* positively (*Letters* VII: 27). Literary surveys of contemporary literature would generally include Lawrence and he was also the subject of articles: 'Somebody sent me the first sheet of the *N [ew] Y [ork] Tribune* with Stuart P. Sherman's article on me. It amused me rather. But a beard is a thing that cultivates itself: if you'll let it. I must get the second leaf, and see what he says about *St Mawr*' (*Letters* V: 272) – to explain, Sherman's article was called, strangely, 'Lawrence Cultivates His Beard'. So Lawrence was not always combative in the face of professional criticism, and he supported Edward McDonald's endeavours to compile a complete and detailed bibliography of his work, which was published in 1925 as *A Bibliography of the Writings of D.H. Lawrence* ('It seems to me wonderfully complete, and *alive*: marvellous to make a bibliography lively' [*Letters* V: 272]).

Towards the end of his life his letters show him putting a great deal of energy into locating manuscripts and typescripts of his works because he now recognized their value as part of his legacy to Frieda Lawrence, who was clearly going to outlive him. If he knew this, Lawrence must have realized the part critics would play in establishing his cultural value. Lawrence was, too, a literary critic himself, and his essays on the novel in particular have enjoyed, and continue to enjoy, a high status in twentieth-century literary studies **[104; 108]**. His singular vision for his own writing dominates his responses to others' work, formally and informally, so that on many occasions his commentaries on the writing of his contemporaries approaches self-criticism (in the best sense).

In May 1927 Lawrence wrote to Richard Aldington thanking him for a copy of his short 'homage', *D.H. Lawrence: an indiscretion* and offering idiosyncratic comment on it. Insomuch as this is not a memoir (in 1950, Aldington satisfied that need with *Portrait of a Genius, But ...*), it differs from most of the other books produced about him by Lawrence's friends. In the ten years or so after his death high numbers of memoirs and reminiscences were published (by the Brewsters, Brett, Carswell, Chambers, Corke, Dodge Luhan, Ada Lawrence, Murry *et al.*) **[30]**. The novelist and journalist Rebecca West attempted to summarize Lawrence's lasting importance as a writer in an extensive obituary which was published as a volume by Secker in 1930. She begins by recording her disappointment at the press obituaries which preserve the crassest myths about their subject, and quotes extensively from an anonymous piece in the *Times Literary Supplement* which, she finds, does some kind of justice to Lawrence's vision and achievement. An anecdote, based on her personal experience of Lawrence, obliquely compares him to Dante and St Augustine, and she concludes that his novels – which she regards as written in a highly personal symbolic mode that makes their meaning often difficult to grasp – achieve an unsurpassed proximity to 'truth', even when they are flawed. Of *Women in Love*, she writes:

> he cannot tell his story save by the clumsy creation of images that do not give up their meaning till the book has been read many times. But even these struggles are of value, since they recall to one the symbolic nature of all thought. Knowledge is but a translation of reality into terms comprehensible by the human mind, a grappling with a mystery. None undertake it with the courage of Lawrence unless they very greatly care.
>
> (West 1930: 39)

Of another 'failure', *Lady Chatterley's Lover*, she declares: 'He laid sex and those base words for it on the salver of his art and held them up before the consciousness of the world, which was his way of approaching creation' (40). Her choice of works to refer to here are interesting, as they were among the least acknowledged by Lawrence's contemporary commentators. West is insightful in her account, as she anticipates the critical response that would follow, decades later, to these controversial texts. E.M. Forster was similarly positive about Lawrence's achievement in the face of negative criticism from T.S. Eliot in particular; and Arnold Bennett, with whom Lawrence had had a few spats, also mounted a spirited defence of his work.

Lawrence had worked hard to succeed in an American market after the disastrous reception of *The Rainbow* in Britain [19; 49–56], and so it is not surprising that the first detailed studies of his writing came out in America. In Britain, the first notable full-length commentary was John Middleton Murry's book, *Son of Woman*, published in 1931, shortly after Lawrence's death. As most of the later biographies of Lawrence make clear, implicitly or explicitly, Murry was seen by Lawrence's allies and champions as barely suitable to publish a major work of criticism on his 'friend' [20]. However, the fact of his association with Lawrence made it seem to the reading public that he wrote with authority about this difficult and rebellious figure who was associated primarily with some highly unorthodox views about sex. Lawrence's reservations about Murry's conservatism were not widely known outside their circle, and Murry was, anyhow, well respected nationally as a critic and man of letters.

Son of Woman (which T.S. Eliot reviewed positively in the *Criterion*) certainly added weight to the tendency to read Lawrence's *oeuvre* as principally autobiographical, and much of Murry's critical energy is expended in diagnostic episodes which emphasize the crippling effect of his mother's love for Lawrence, and the subsequent difficulties he experienced in relationships with women. Murry starts his book with excessive praise of *Fantasia of the Unconscious* and brings his familiarity with that work to bear on his readings of the fiction and poetry. He addresses the writing as symptomatic of the life; how Lawrence worked out his problems or fantasies usually around the issues of masculinity and power. Of *Women in Love*, a novel which Murry reviewed negatively ('turgid, exasperated writing impelled towards some distant and invisible end' [Draper 1970: 169]), he offers an interpretation with which many feminist critics, decades later, might be in some agreement:

> To annihilate the female insatiably demanding physical satisfaction from the man who cannot give it her – the female who has thus annihilated him – this is Lawrence's desire. To make her subject again, to re-establish his own manhood – this is the secret purpose of *Women in Love*. In imagination, he has his desire. He creates a sexual mystery beyond the phallic, wherein he is the lord; and he makes the woman acknowledge the existence of this ultra-phallic realm, and his own lordship in it. He triumphs over her in imagination, but not in life.
>
> (Murry 1931: 118)

So it is that Murry both anticipates interesting debates about sexuality and power in Lawrence *and* manages to settle a few old scores by emphasizing what he perceived to be Lawrence's rigid mania for theorizing sexual relations around his own inadequacies. Murry also, it might be noted, since he chooses to write in part about Lawrence's representation of women, had strong feelings for Frieda Lawrence which were brought to some kind of resolution immediately after Lawrence's death (Ellis 1998: 534). Murry then, is one of the few of Lawrence's important critics to have had a significant, long-term involvement in his life and relationships which made impartiality quite impossible, but that does not exclude the occasion of insightful commentary.

Probably because he took exception to Murry's version of Lawrence, Aldous Huxley (who satirized Murry in his novel *Point Counter Point* [1928] where Lawrence also appears as the character Rampion) sought to be corrective in the introduction to his edition of Lawrence's letters published in 1932. Murry's representation of Lawrence, argued Huxley, was largely 'irrelevant' because it overlooked the fact that Lawrence required evaluation principally as an artist, 'and an artist with a particular kind of mental endowment'. Huxley's importance to early Lawrence criticism is in large part his resistance to the predominance of the biographical approach. He was interested in the philosophical parameters of Lawrence's thought and acknowledged his value as a thinker. Huxley's introduction to the letters is couched in terms that Lawrence probably would have approved. He is the first commentator properly to represent Lawrence's preoccupation with 'modes of being'. Huxley also hints at Lawrence's dissatisfaction with the Cartesian split of mind and body in Western thought, describing this in terms of his subject's 'mystical materialism' with its insistence on the necessity of the 'resurrection of the body', which is also the rebirth of the self, through sensitive contact with the external world. He quotes at length from a document which was to become central to readings of Lawrence thereafter, the letter about character in the novel written to his mentor, Edward Garnett, on 5 June 1914 (*Letters* II: 182–4) **[54]**. Lawrence's position, Huxley asserts, which is brilliant and radical, explains the 'strangeness of his novels', but he is not afraid to point out that many of those novels, often in their language, fail – or are at the very least flawed. He refers to modes of expression in Lawrence, with some justification, as having 'certain qualities of violent monotony and intense indistinctness' (Huxley 1932), but his sense of Lawrence's lasting contribution to the development of the modern novel as moral is uppermost.

T.S. Eliot was the next major figure to pass judgement on Lawrence, notably in his limited representation of Lawrence's motives and values (in a comparative context) in the series of lectures published as *After Strange Gods* (1934). Lawrence's defenders frequently alight on the hostile remarks made by Eliot here and reprint them out of context, so that the negative judgements are presented at a remove from Eliot's attempts to establish exactly how Lawrence is a valuable and important writer: important despite – or perhaps because of – his position as one 'wholly free from any restriction of tradition or institution' (Eliot 1934: 59). According to the criteria promoted by Eliot in *After Strange Gods*, Lawrence is a writer who misdirected his talent because he could not overcome the disadvantages of his birth and education: the criticism of his 'insensibility to ordinary social morality' (59) communicates more about Eliot than Lawrence. Despite the acknowledgement of his literary significance it is Eliot's negative commentary on Lawrence which is remembered and repeated and it was Eliot, a highly influential critic, who carried much of the Establishment with him against Lawrence in the 1930s and later. F.R. Leavis, as he championed Lawrence, and even while he respected Eliot as a critic, would write most forcefully against Eliot's judgements – in his first book-length study of the novels he refers to 'the insistent leading part played by Eliot in retarding the recognition of Lawrence' (Leavis 1955: 18). Eliot failed to identify the Nietzschean Lawrence who was positively in favour of the revaluation of all values. Instead, he identified a 'sick' vision divorced from the 'tradition' which Eliot valued so highly. Lawrence produced other conflicting responses at the time Eliot was writing: some associated him with proto-fascism, while others read him as accommodating the values of the Left (for a discussion of Lawrence's impact which was written in the 1930s, see William York Tindall 1939: chapter 6).

Eliot's dominance of the critical scene after Lawrence's death is a fact. Less influential judgements at this time came from Horace Gregory, *Pilgrim of the Apocalypse: A Critical Study of D.H. Lawrence* (1933), and Stephen Potter, *D.H. Lawrence: A First Study* (1930). Also of this period is Tindall's critical study of Lawrence's attempts to establish his 'private religion', *D.H. Lawrence and Susan His Cow* (1939). However, this is a period when 'English studies' is relatively young and the methodologies of literary criticism itself under close scrutiny. In John Crowe Ransom's *The New Criticism* (1941) the critical practice of T.S. Eliot is discussed alongside that of I.A. Richards (whose book *Practical Criticism: A Study of Literary Judgment* [1929] includes Lawrence's poem 'Piano' among its texts for analysis), and William Empson (author of *Seven Types of Ambiguity* [1930]). Although those given consideration by Ransom did not all welcome the description of 'New Critic' as a generic term, the appellation is associated with a mode of close reading and a concentration on literary language which challenged the dominance of earlier kinds of historical analysis. American scholars who became associated with New Criticism – not always unproblematically – include Cleanth Brooks (*The Well-Wrought Urn* [1947]), Allen Tate, Robert Penn Warren and Yvor Winters, like their British counterparts, politically conservative. In 1935 their contemporary, R.P. Blackmur, wrote an authoritative criticism of Lawrence's poetry ('expressive form') judging it difficient in formal rigour and, as we have seen, Eliot had similar misgivings. Nevertheless, out of the broad 'church' of these approaches emerged, in the English academy, F.R. Leavis, and it is to Leavis, and his profound effect on the critical estimation of Lawrence, that we must turn.

(b) F.R. LEAVIS AND THE 1950s

Leavis was identified from the 1930s with the Cambridge-based literary journal *Scrutiny* and he lost no time in writing critically, cognizant of Murry and Eliot, about Lawrence's positive contribution to English literature. He writes as a self-confessed admirer, insistent about Lawrence's 'genius' and contemporary significance. In doing so, he was moving counter to T.S. Eliot's version of an 'heretical' Lawrence (in *After Strange Gods*), viewed as incapable of effective cultural analysis because of his partiality, insufficiently educated to be a custodian of meaning, and negatively anti-tradition. Aside from a considerable number of essays and commentaries, Leavis's principal and influential defence of Lawrence came in 1955 with a full-length study, *D.H. Lawrence: Novelist*. Although he returned to Lawrence in *Thought, Words and Creativity: Art and Thought in D.H. Lawrence* (1976), it is the volume of 1955 which is acknowledged to have had the most impact in its positive reassessment of Lawrence's fiction. For an understanding of the terms in which Leavis attempted to establish his version of a literary tradition in English writing, with specific emphasis on the novel, it is useful to turn to *The Great Tradition* (1948), and in particular the synoptic first chapter of that book.

It is in the context of looking for signs of literary greatness in an individual writer after Conrad (about whom Lawrence himself, incidentally, had reservations) that Leavis places so much emphasis on Lawrence's fiction. His praise is given in the most glowing terms: 'he was, as a novelist, the representative of vital and significant development' (Leavis 1948: 35); 'He is a most daring and radical innovator in "form", method, technique. And his innovations and experiments are dictated by the most serious and urgent kind of interest in life' (36). Building his argument, Leavis quotes at length from letters to Edward Garnett in which Lawrence comes close to expressing what are perceived to be central aspects of his personal philosophy and abiding aesthetic principles. These are letters on which later critics have barely ceased to draw.

Leavis was also keen to demonstrate a high degree of responsiveness to Lawrence's language. *D.H. Lawrence: Novelist* would transform the way Lawrence was received for at least a generation with the emphasis often on the uniquely creative power of Lawrence's prose. Although capable of acknowledging a capacity in Lawrence for 'jargon' and the occasional failure of artistry, if not vision, Leavis saw an integrity which he could only praise in the most elevated terms: Lawrence's 'supreme vital intelligence is the creative spirit – a spirit informed by an almost

infallible sense for health and sanity' (1955: 81). In moral understanding, Leavis argues, Lawrence is unsurpassed. His readings of the
novels also institute a new order, or hierarchy, of value within the *oeuvre*:
the Brangwen novels, *The Rainbow* and *Women in Love*, are reassessed
and placed high among Lawrence's achievements, technically more
radical than *Sons and Lovers* with which Leavis deals rather as a necessary
preliminary to more impressive, more profound, writing to come. In
the 1930s and 1940s the Brangwen novels had not been rated particularly highly – the suppression of *The Rainbow* and the accompanying
judgements had left their mark, and the influential Murry had been
very negative about *Women in Love* – but these books become central to
Leavis's evaluation of Lawrence's 'poetic', and he won a new readership
for them. While he had the authority he was at liberty to consign *The
Plumed Serpent* and early works like *The White Peacock* and *The Trespasser*
to a back shelf. Of the novellas and short stories he considered *St Mawr*
to have exceptional qualities. Readings of *St Mawr* and *Women in Love*
had appeared in *Scrutiny* in a series called 'The Novel as Dramatic Poem',
a context which throws into relief Leavis's sense of Lawrence's technical
mastery.

Leavis, who also highlighted the importance of Lawrence's writing
on Englishness, class (see his analysis of 'Daughters of the Vicar') and
'the malady of industrial civilization' (82), was keen to underline
Lawrence's value as a cultural critic, seeing in his work a profound and
extended commentary on the spiritual (and social) crises of the era (if
he was a 'prophet' it was inasmuch as his warnings about a degenerate
civilization had been proved by the Second World War to be worth
taking seriously). Hence, Lawrence was for Leavis a writer of great
moral intelligence, but largely, it has been argued (especially as Leavis's
influence has declined), because he seemed to confirm the critic's view
of the world. As Michael Black perceptively notes when writing about
the impact of the 1955 volume:

> The Lawrence who emerges [in *D.H. Lawrence: Novelist*] is Leavis's
> Lawrence. Given what had been written and accepted about
> Lawrence until then, it was a positive transformation, indeed an
> apotheosis; nonetheless it is also an appropriation, as any very
> distinctive criticism is likely to be.
>
> (Black 1995: 18)

The partiality of this assumption in Leavis that Lawrence's writing
expressed 'life values' was not authoritatively challenged, in literary
criticism, for some time.

Other monographs on Lawrence published in or just after the year of *D.H. Lawrence: Novelist* include Mary Freeman's *D.H. Lawrence: A Basic Study of His Ideas* (1955). Freeman acknowledges the *Scrutiny* articles by Leavis, and cites Stephen Spender in *The Creative Element* (1953), among others, as offering equally important insights. Interested in the hostility directed at Lawrence in the 1930s, Freeman's study includes a chapter on Lawrence and fascism which focuses in part on his relationship to Italian futurism. In a chapter which considers Lawrence's stated views and representations of Jews, women, of democracy and leadership, she argues that attempts to link Lawrence's pronouncements doctrinally with European fascism (a view of Lawrence which still has some currency) are misguided. Elsewhere, Freeman develops her analysis of Lawrence's relationship to modernist avant-gardes and the intersection of aesthetic and social topics: class and capital, modernity and revolution, 'dissolution' and 'resurrection'. She anticipates others in giving some attention to the expository writing including 'The Crown'.

Mark Spilka's more thematic emphasis in *The Love Ethic of D.H. Lawrence* (1955) has had greater influence than Freeman, as has Graham Hough's *The Dark Sun: A Study of D.H. Lawrence* (1956), which felt itself to be in the shadow of Leavis's strong defence of Lawrence published the year before. Spilka, discussing the fiction, concentrates on a religious impulse in Lawrence's writing identified in the vital transformations undergone by, or arrested in, his principal characters as a result of their interactions with others. Like Leavis, he regards Lawrence as being in possession of an affirmative moral philosophy in which the regeneration of the arrested individual is always at stake. That Spilka (more in the spirit of New Criticism than Hough), chooses in part to concentrate chapters on the imagery and meaning of *The Rainbow* and *Women in Love* shows some sympathy with Leavis's rehabilitation of these works. There is also some implicit acknowledgement in Spilka's position of Murry's earlier assessments of a religiosity in Lawrence, and Spilka is comfortable with the idea of a 'prophetic' Lawrence who can teach the sensitive reader a moral value (see discussion of Moore below). Hough, writing as Spilka is not, from Cambridge (Leavis's home ground), acknowledges the territory won by Leavis in discussions of Lawrence and commends his work in particular on *The Rainbow* and *Women in Love*. The organization of his study shows an interest in Lawrence as a poet as well as a writer of fiction (the dramatic work is still, at this time, getting little serious critical attention). Of significance is Hough's decision to give a section of his book over to what he calls 'the doctrine'.

In an assessment of 'Fiction and Philosophy' *The Dark Sun* attempts to show how far these categories overlap in the prose. As many commentators will do after him, Hough quotes from the preface to *Fantasia of the Unconscious* to show their joint significance to Lawrence: 'even art is utterly dependent on philosophy: or if you prefer it, on a metaphysic.' This final part of Hough's book attempts to trace the principal areas of Lawrence's *Weltanschauung*, concluding that the thought was 'virtually complete' by 1923 with *Studies in Classic American Literature* and the two books on the unconscious, and that most of what came later was re-statement with little useful revision. The dominant tone of Hough's critique is defensive, writing against perceived vulgarizations of Lawrence's thought with a sense being conveyed that, even in 1956, Lawrence was in fact largely unread:

> Criticisms of Lawrence are commonly criticisms of his psychology, his morals or his politics; and these are all indeed open to criticism. But such attacks must remain partial and inconclusive unless it is seen how all these particular doctrines arise from a few central ideas.
>
> (Hough 1956: 223)

What follows is a sense of Lawrence, which owes much to Leavis, as the originator of a highly idiosyncratic philosophy based on the 'will-to-live' ('Certainly [Lawrence] is a vitalist ... but it is hardly appropriate to use modern analytical terminology at all' [224]). Lawrence's thought is variously referred to as 'pantheism', 'animism' and elsewhere his 'materialist' concentration is underlined. What is interesting in Hough's critique is the evident problem posed by Lawrence's terms, by his language, although Hough does not focus on the way that language is a central *theme* in Lawrence's writing (fictional and discursive). His reading, however, as it unfolds, continually exposes the difficulties posed by Lawrence's main modes of expression. With less emphasis than this might suggest on Lawrence's relationship to his medium, Hough's intention is to delineate the main ideas, and so he concentrates on the 'blood', on Lawrence's dualism and his 'oppositional' thinking, on relationships, community and the individual. He concludes with a section on 'The Quarrel with Christianity' (see also Fr. William Tiverton, *D.H. Lawrence and Human Existence* [1951]) which examines Lawrence's analysis of different kinds of love, Platonic, Romantic, Christian. An emphasis on Lawrence's 'power to show' asserts the value of the 'prophetic' tendency in his writing (which dominated thought on Lawrence in the 1950s).

Hough's study is comprehensive, which is where its main virtue lies, and he is among the first, if not *the* first critic, to examine the relationship between the fiction and the discursive writing in a detailed way. There are omissions. Like Leavis, and most of his contemporaries, he dismisses *The Trespasser* (unhappily for Hough it has 'the second-hand poetry of the woman's magazine' [34]), while he is not overly impressed, either, with *The Lost Girl*. However, *The Dark Sun* provides, on the whole, a measured survey of the *oeuvre* – drawing a great deal on the material available in *Phoenix*, and keeping the autobiographical aspects of Lawrence's literary production in view – and it complements Leavis's more influential study.

In the post-war period, much of Lawrence's writing was re-issued in Britain and America, which both suggested and created a larger audience than the pre-war readership, and the 1950s figure significantly in the history of the reception and criticism of his work. In particular, the tendency for critical biography continued, derived from the academy rather than from the community of Lawrence's friends and acquaintances who, in the main, published their reminiscences before the war. In 1951, Harry T. Moore's *The Life and Works of D.H. Lawrence* was published, followed by *The Intelligent Heart* in 1954 (revised and re-issued as *The Priest of Love* in 1974). Moore, in *The Life and Works*, provides a conclusion to which the next decade of critics and commenta-tors – Leavis among them – would remain largely faithful. 'Literature', announces Moore, 'is the autobiography of humanity'(246). Moore:

> The important writer, the truly creative man who works from internal compulsion, comprehends in his vision the elements that make up the different departments of life, and in expressing them and their impact upon mankind, he uses the medium of fable. Whether the fable takes the form of the epic, the drama, or the novel will depend on which of these is the living form of the age, as the novel is of ours. The important thing is that the fable presents experience in the fullest and richest way.
>
> (Moore 1951: 246)

Here, Lawrence's belief in the novel as 'the one bright book of life' finds its echo.

Following Huxley's example, Moore (in 1962) continued his work by publishing *The Collected Letters of D.H. Lawrence*. In 1957, Edward Nehls began the publication of his three volume *D.H. Lawrence: A Composite Biography*, dedicated to Frieda Lawrence Ravagli (she married again), and bearing her Foreword. Nehls' work, which is still an extremely useful resource, presents and contextualizes selections from Lawrence's letters alongside excerpts from a range of memoirs by people from all phases of his career. In her Foreword Frieda Lawrence suggests that the young generation who had passed through the years of the Second World War were more ready to read and re-read Lawrence, more open to his warnings about a self-destructive civilization in need of regeneration, than his audience a generation earlier. Certainly, the 1950s was a decade that made all sorts of extra-literary claims about Lawrence's work. There was a vast increase of critical material published at this time, compared with the pre-war period (see *A D.H. Lawrence Miscellany*, edited by Harry T. Moore [1961]), and a great deal of energy was directed into the preservation of accurate biographical and bibliographical records. This activity was largely, but not exclusively, confined to Britain and America.

(c) RADICAL LAWRENCE

As a response to the emergence of a considerable audience for Lawrence, as well as a thriving critical and academic interest in America and Europe, Penguin Books took the decision to publish an unexpurgated version of *Lady Chatterley's Lover*, giving rise to the obscenity trial in London in 1960 **[75]**. There had been legal action in America the year before, indeed, the case against Penguin Books in Britain was one example of several proceedings against the publication of the novel in other parts of the world. In English law Lawrence's was the first novel to be prosecuted under the Obscene Publications Act (1959). The prosecution concentrated on representations of sexual acts and the use of verbal 'obscenities'. Witnesses for the defence included critics and intellectuals – Graham Hough, Helen Gardner, Vivian de Sola Pinto and Richard Hoggart among them (Leavis did not participate) – as well as distinguished writers like Rebecca West and E.M. Forster. Rebecca West was able in court to represent the novel in allegorical terms:

> Here was culture that had become sterile and unhelpful to man's deepest needs, and he [Lawrence] wanted to have the whole of civilization realizing that it was not living fully enough, that it would be exploited in various ways if it did not try to get down to the springs of its being and live more fully and bring its spiritual gifts into play. The baronet [Sir Clifford Chatterley] and his impotence are a symbol of the impotent culture of his time; and the love affair with the gamekeeper was a calling, a return of the

soul to the more intense life that he felt when people had had a different culture, such as the cultural basis of religious faith.

(Rolph 1961: 67)

The acquittal of Penguin Books was no great surprise. The interest stimulated by the trial guaranteed a new audience for the book and ushered in a decade in which Lawrence's cultural value was high, and in which popular movements could appropriate him in their rejection of an certain stifling orthodoxies. If in the 1950s the volume of critical writing on Lawrence increased dramatically, from 1960 (not only, it must be said, as a result of the Chatterley trial) a 'Lawrence industry' took off. A great deal of Lawrence's discursive writing was made available in a reprint of *Phoenix* and the publication for the first time of other material in *Phoenix II* and *The Symbolic Meaning* (early versions of the essays in *Studies in Classic American Literature*). Apart from the ready availability of the prose, *The Complete Poems*, edited by Vivian de Sola Pinto and F. Warren Roberts, was published in 1964. In 1965 (the year of the Royal Court revivals [37]) Heinemann brought out (unfortunately without introduction or commentary) *The Complete Plays of D.H. Lawrence*. For a more minority interest, Mervyn Levy edited a volume, *The Paintings of D.H. Lawrence* (1964). There was still clearly a market for reminiscences which enjoyed something of a revival with E.W. Tedlock's *Frieda Lawrence: The Memoirs and Correspondence* published in 1961.

At this time, even though the dominance of Leavisite thought on Lawrence's value and *oeuvre* was largely unchallenged, interpretative variations were offered. Book-length studies in this vein include Eliseo Vivas's study, *D.H. Lawrence: The Failure and Triumph of Art* (1960), with its concentration on the form and organization of the novels. Like Leavis, Vivas acknowledges the elusiveness of the principles of organization in a work like *Women in Love*, and much of the time his readings set out to show the complex interrelation of imagery and event which produces the formal contours of each text. Vivas also adheres to Leavis's notion of a shifting scale of artistry throughout the *oeuvre*, so that *The Rainbow* and *Women in Love* still constitute the 'triumphant' achievements of the title of his book in contrast to the flawed performances represented by the others (*Sons and Lovers* is an exception among the novels, but is not regarded as a work of maturity). However, Vivas is less persuaded than many by the consistently affirmative, even visionary, version of Lawrence created and sustained by Leavis and consequently his study shows a greater willingness to examine a negative power in Lawrence.

Eugene Goodheart in his study of Lawrence's 'utopianism' (achieved by the intersection of 'art' and 'idea'), *The Utopian Vision of D.H. Lawrence* (1963), criticizes a naivety in Lawrence for confusing the visionary with the ethical. Like Kingsley Widmer in *The Art of Perversity* (1962) and E.W. Tedlock Jr., in *D.H. Lawrence: Artist and Rebel* (1963) Goodheart points to this fundamental problem in Lawrence:

> When Lawrence converts his vision into doctrine and turns prophecy into moral prescription, he betrays a confusion about his achievement. The visionary habit is alien to the moral life, because it refuses to accommodate itself to anything different from it.
>
> (169)

He also seeks to correct Leavis's denial of a properly European context for Lawrence: '[i]n the effort to reveal the revolutionary implications of Lawrence's utopianism both in his art and in his thought, I go against the prevailing tendency, most significantly exemplified by F.R. Leavis, *to confine Lawrence within English ethical and artistic traditions* (1, emphasis added). In underlining the importance of bringing Nietzsche and Freud to bear on readings of Lawrence, Goodheart anticipates the direction of much criticism to follow.

These analyses had the self-confidence to acknowledge and explore ambiguity and contradiction in the fiction and discursive writing, and to make examination of the reliance in Lawrence's thought on contrasting principles (of deathliness as much as of 'life') a feature of writing about him. In his book *The Forked Flame* (1965), H.M. Daleski draws attention to 'Study of Thomas Hardy' for a reading of the major novels, and in particular Lawrence's insistence on a model of dualistic thought based on 'two principles' in productive tension, or opposition, as providing the underlying grammar of his 'metaphysic' **[99–101]**. Acknowledging the importance of Daleski's thesis, and concentrating on the language of the drafts which were to become *The Rainbow* and *Women in Love*, Mark Kinkead-Weekes similarly draws on 'Study of Thomas Hardy' (and 'The Crown') although to different ends. Kinkead-Weekes emphasizes the exploratory nature of language in Lawrence. His 'Art'

> must contain a dialectic of opposites, a real conflict in which both sides are allowed to assert themselves fully, and the scales are never weighted. Furthermore it must both Be and Know – must contain, as it were, a continual 'systole' and 'diastole' of poetry and analytic

prose, exploration and understanding. Most of all, the Supreme Art must move through thesis and antithesis to try to see beyond.
(Kinkead-Weekes 1968: 384–5)

The emphasis in this influential essay is to demonstrate the validity of the main claim with close reference to Lawrence's practice. 'The Crown' is evoked in part as a re-statement of the central argument of 'Study of Thomas Hardy' although in places, as in the sub-section called 'The Flux of Corruption', negative terms must come to the fore *creatively*. Disintegration ('corruption') and consummation, argues Kinkead-Weekes, are represented in the novels in a dialectical relationship in order that Lawrence can imagine regeneration (his personal symbol was the phoenix). As always with Lawrence issues of language are central. Kinkead-Weekes asserts that 'the word "corruption" itself carries no overtones of judgement' and he quotes from 'The Crown': '"Destruction and Creation are the two relative absolutes between the opposing infinities. Life is in both"' (397).

Colin Clarke is less convinced that 'Life is in both'. His study, *River of Dissolution* (1969), emphasizes the dark side of rebirth in Lawrence now located in the tradition of English Romanticism. With particular reference to the language of *Women in Love* he draws attention to the prevalence of images of decay and disintegration in the processes which lead to renewal. He pursues the internal logic of these images of decay and corruption, and directs the critical emphasis to the centrality of destruction in Lawrence's personal philosophy. Clarke is less interested than his predecessors in Lawrence's general cultural position than in the grain of his philosophy and the expression of his 'metaphysic'. Although he had his detractors, in the 1960s (and beyond) it was no heresy to insist on the 'darker' side of Lawrence's writing.

(d) LAWRENCE AND PSYCHOANALYTIC CRITICISM

Freud described the formation of the subject in terms of the psycho-sexual dramas of the family based on the child's rivalry with a parent. Initially in agreement, C.G. Jung departed from Freud's ideas directing his attention towards 'analytical psychology' and studies of the personality, developing ideas, among many, of 'archetypes' and the 'collective unconscious'. Lawrence acknowledges debts to both Freud and Jung in the Foreword to *Fantasia of the Unconscious*, slightly playing down his rejection of Freud in the earlier book, *Psychoanalysis and the Unconscious*

[102–4]. Critics have long found in Lawrence's work echoes of Freudian themes, and this has resulted in 'Freudian', or more broadly, psychoanalytic, readings of specific texts.

Lawrence's resistance to this kind of reading is well-documented even though he appropriated Freud's terms *and* developed his own vocabulary to describe 'unconscious' functioning. He hated reviews of his work which sought to understand them in terms of popular Freudianism (in particular Alfred Booth Kuttner's reviews of *Sons and Lovers* in *New Republic*, 1915 [Draper 1970: 76–80], and in 1916 in the *Psychoanalytic Review* [Salgādo 1969: 69–94]) **[44]**. Murry claimed in *Son of Woman*, and elsewhere, that Lawrence's writing on psychology was about the most significant thing he had achieved, and argued, furthermore, that psychoanalysis was the starting point (but only this) for many of Lawrence's perceptions: in a review of *Fantasia* he noted that 'The language and conceptions of the psycho-analysts were useful to [Lawrence] sometimes in giving expression to his own discoveries; but his discoveries were his own' (Draper 1970: 186).

Frederick J. Hoffman wrote the first extensive discussion about Lawrence's reception of Freud's ideas, and more broadly the relationship between psychoanalysis and literature, in his book *Freudianism and the Literary Mind* (1945). Hoffman finds Lawrence at least acknowledging the general significance of Freud to his contemporaries, even while his opposition to a psychoanalytic mode of understanding was everywhere apparent in his discursive writing. Hoffman's main chapter on Lawrence, called 'Lawrence's *Quarrel* with Freud' (my emphasis), suggests that his objections operate principally at a doctrinal level, which is to miss the point about Lawrence's attack on Freud's *terms*, that is, the language of psychoanalysis and its insistence on the locus of the unconscious 'in the head' (this aspect of Lawrence's departure from Freud is at the heart of both *Psychoanalysis and the Unconscious* and *Fantasia of the Unconscious*). However, many of Hoffman's conclusions are astute, and he rightly draws attention to Lawrence's favourable reception of Trigant Burrow's book, *The Social Basis of Consciousness* with its emphasis on the social group rather than the individual (Lawrence's review is reprinted in *Phoenix*, 377–82) **[104]**.

A later study, Daniel A.Weiss's book, *Oedipus in Nottingham* (1962), offers a Freudian analysis of Lawrence. In it attention is focused on the posited Oedipal crisis which underpins *Sons and Lovers* and, indeed, the later novels, as a problem which Lawrence fails to resolve in himself. As the title suggests, Weiss's study tends to be diagnostic. The psychoanalytic theme, however, was developed later by David Cavitch in *D.H. Lawrence and the New World* (1969). Cavitch draws attention to the importance of the discounted 'Prologue' to *Women in Love* and concludes, by an analysis of Birkin's feelings for Gerald Crich, that an exploration of Lawrence's sexuality is at the heart of the novel. In the final version of *Women in Love*, argues Cavitch, Birkin's sensations are given to Gudrun in her relationship with Gerald (and later Loerke), and this 'shifts the atmosphere of perversion on to heterosexual relations, alleging them to be hopelessly complicated by homosexual ambivalence' (68). In the Prologue Gerald's crisis is due to his denial of 'manly love', while Birkin 'tormented' (66) has at least learned to acknowledge his feelings. Gerald's rejection of Birkin's version of blood brotherhood, and his death – which represent to Cavitch 'the failure of the homoerotic ideal in *Women in Love*' (75) – explain Lawrence's ambivalent attitudes towards women in the later novels **[56–65]**.

Generally, the tendency in the earlier psychoanalytic criticism is to seek out Freudian correspondences or variations. A range of interesting studies also focus on the genealogy of the unconscious in Lawrence's discursive and fictional writing in contexts which more broadly examine the relationship of literature and science. Daniel Schneider (1984), concerned with influences on Lawrence when he discusses dreams in *Fantasia of the Unconscious*, cites Piaget, Freud and Jung. Others concentrate on the psycho-biology articulated by Lawrence in the books on the unconscious and elsewhere (it is worth looking at *The Symbolic Meaning* [1962] in this context). Useful studies include Evelyn Hinz's 'The Beginning and the End: D.H. Lawrence's *Psychoanalysis* and *Fantasia* (1972) which contrasts the 'scientific mode' of *Psychoanalysis and the Unconscious* with the 'archetypal mode' of *Fantasia of the Unconscious*. Working in a similar area, Patricia Hagen considers Lawrence's language and non-analytic modes of understanding in 'The Metaphoric Foundations of Lawrence's "Dark Knowledge"' (1987). With an interest in a 'materialist' Lawrence are Katherine Hayles' 'The Ambivalent Approach: D.H. Lawrence and the New Physics' (1982) and 'Evasion: The Field of the Unconscious in D.H. Lawrence'(1984), as well as David Ellis, 'Lawrence and the Biological Psyche' in *D.H. Lawrence: Centenary Essays* (1986), and Christopher Heywood in '"Blood-Consciousness" and the Pioneers of the Reflex and Ganglionic Systems', published in *D.H. Lawrence: New Studies* (1987). It is also worth turning to James Cowan's *D.H. Lawrence's American Journey: A Study in Literature and Myth* (1970). These studies focus on the 'doctrine' and on Lawrence's terms, that is to say, on his idiosyncratic (and paradoxical) mimicry of scientific exactness. They may not constitute psychoanalytic readings of Lawrence, but they offer detailed responses to his writing on 'psychology', directly related to the problem of 'knowledge' in his work.

More recently, Linda Ruth Williams has combined a psychoanalytic approach with feminist film theory to examine gendered identity in Lawrence in her book *Sex in the Head*. Like some of the earlier studies it has a diagnostic foundation – 'Lawrence ... likes the wrong things, writing and looking against-himself' (Williams 1993: 149) – but the result is a fresh reappraisal, using theories of the gaze, of Lawrence's sexual politics. While some critics have a more polemical purpose, like Angela Carter in 'Lorenzo as Closet Queen' (1982), most, like Judith Ruderman in '*The Fox* and the Devouring Mother' (1977), Judith Arcana in 'I Remember Mama: Mother-blaming in *Sons and Lovers*' Criticism' (1989) and Carol Sklenicka (1991), attempt to combine Freudian and some post-Freudian perspectives with close reading in a deliberately objective way. A related study by Ruderman, *D.H. Lawrence and the Devouring Mother* (1984), considers the theme of masculinity in the writing of the 1920s. It can usefully be read alongside Schneider's study of the same year. Margaret Beede Howe concentrates on Lawrence's play with the concept of personality in *The Art of the Self in D.H. Lawrence* (1977) which, with a different inflection is also the case in Daniel Albright's comparative study *Personality and Impersonality: Lawrence, Woolf and Mann* (1978). This shifting of the perspective inwards is countered by Anne Fernihough's 'The Tyranny of the Text: Lawrence, Freud and the Modernist Aesthetic' (1990), which historicizes Lawrence's conflict with Freud in the context of literary modernism. Finally, Deleuze and Guattari (1984) celebrate Lawrence as a 'de-oedipaliser' by means of an analysis of the radical metaphoricity of his language.

Evidently, much of Lawrence's critical writing can be viewed as 'psychoanalytical' even while he eschews the psychoanalytic as a literary approach. Elizabeth Wright (1989) makes this valuable point in her discussion of Lawrence's critique of American writing and culture in *Studies in Classic American Literature*, the text where he makes his claims for 'art-speech' (duplicitous and elusive, 'out of a pattern of lies art weaves the truth' [SCAL 8]). Lawrence, we remember, persisted in regarding American literature and tendencies in American culture in terms of psychic drama: 'There is a "different" feeling in the old American classics. It is the shifting over from the old psyche to something new, a displacement. And displacements hurt' (SCAL 7–8) **[104–8]**.

Michael Ragussis (1978) also cites Lawrence's critique of the American writers and the comments on 'art-speech', but he underlines the centrality of Lawrence's comments not simply to the act of reading but to writing as well, exploring in his study the idiosyncratic 'art-speech' of *Women in Love* (see 'Lawrence and Language' **[149]**). He begins his study by situating Lawrence as a psychoanalytic critic in spirit, despite the suspicion of Freud. He makes the valuable point that both Freud and Lawrence, independently, use the phrase 'verbal consciousness' as each struggles to bring his philosophy into language. Referring to Lawrence's often quoted dictum that 'one sheds one's sicknesses in books', Ragussis suggests that

> Lawrence ... imagines this curative process to be like the "talking cure" of psychoanalysis, which posits as a cure the coming into full consciousness, and thereby a freedom to direct one's own destiny, through the articulation, to the analyst and to oneself, of one's deepest emotions and thoughts. Freud and Lawrence even use the same term – "verbal consciousness" – to describe this process.
>
> (Ragussis 1978: 4)

Ragussis also reminds us that the post-structuralist thinker, Jacques Lacan, Freud's principal re-interpreter whose work on language and the subject has influenced a generation of literary theorists, and the philosopher Paul Ricoeur who has worked on metaphor, link the unconscious with language in ways which enable productive re-readings of Lawrence. 'Lacanian' analyses have produced, and continue to produce, interesting responses to his work.

(e) LAWRENCE AND SOCIETY

Lawrence wrote on social issues in essays like 'Democracy' (1919; 1936) and 'Education of the People' (1936) (RDP 63–83; 87–166) as well as his prefaces and introductions (in, for example, *Movements in European History*). His political novels, *Aaron's Rod*, *Kangaroo* and *The Plumed Serpent*, even *Lady Chatterley's Lover*, test out ideas of social reform but ultimately give expression to a scepticism with regard to the political over and above the personal. F.R. Leavis had argued strenuously that the existence of 'class-feeling' in Lawrence was in harness to his larger theme of life, lived, over and above a specific social interest: in this context he raises a comparison of his achievement with that of George Eliot. Much of the value of *The Rainbow*, asserts Leavis in *D.H. Lawrence: Novelist*, resides in the broad-brush analysis which it offers of contemporary civilization. For Leavis, Lawrence evokes in the 'great' novels an irrefutable kind of Englishness and irrefutable truths about community, and he does so because of his own formation: 'Lawrence knows and renders ... what have been the conditions of his own individual development; to be brought up in the environment of a living tradition – he is recording, in his rendering of provincial England, what in the concrete this has meant in an actual civilization' (Leavis 1955: 107). Leavis, at this level, is reading *The Rainbow* as a novel about England, or more specifically a certain vision of Englishness. The partiality of that vision, or what it leaves out, is not examined by Leavis. A useful comparison can be made with Raymond Williams' exploration of Lawrence and English culture, and the ways in which his reading is subtly different from Leavis's retrieval of a humanist agenda in Lawrence. Williams, a leading exponent of Marxist literary criticism in the British academy (*Marxism and Literature* [1977]), originator of cultural materialism, discusses Lawrence's fiction in *The English Novel from Dickens to Lawrence* (1970) and has influenced subsequent studies of Lawrence, quite recently Tony Pinkney's examination of Lawrence's modernist credentials (1990). Williams is more interested than Leavis in the external conditions which affect changes in the subject and, thereafter, literary representation (see *Culture and Society, 1780–1950*).

Writing in *Keywords* (1976) about 'community', Raymond Williams draws attention to a dynamic term characterized by its positive use:

> Community can be the warmly persuasive word to describe an existing set of relationships, or the warmly persuasive word to describe an alternative set of relationships. What is most important, perhaps, is that unlike all other terms of social organization (*state*, *nation*, *society*, etc.) it seems never to be used unfavourably, and never to be given any positive opposing or distinguishing term.
> (Williams 1976: 76)

This exploration of meaning and the sublest of distinctions here uncovered bears directly on Williams' reading of Lawrence as the first novelist in English effectively to conjoin his own language with that of his characters: this has everything to do with the reference his writing makes to Lawrence's social origins. In *Culture and Society, 1780–1950*, Williams draws attention to the anti-industrial ethos in Lawrence, aligning him with the nineteenth-century intellectuals Thomas Carlyle and Matthew Arnold. In his book, *The English Novel from Dickens to Lawrence*, he continues to argue for Lawrence's importance in the context of almost three generations of writers in whose hands the novel form represents 'the exploration of ... the substance and meaning of community' (Williams 1970: 11). Beginning his volume with a critique of Dickens, Williams identifies a period in which what it means to live in a community is more uncertain, more critical, more disturbing as a question put both to societies and to persons than ever before in history. The underlying experiences of this powerful and transforming urban and industrial civilisation are of rapid and inescapable social change; of a newly visible and conscious history but at the same time, in most actual communities and in most actual lives, of a newly complicated and often newly obscure immediate process. These are not opposite poles: they are the defining characteristics of the change itself. People became more aware of great social and historical changes which altered not only outward forms – institutions and landscapes – but also inward feelings, experiences, self-definitions.

(Williams 1970: 12)

This description of social and economic change, and of a corresponding alienation at the level of individual consciousness, which for Williams applies from around the 1840s, recalls Lawrence's description in *The Rainbow* that, 'About 1840, a canal was constructed across the meadows of the Marsh Farm . . .' (R 13). A description of modernization, this is a point in the text which indicates a significant alteration in narrative tone (and social relations). It directs attention to 'public' 'official' history aside from the intimate community consciousness which has represented the Brangwens up to this moment of major change (and the narrative will move from the inclusiveness of community to the new condition of alienated individual consciousness, finally achieved with Ursula's story) **[49–56]**. The way this novel maps the shift from an agricultural to an industrial society, foregrounded here, is also noted by Leavis. *The Rainbow*, however, with its origins in a time of particular social crisis, comes to signify for Williams a new form in the novel: one that represents 'the experience of community ... and then of its breakdown' (Williams 1970: 178). He traces, in the changing language of that novel, a shift between two kinds of reality which he relates to Lawrence's sense of the pressures wrought by social change:

The given reality of men and women is the experience and the method of the early chapters, and then under pressure – the pressures of altering ways of life, economic and social and physical changes – such a reality, radical and irreducible, has to be made or found; it is not given. It is then made and found – attempted to be made and found – in certain kinds of relationship: physical certainly but physical mainly as a discovery of being, of spirit. Other people drop away. They become increasingly irrelevant to this intense and desperate effort. Just because the reality is no longer given – and that loss is explicit; a social system, industrialism, has destroyed given reality by forcing people into systematic roles – the new reality, that which in its turn is irreducible and radical, has to be fought for – the strain and the violence are obvious.

(Williams 1970: 178)

In that book's sequel, '[e]ffective community has gone' ... 'Women in Love is a masterpiece of loss' (180, 182). This is the basis of the significant position held by Lawrence in Williams' critical history of the novel form.

The feeling of, or perhaps for, community that is indicated in these statements has its finest expression for Williams in Lawrence's early work, principally in 'Odour of Chrysanthemums' and other short stories roughly contemporary with it, as well as in the first three plays and *Sons and Lovers*. What Williams appears to value highly in these is the vernacular, a shift in narrative language 'to the colloquial and informal from the abstract and polite' (173). What is at stake here is a representation of a social vision; the individual relationships expressed in the writing are not separable from the experience of community that underpins, even creates, them. For Williams this continues to be the case in Lawrence's last novel, *Lady Chatterley's Lover*, where post-war England defined by familiar class inequalities and iniquities, is the community in which radical, more positive, relationships than those of mechanistic modernity have to be formed. The alteration of 'outward forms' as not separable from the transformation of 'inward feelings', to use Williams' terms, is Lawrence's principal theme. However, for many critics *Lady Chatterley's Lover* fails to remain true to the political consciousness which, from the outset at least, it seems is going to determine that novel. Principally, they argue, *Lady Chatterley's Lover* is a novel about class, but the way in which personal relations are resolved in the book actually show Lawrence in flight from political realities and resorting to a sexual 'philosophy' in such a way which ignores the imperatives of history (Lawrence, who saw his book as 'defiant', answers in 'A Propos of *Lady Chatterley's Lover*' that 'if the lady marries the gamekeeper – she hasn't done it yet – it is not class spite, but in spite of class' [LCL 334]). Unconvinced, Graham Holderness in *D.H. Lawrence: History, Ideology and Fiction* (1982) and Scott Sanders, *D.H. Lawrence: the world of the major novels* (1974), perceive in statements like this a troubling resistance in Lawrence to his own evident consciousness of the politics of class, which Williams does not fully debate. In a wide-ranging analysis of Lawrence's 'literary dissidence', Drew Milne discusses these critical perspectives in detail but perceives in Lawrence a much greater sense of hesitancy towards the rightness of his philosophy of 'sexual transcendence' than these earlier critics acknowledge. More in keeping with Peter Scheckner (1985), he identifies a genuine self-questioning at work in Lawrence's writing and urges some greater recognition of 'the extent to which the novels are critical of sexual solutions to the political problems represented in the novel [*Lady Chatterley's Lover*]' (Milne 2001: 212).

Graham Holderness is less inclined to see the achieved results of dialectical process in Lawrence. Quite apart from the ideological blindspots of *Lady Chatterley's Lover*, for him the 'mythic' and the 'historical' are self-consciously opposed values which are set up particularly problematically in *The Rainbow*. Holderness argues convincingly and cogently that the vision of the folk working the land at the opening of *The Rainbow* – the writing which is often referred to as the novel's 'prologue' – is mythic in a facile sense, disturbingly anti-real. An 'alternative to history' is represented which, in its denial of genuine conflict (between social classes; between man and nature) is a sham. Holderness disagrees that the 'prologue' is a sketch of pre-industrial England with any basis in actuality, calling it, rather, a strategic 'distortion of history' on Lawrence's part. If the relationship or connection between the community and the land (referred to metonymically as 'Marsh Farm') is to be perceived as 'organic', it is so in order to establish a contrast with the mechanized civilization of the pit town (at the end of the novel) and the alienated workers which populate it. However, for Holderness, the pastoral ideal of the 'prologue' and the promise contained in the rainbow (as symbol for the regeneration of industrial England), are both fictions which show Lawrence ignoring the crisis of history out of which, in 1914, he writes. This interpretation (which owes something to Williams) forcefully exposes the deluded spirit of Leavis's humanism, and the distance from history which his reading (at least of *The Rainbow*) actually represents. If Holderness has produced the principal sceptical reading about the nature of the social vision in Lawrence's work, he can usefully be read alongside Peter Scheckner's later study, *Class, Politics and the Individual* (1985) and Tony Pinkney's *D.H. Lawrence* (1990).

Mark Kinkead-Weekes is less exercised than Holderness by the lack of historical reference in the representation of the first generations of Brangwens in *The Rainbow*, and insists on its status as an historical novel (Kinkead-Weekes 1989: 121). He shows, in part to refute Holderness's argument (by means of opening quotations from Karl Jaspers and Georg Lukács), how Lawrence constructs the private histories of the Brangwens – including the minor characters – around specific historical events. These comprise education acts, domestic legislation and related social change; specific effects of the Industrial Revolution (in Nottinghamshire); the introduction of the automobile and its impact on the country; changes in levels of prosperity and aspiration across social classes; female emancipation and the 'new woman'. History in Lawrence, according to Kinkead-Weekes, is everywhere available in the attention paid to this kind of detail, but underpinning the 'historical' is an 'archetypal' vision, directly related to the main principles of the 'metaphysic'. Without this understanding, he argues, much is lost.

(f) LAWRENCE AND FEMINIST LITERARY CRITICISM

Some of the most developed and influential political critiques of Lawrence are the product of feminist literary criticism and, latterly, include work in the broad area of gender studies. Under scrutiny has been the representation of women in Lawrence's writing, and the specific implications of his sexual politics. This emphasis gave rise to influential arguments in the early 1970s which sought to unmask his misogyny, and to draw attention to the oppressive operations of patriarchy in his work. Feminist literary and cultural criticism is diverse and draws on a number of traditions. In attending to Lawrence, feminist critics since 1969 have successfully challenged the complacency of decades of Lawrence criticism, and subjected Lawrence's work to some of its most rigorous tests. Within feminism, of course, a range of views co-exist.

Sheila MacLeod introduces her book, *Lawrence's Men and Women* (1985), with a personal observation:

> Since the early 1970s feminists have been attacking Lawrence as the epitome of sexism and his theories of sexuality as male-centred and insensitive or dismissive towards women. I have scarcely been able to find a woman in the 1980s who has a good word to say for him.
>
> (MacLeod 1985: 11)

Her comments bear witness in part to the success of that rare thing, the best-selling work of literary criticism: MacLeod's principal target throughout her book is Kate Millett, author of a highly influential study,

Sexual Politics (1969), which, alongside chapters on Henry Miller, Norman Mailer (who replied with a 'defence') and Jean Genet, includes a chapter on D.H. Lawrence. Both these studies will be examined later in this sub-section. First, however, it is important to explore the context of feminist readings of Lawrence prior to Millett's forcible book, and to get a sense of the main arguments. In doing so, it is fair to note that Lawrence is a writer about whom few readers actually feel indifferent, and that feminist scholarship has succeeded most in stimulating energized debates about the 'doctrine' and the work.

Lawrence stated, in a letter to Edward Garnett about *The Rainbow*, that it showed 'woman becoming individual, self-responsible, taking her own initiative' (*Letters* II: 165). This need not be taken as a sign of his support for the feminist politics of his time, but rather as an indication of his idiosyncratic approach to the relations between men and women (defining and defined by their culture) which increasingly concerned him in his writing. A great deal more is at stake for Lawrence in the phrase 'becoming individual' than the issue of votes for women, equal representation and fair pay. Sexual metaphors predominate in the discursive writing: the abstract 'male' and 'female' principles in the early exploratory prose give way to a more coherently expressed sexual 'metaphysic' which is at the heart of his explorations of masculinity, selfhood, marriage, for example. And increasingly, the 'woman question' that absorbs Lawrence is articulated in terms of sexual violence ('The Princess', *The Plumed Serpent*, 'The Woman Who Rode Away'). His exhortations to husbands and wives in *Fantasia of the Unconscious* (see the chapter called 'The Lower Self'), have irritated numberless readers, as has the tone of his return to the themes of mothers and mothering and the education of children (he insists that the sexes should be kept apart). The 'Study of Thomas Hardy' had included a chapter on suffrage (and the pointlessness of women having the vote – at best, a collusion with patriarchy), but the later essays like 'Women Are So Cocksure' (*Phoenix*), 'Ownership', 'Master in His Own House', 'Matriarchy' and 'Cocksure Women and Hensure Men' (*Phoenix II*) are more aggressively critical about aspirational 'modern' women.

In *The Second Sex* [*Le Deuxième Sexe*] (1988), French novelist and essayist Simone de Beauvoir, writing about myths of the feminine in literature, includes a section on Lawrence called 'D.H. Lawrence or Phallic Pride'. It is an argument which gets considerable restatement in the 1970s. Through extensive quotation of *Fantasia of the Unconscious*, and with reference to the novels (principally *Women in Love*, *Lady Chatterley's Lover* and *The Plumed Serpent*), de Beauvoir finds Lawrence rediscovering the traditional bourgeois conception of sexual relations wherein 'Woman should subordinate her existence to that of man' (1988: 250). Her conclusion is that, 'It is once more the ideal of the "true woman" that Lawrence has to offer us – that is, the woman who unreservedly accepts being defined as the Other' (254). This conclusion is reached via a close examination of the various stages of Lawrence's thought on women and men with particular attention paid to his anti-Cartesianism, his philosophy of marriage and the 'psychophysiology' of the books on the unconscious. Where de Beauvoir's response is a reaction to Lawrence's discourse it focuses on the phallocentricity of his thought and language – hence the title to the piece. Hers is an interesting and sharply observed critique which usefully parallels the essay earlier in her book – although she does not make the connection more explicit than their co-incidence in the volume – of Freudian psychoanalysis.

Kate Millett's reading of Lawrence in *Sexual Politics* is in many respects a restatement of de Beauvoir's insights but it constitutes a much more thorough reading of the fiction than de Beauvoir's study permitted, and it asserts straightforwardly the assumption in Lawrence of the relationship in his culture (which he reproduces) between sex and power. Millett concurs with critics who provide a Freudian explanation of *Sons and Lovers* but her assessment of that novel is most concerned with the nature of power which gets expression in Paul Morel's relationship with, in particular, Miriam. The transition to a male supremacism is then traced in *The Rainbow* and *Women in Love*. However, it is *Aaron's Rod*, in Aaron's rejection of women and his return to a superior form of masculine friendship offered by Rawdon Lilly, which represents a much more open statement of Lawrence's 'fraternalism' than *Women in Love*. Millett's reading shows the self-assuredness of Lawrence's anti-egalitarianism (which in *Aaron's Rod* is articulated through Lilly). It is the political model offered by that book (of the superior man having a real responsibility for his culture and himself, not permitted by democracy) which makes possible the idea of 'messianic' male supremacy. Its formation continues in *Kangaroo*, argues Millett, and in *The Plumed Serpent* where religious and political ideologies dovetail. Millett's view of that novel's heroine, Kate Leslie, that she is a 'female impersonator', could be said of many of Lawrence's heroines. The point is that in *The Plumed Serpent* a dubious substitution is performed: 'Through the device of the heroine, Lawrence has found a vehicle to fantasize what seems to be his own surrender to the dark and imperious male in Cipriano' (284). What Millett arguably resists in her reading of the novels is an acknowledgement of the ambitious objectives which Lawrence had for the novel form, and his sense of his own novels' frequent failure. However, it is to the short story, 'The Woman Who Rode Away', that she most memorably turns, and provides one of the best-known readings of the text which inevitably comes to stand as a comprehensive criticism of its creator.

In her interpretation of the sexual politics of 'The Women Who Rode Away' Millett makes Lawrence the proper object of feminist hostility by showing what 'phallic-consciousness', foregrounded by de Beauvoir, really means. The climax of the tale is the ritual murder by tribal priests of the white woman **[96]**. Millett:

> The act here at the center of the Lawrencean sexual religion is coitus as killing, its central vignette a picture of human sacrifice performed upon the woman to the greater glory and potency of the male. But because sexual potency could accomplish little upon a corpse, it is painfully obvious that the intention of the fable is purely political.
>
> (Millett 1969: 292–3)

Not only does Lawrence link sex and death but his tale enjoys the enactment, the spectacle, of man's power over woman. R.P. Draper (1966 [1988]), writing earlier than Millett and with Lawrence's style principally in mind, typically overlooks the political, and comments on the 'orgasmic effect' of the last scene in 'The Woman Who Rode Away', suggesting its importance as a precursor of *Lady Chatterley's Lover* and 'The Man Who Died' (written, says Draper, after Lawrence's animosity towards feminists had lessened!). With the focus on equivalences, Draper's conclusions are not to be reconciled with those of de Beauvoir and Millett but, it could be argued, in all three a judgement is passed without proper accommodation of Lawrence's sense of the difficulty of his task if that is to be viewed as an attempted revaluation of sexual values. Sheila MacLeod makes a play for balance and intends to be corrective in her study (1985). 'Men', 'Women' and 'Marriage' are the organizing principles of that book which concentrates on the fiction. MacLeod's analysis of 'The Woman Who Rode Away' self-consciously addresses Millett's persuasive but, in some quarters, controversial interpretation.

With an eye on Lawrence's cherished theme of resurrection, MacLeod calls this tale a 'modern fertility myth' (145) and aligns it with 'The Man Who Died' (also called 'The Escaped Cock'). Like Millett she sees the woman, who remains nameless, as symbolic, but she argues that her journey is a 'religious quest' (141) and in 'losing' herself she paradox-ically 'finds' herself. MacLeod draws attention to the woman's desire for freedom from a marriage and family life which has seemed to arrest her spiritual development. Sexual identity, she argues, is that which is being rejected *by the woman*, so that a mythic identity – free from the ordinary demands of her sexualized existence – may be taken on:

> Contrary to Kate Millett's claim in *Sexual Politics*, there is no evidence here of the white male fantasy that dark-skinned men are inordinately attracted to white women. It is repeatedly stressed that the Indians find the woman sexually repulsive. Something quite other is happening: one of the last vestiges of her identity, the double pride in her whiteness and the power of her sexuality, is being shed.
>
> (MacLeod 1985: 140)

The radical aspect of the tale in MacLeod's view resides in the depiction of a female Christ-figure who combines the sacrificial imperative with a concept of (self-) salvation: she is the female equivalent of 'the man who died'. It is in arguing this point that MacLeod seeks to accommodate the central aspects of Lawrence's personal philosophy to do with notions of rebirth (of the self). Her account therefore attempts a greater responsiveness to Lawrence's *stated* aims than Millett's, but the text supports both readings. Millett grounds her interpretation more obviously than MacLeod in questions of class, gender and race, where MacLeod's assessment of the Lawrencean subject is based more on her apprehension of Lawrence's 'symbolic meaning'. MacLeod is perhaps happier to read Lawrence in, and on, his own terms but Millett's scepticism remains an important, influential and pervasive counter-voice.

As the survey of critical writing provided in Part III of this *Guide* shows, most book-length studies until 1969, largely but not exclusively in an Anglo-American intellectual tradition, ignore gender. Thereafter, studies of the representation of women in Lawrence are not necessarily feminist in approach. Many return to well-worn critical themes such as Lawrence as son/lover using fiction in order to work out a troubled sense of mothering. Carol Dix (1980), having asserted that hers is a personal rather than 'academic' response, seeks, rather ineffectively, to counter Millett's influential position, mounting a defence of Lawrence by arguing that he offers as many positive views of women as negative. Hers needs to be read in tandem with other more exploratory and expansive studies. Hilary Simpson's *D.H. Lawrence and Feminism* (1982) examines the historical contexts for the development of Lawrence's attitudes, and feminist reassessments, and can also be usefully read alongside Cornelia Nixon's *Lawrence's Leadership Politics and the Turn against Women* (1986) which returns to the treatment of masculinity, sex and power in the later writing. Peter Balbert, in *D.H. Lawrence and the Phallic Imagination: Essays on Sexual Identity and Feminist Misreading* (1989) strikes a counter-note.

Anne Smith's edited collection *Lawrence and Women* (1978) brings together diverse essays on the theme of gender relations. Smith's introductory essay follows the biographical imperative and assumes that when Lawrence writes about women he seeks 'his own sexual identity' (10). Drawing heavily on the correspondence, she strives to illustrate Lawrence's preoccupation with male-female relations, latterly in terms of his marriage. Most of the essays in this volume show a concentration on the fiction. Faith Pullin writes on the representation of women in *Sons and Lovers*, while Lydia Blanchard examines mother-daughter relations in *The Rainbow* and some of the shorter works. Mark Kinkead-Weekes' 'Eros and Metaphor: Sexual Relationship in the Fiction of Lawrence' ([1969] reprinted from another source), concentrates on the language of sexual description in episodes from *Sons and Lovers*, *The Rainbow*, *Women in Love* and *Lady Chatterley's Lover* to show Lawrence's awareness of 'process' in terms of both sexual and 'verbal consciousness'. This is not an example of feminist literary criticism, but of criticism, like much in Smith's book, which shows a concentration on men, women and sex in Lawrence. Also in this volume, Philippa Tristram examines the polarization of life and death as 'male' and 'female' principles in the Brangwen novels and *Aaron's Rod*, drawing on Freud and *Psychoanalysis and the Unconscious* and *Fantasia of the Unconscious*. T.E. Apter offers a reading of *The Plumed Serpent* which can be usefully aligned with later critiques of Lawrence's sexual politics and primitivism. Harry T. Moore's 'Bert Lawrence and Lady Jane' is an overly defensive response to Millett's 'distortions' (180) and 'misreading' (181) which does not provide an effective counter-argument. Mark Spilka's 'On Lawrence's Hostility to Wilful Women: The Chatterley Solution', argues that Lawrence's accommodation of 'tenderness' and vulnerability as an aspect of Mellors' 'maleness' is an antidote to old ideas of aggressive masculine dominance in his writing.

Linda Ruth Williams' more recent study *Sex in the Head* (1993) productively alters the tenor of the debate about Lawrence's sexual politics by combining it with a critique of the politics of 'looking', largely in the fiction (see 'Lawrence and Psychoanalytic Criticism' **[134]**). Her book theorizes a palpable ambivalence in Lawrence's thought about sex by bringing feminist film theory to bear on the convergence in Lawrence of stated hostilities both to 'modern' women and to modern(ist) visual culture – he was notably critical of cinema which he thought of queasily as a masturbatory pleasure – and focuses on the apparently contradictory fondness for spectacle in his narratives. (The other principal monograph on the visual in Lawrence, with very different theoretical foundations from Williams' study but worth highlighting here, is Keith Alldritt's *The Visual Imagination of D.H. Lawrence* [1971]).Williams has also written the 'Writers and their Work' series volume on Lawrence (1997) in which she argues that, in his desire to 'identify' and perhaps 'police the boundary between the sexes' (67) he shares one of feminisim's aims. This is a typically refreshing view from a critic who 'theorizes' Lawrence more successfully than most. She too eventually turns to 'The Woman Who Rode Away' drawing attention to the fact that the story is as much about the deferral of desire than its accomplished ends: the narrative concludes in the moment before the woman is executed having dwelt in detail on the elaborate preparations made for her sacrifice. Drawing on Freud, Williams therefore reads the tale as enacting the '"foreplay" of suspense' (106): it is an 'exercise in perversity' (107) either in terms of the woman's action in inviting and embracing her spectacular destruction (which is masochism), or through the writer's delight at detailing her humiliation (which is sadism).

So it is that gender remains a key issue for Lawrence critics. Alongside book-length critical studies, a vast number of essays and articles have been written around the broadest issues of Lawrence's 'sexual politics': from analyses concerned with the re-invention of Lawrence as a liberationist after the *Chatterley* trial to more theoretically challenging assessments of specific texts and tendencies in his writing. Feminist criticism, in its diversity, continues to intersect with other theoretical approaches, historical, psychoanalytical, post-structuralist, in its assessments of Lawrence.

(g) LAWRENCE AND LANGUAGE

Prior to 1970, there is a tendency in criticism to draw attention to issues of narrative technique and problems of style in evaluations of Lawrence's craft, particularly with reference to the fiction. Since then, several studies have taken more than a sideways glance at those idiosyncrasies of style and expression which have prompted extreme responses to what is a highly personal lexicon, as the 'metaphysic' is articulated and 'verbal consciousness' (W 486) attempted. Mid-century, Dorothy Van Ghent (1953), in a comparative study, acknowledges Lawrence's radical writing practice in *Sons and Lovers*. Comparable commentaries include Roger Sale's essay, 'The Narrative Technique of *The Rainbow*' (1959), Frank Baldanza's essay, 'D.H. Lawrence's *Song of Songs*' (1961), and Dorrit Cohn's comparative study which begins with a short piece of textual analysis of a passage from *The Plumed Serpent* (1966) but in fact concentrates more on Lawrence's contemporaries. Daleski (1965) and Kinkead-Weekes (1968), in writing about the ideas that underpin the 'metaphysic', inevitably acknowledge both the strangeness and the importance of Lawrence's principal modes of expression – for instance Kinkead-Weekes draws attention to the exploratory forms of Lawrence's language, when he refers to 'a continual "systole" and "diastole" of poetry and analytic prose, exploration and understanding' (Kinkead-Weekes 1968). For neither of these critics can the fiction be properly understood without recourse to the ideas, and the language, of the discursive writing, in particular 'Study of Thomas Hardy' and 'The Crown', while reference is also made to the 'quasi-Biblical' language of the Foreword to *Sons and Lovers* which many critics find awkward and impenetrable **[99; 101; 47]**. Of course, Lawrence was concerned early on to find his own voice and a style which suited the substance of what needed to be said, but he is also important as a writer who makes language a major theme, especially in the novels.

A useful study of Lawrence's language in this context is Michael Ragussis's comparative work, *The Subterfuge of Art: Language and the Romantic Tradition* (1978) (see 'Lawrence and Psychoanalytic Criticism' **[134]**). His principal chapter on Lawrence concentrates with great attention to detail on the life of particular words and phrases in *Women in Love* (words which amount to a 'new vocabulary'), noting the extent to which Lawrence makes individual words *mean* differently according to their place and context in the narrative. The philosophers Maurice Merleau-Ponty (*Phénoménologie de la perception* [1945]) and Friedrich Nietzsche, and the structural linguistics of Ferdinand de Saussure, provide some of the intellectual background to Ragussis's work. To support his argument he examines Lawrence's discursive writing on the novel form, highlighting Lawrence's anxiety about the gulf which he perceives to have opened up between fiction and philosophy in the modern novel, and his reading of the classic American texts where Lawrence formulates his views on 'art-speech'. 'Art-speech' is the phrase to which Ragussis then returns in his critique of the language – and the language theme – of *Women in Love*. He discusses a tendency in Lawrence's language use which is predicated on the movement of a range of meanings (often opposing meanings) through single words as

Lawrence deploys and redeploys them in a variety of contexts. It is in this sense, he argues, that

> *Women in Love* constructs a new vocabulary, so that when the reader first sees these words he realizes that he is to learn their meaning and to proceed. What is baffling about this novel's vocabulary is that it seems deliberately to defy our educative powers. The reader is more surprised, not when he sees a fairly common word like 'inhuman' used in a special way, but rather when the word is repeated later and he realizes that it now has an additional, and sometimes antithetical, meaning. It is, in short, a vocabulary that seems not to respect our understanding of vocabulary.
>
> (Ragussis 1978: 179)

So it is that Ragussis helps to draw attention not only to a highly personal lexicon in Lawrence's writing but, within that, to the drama of meaning contained in single words – words like 'inhuman' and 'love', for instance, which take on a life of their own in *Women in Love*. Through a concentration on the play in Lawrence with definitions, Ragussis is able to claim that 'Lawrence ... gives a Saussurian test of difference, suggesting that words attain meaning, not through the notion of similarity, but difference' (183). His study brings together a range of useful observations based in the first instance on structuralist perceptions and supported by close reading.

Avrom Fleishman (1985) acknowledges the positive contribution of Ragussis in his critique of *St Mawr* which begins with a statement about the otherwise parlous condition of critical writing on Lawrence's style:

> A nonspecialist coming to D.H. Lawrence studies must be moved by the intensity with which his ideas are debated but surprised at how little is made of his stylistic achievements. When attention is paid, it is usually to deride or defend the universally acknowledged *badnesses* – the purple passages, the swatches of slack dialogue and careless narration, the lapses into self-indulgent vituperation
>
> (Fleishman 1985: 162)

As the title of the piece indicates ('He Do the Polis in Different Voices: Lawrence's Later Style'), Fleishman is interested in demonstrating the polyphonic quality of the prose writing of the later 1920s via an understanding of Lawrence both as a polyglot and a translator – he translated the Sicilian writer, Giovanni Verga between 1922 and 1927, a detail which Fleishman privileges **[23; 69]**. Stressing the importance of the discourse theorist Mikhail Bakhtin's concept of the dialogic, Fleishman produces a reading of *St Mawr* in which, it is argued, 'Lawrence manages an extended construction in what Bakhtin calls "dialogized hetero-glossia", the interchange and opposition of competing languages or linguistic registers' (169). The work cited to produce this reading is Bakhtin's 'Discourse in the Novel' in *The Dialogic Imagination* (1981). In the rhetorical analysis which ensues, Fleishman produces a sense of multiple linguistic registers at work in the text and seeks to relate Lawrence's search for a 'new language' (169) to the crises of his historical moment. This approach to Lawrence's language is continued in David Lodge, 'Lawrence, Dostoyevsky, Bakhtin: D.H. Lawrence and dialogic fiction' (1985), and in Fleishman's later essay 'Lawrence and Bakhtin: Where Pluralism Ends and Dialogism Begins' (1990).

Rhetorical analyses of Lawrence's writing which stress opposition-ality and ambivalence are often indebted to the influence and insights of post-structuralist thought about language. Gerald Doherty is a critic who argues for Lawrence as embodying a deconstructive sensibility after the philosopher Jacques Derrida, and, with the linguistic mobility of *Women in Love*, he becomes 'an ardent deconstructor of logocentric modes of completion and closure' (Doherty 1987: 477). Another article reads *The Rainbow* in the same tradition (Doherty 1989), stimulated by a particularly Lawrentian take on the 'metaphysics of presence'. For some, the emergence of a deconstructive Lawrence might seem difficult to sustain, or Lawrence himself might seem to disappear under the claims that it is in the anticipation of a post-structuralist response to language that his importance lies. Even so, it is unnecessary to argue that such perspectives have nothing to offer the reader of Lawrence. They may in fact profitably help to shift the critical emphasis away from the biographical, life-to-art, approach which has dominated Lawrence studies.

Diane Bonds describes her analysis of Lawrence's language as charac-terized by the 'deconstructive operation' (1987: 1) inasmuch as she concentrates (like Ragussis and Fleishman in intention, if not quite in approach) on the oppositional play of meaning in Lawrence. Drawing on the literary-philosophical work of theorists Barbara Johnson and J. Hillis Miller, Bonds makes claims for the 'self-deconstructive' and 'self-interrogative' characteristics of Lawrence's prose, and links the existence of a 'theory' of language in Lawrence to his treatment of self-hood. Bonds' study draws attention to what she calls 'differential' models of language and the self, which contradict the logic of Lawrence's stated interest (in the discursive writing) in 'organic' models, both of self and language. Hence, for instance, writing of the beginning of *The Rainbow* (i.e. the 'prologue' which for Graham Holderness is weakly quasi-mythic ('Lawrence and Society **[138]**), while for F.R. Leavis it constitutes a fine evocation of 'traditional country life'), the claim is made that

> the relations of the Brangwen men and women mirror two alter- nate theories of the linguistic sign, one in which the sign is viewed as a unity of signifier and signified (the symbolic conception of the sign) and one in which the sign is viewed as a signifier that has its significance in its relation to other signifiers (the differential conception of the sign).
>
> (Bonds 1987: 56)

She uses this conceptual model (which refers to the language of structural linguistics) to argue that '*The Rainbow* sets up considerable resistance to the differential conception of the sign (and of language and of reality)' (56). The accompanying analyses of *Sons and Lovers* and *Women in Love* pursue the idea of a 'differential metaphysic' (93) with considerable attention to the textual detail of each work. The paradox of language which underpins her argument is Lawrence's exploration of the fact that 'language might be said both to liberate the self (from what Lawrence calls "the unconscious" into conscious being) and to imprison it' (7). For all her concentration on the relation between self (mind) and 'reality' (or 'world'), Bonds does not overtly explore Lawrence's reaction against Cartesian idealism, a question that later critics, also with an interest in Lawrence's language, have taken up.

Aidan Burns, in *Nature and Culture in D.H. Lawrence* (1980) – his title reflects another dominant binary structuring Lawrence's thought – is also interested in the relation of self and language in the novels. He concludes his book with this observation:

> The danger in the use of the language of transcendence arises when we assume that because we can find limits to any conceptual frame- work in which we try to grasp the self, we can therefore do without any framework at all. This is a mistake. For the self is only found, indeed is only constituted, in language, even in a language it trans- cends. ... there is no archimedean point outside society or outside language to which we can escape. The relative ones we have are the only ones there are and they form the conditions in which political and social life become possible.
>
> (Burns 1980: 122)

That the self is constituted in language engages Michael Bell, whose study of Lawrence (1992) is less preoccupied than Bonds with bringing theories of language to bear on Lawrence, in preference to seeing if an appropriate way of reading Lawrence will emerge out of his evident concern with language and its limitations in his writing. Bell's *D.H. Lawrence: language and being* also emphasizes the importance of German thought – Ernst Cassirer, Martin Heidegger, Nietzsche – in a considera- tion of the fiction. Like most recent assessments of Lawrence's language, Bell's study cites the now familiar comments in *Studies in Classic American Literature* on 'art-speech' and acknowledges the difficulties of writing about Lawrence's 'struggles' with language. In the introductory comments which precede his detailed analysis of the linguistic modes of the key works, Bell outlines the philosophical understanding which informs his reading of the texts and the 'metaphysic', and explains the importance, in the first instance, of Heidegger:

> Like Lawrence, Heidegger had a powerful vision of a pre-metaphy- sical mode of being which he struggled to express in modern terms, even though it was part of his point that it could not be so trans- lated. And part of the outcome, as with Lawrence, was to give him a heightened sensitivity to the relative nature of our own habitual world. Heidegger's term 'world' is the philosophical equivalent of the constantly modulating and relational representa- tion of 'external' existence in Lawrence's fiction. In the Heidegger- ean, as in the Lawrencean, conception there is no external world separable from human being in the world ... The special term 'world' denotes a radical opposition to Cartesian dualism; an opposition which does not merely differ but offers a comprehensive aetiology of that dualism. Overt philosophising would distract from, and undermine, the holism of Lawrence's presentation of states of being but his presentation subsumes an ontological under- standing every bit as subtle and comprehensive as Heidegger's.
>
> (Bell 1992: 10)

Hence Bell's title 'language and being'. What he refers to as Lawrence's 'ontological' theme (an emphasis on 'states of being' explored in relation to the external 'worlds' of each book) is not always successfully accom- modated, so Bell argues, by the narrative language of the fiction: indeed in the later writing *The Plumed Serpent*, especially, can be seen as an inadvertent parody of the attention to 'world' subtly achieved in the travel writing, for example, of the same period. The issue here, then, is language and the novel form (and often its failure), that is to say, its suitability or adaptability to Lawrence's philosophy of self and place. In his attempt to understand Lawrence on Lawrence's own terms (something we noted with MacLeod [1985]), Bell produces an account of the fiction that makes useful observations about how language enacts (creates) the central relationship between self and world. He concludes that this is either beautifully achieved (*The Rainbow*) or disastrously over-conscious (*The Plumed Serpent*).

Other critics in the 1990s who have developed the Heideggerean, and other philosophical, parallels with Lawrence include Anne Fernihough, *D.H. Lawrence: Aesthetics and Ideology* (1993), which demonstrates common ground in the thought of Lawrence and Heidegger on the work of art (Fernihough also conducts here the most extensive recent debate on authority in her chapter on Lawrence and fascism); Robert E. Montgomery who, in *The Visionary D.H. Lawrence: Beyond philosophy and art* (1994), examines Lawrence alongside Schopenhauer, Nietzsche, Heraclitus and Boehme; Fiona Becket, *D.H. Lawrence: The Thinker as Poet* (1997), which is an examination of metaphor as a mode of understanding in Lawrence. These studies concentrate on the fiction and the discursive writing. Allan Ingram, in *The Language of D.H. Lawrence* (1990), moves away from obvious philosophical parallels but usefully contrasts the style of Lawrence with his modernist contemporaries, and revives the question of form. In the same year, John B. Humma turns his attention to rhetorical issues, again in the fiction, with *Metaphor and Meaning in D.H. Lawrence's Later Novels* (1990).

Shorter-length studies than these attempt a concentration on genres apart from the fiction, seeking effectively to dovetail questions of language and other areas of theorized debate, or revisiting important discussions around issues of narrative, style and *knowledge*, a key term in Lawrence. Michael Squires examines 'Recurrence as a Narrative Technique in *The Rainbow*' (1975) and returns to the issue of narrative strategies in 'D.H. Lawrence's Narrators, Sources of Knowledge and the Problem of Coherence' (1995). Garrett Stewart explores Lawrence's ontological themes, and his chosen terms, in 'Lawrence, "Being," and the Allotropic Style' (1975). Catherine Stearns examines 'Gender, Voice, and Myth: the Relation of Language to the Female in D.H. Lawrence's Poetry' (1987), while Hagen (1987) considers Lawrence's use of metaphor. Jack F. Stewart focuses on Lawrence's most dialogic novel in 'Dialectics of Knowing in *Women in Love*' (1991). With a different emphasis, David J. Gordon considers discourses of desire in 'Sex and Language in D.H. Lawrence' (1981). These studies indicate the extent to which considerations of Lawrence's language cross over into other debates. So vast is the quantity of recent criticism on Lawrence, and indeed with a focus on language, that this highly selective synopsis can at best provide only a snapshot of the work in the field.

FURTHER READING

General

The purpose of Part III of this volume is to introduce some of the main developments in the criticism of the works of D.H. Lawrence, from the responses of his contemporaries to the present-day. His work has produced such a high level of commentary internationally that the best that can be hoped for in a guide of this kind is to signal certain areas of debate in order that the interested individual can pursue a particular direction from an informed position. It remains to give some further indication of studies which seek to map Lawrence thematically and historically, aside from the critical approaches already signalled in this volume. Occasionally, early studies of Lawrence provide an overview of the contemporary critical reception with the result that present-day readers can gain a sense of who valued what, and when – the introduction to Gregory (1933) is a case in point and, slightly more extensive, is Beal's chapter 'Lawrence's Reputation and Critics' in *D.H. Lawrence* (1961). Mark Spilka (1963) also provides a summary of critical attitudes in his introduction to a volume which offers representative analyses from the 1950s, a decade characterized, he suggests, by 'the best criticism on Lawrence ... much of it by younger men influenced by Leavis, or schooled in the New Criticism and pushing onward' (13). Harry T. Moore (1974) offers a briefer synopsis of the reception of Lawrence (646–9). More recently, Dennis Jackson and Fleda Brown Jackson's 'D.H. Lawrence's Critical Reception: An Overview', in their edited collection, *Critical Essays on D.H. Lawrence* (1988), is extremely thorough and deals with criticism both chronologically according to decade and conceptually. This is supplemented by a more detailed project, *D.H. Lawrence: Critical Assessments*, edited in four volumes by David Ellis and Ornella de Zordo (1992), which prints a range of reviews and evaluations, bringing a diverse body of material usefully together. Peter Preston's 'Lawrence in Britain' (in Iida 1999) deals with the critical history chronologically. Older resources have certainly not outlived their usefulness, and Lawrence scholars have long turned to R.P. Draper's edition of *D.H. Lawrence: The Critical Heritage* (1970) and to Keith Sagar's *A D.H. Lawrence Handbook* (1982). More recently, Takeo Iida's

The Reception of D.H. Lawrence Around the World (1999) provides extensive analytical and bibliographical coverage of the reception of Lawrence since the 1930s in Europe, America, Australia and Asia. This book is a useful point of departure for anyone interested in the study of Lawrence globally.

Companions, chronologies and journals

There are many books which bring together essays from critics representing different approaches and critical traditions. In the present study reference has been made to Spilka (ed.) *D.H. Lawrence: A Collection of Critical Essays* (1963), Kalnins (ed.) *D.H. Lawrence: Centenary Essays* (1986) and Heywood (ed.) *D.H. Lawrence: New Studies* (1987) among others. More recent volumes on Lawrence include Peter Widdowson (ed.) *D.H. Lawrence* (1992) which brings together in one volume some authoritative studies written over several decades; and Anne Fernihough (ed.) *The Cambridge Companion to D.H. Lawrence* (2001) which contains new essays in the field, any of which can supplement the relevant 'Further Reading' sections of the present book. Useful general studies relating to the period include *The Context of English Literature 1900-1930* edited by Michael Bell (1980) and *The Cambridge Companion to Modernism* (1999) edited by Michael Levenson, as well as Levenson (1984). James MacFarlane and Malcolm Bradbury (eds) have produced a detailed introduction to the period in *Modernism 1890–1930* (1976). Useful additional reading about Lawrence in relation to specific kinds of modernist experimentation includes Chapter 1 of Allan Ingram's *The Language of D.H. Lawrence* (1990); A. Walton-Litz in Balbert and Marcus (eds, 1985); Henry Schvey in Heywood (ed., 1987).

Every monograph, essay and article will not fall neatly into the categories of critical history outlined in Part III. There are excellent comparative studies, for instance, that incorporate discussions of Lawrence alongside other writers, as well as studies which focus on textual history such as the task of editing Lawrence. Recently, useful aids to research have also emerged which supplement the established bibliographies, calendars and chronologies, and among these can be counted Paul Poplawski's *The Works of D.H. Lawrence: A Chronological Checklist* (1995) and *D.H. Lawrence: A Reference Companion* (1996). Journal publication also continues, not least with *The D.H. Lawrence Review* (U. S. A.), and the Paris-based *Études Lawrenciennes* both of which acknowledge areas of current research with special 'themed' issues (see Bibliography).

General context

In addition to publications which are dedicated to the study of Lawrence, other related publications are useful. Certain anthologies, for instance, contain helpful material for the study of the period, providing essential historical and contextual information. Of particular relevance are Patricia Waugh's *Revolutions of the Word: Intellectual Contexts for the Study of Modern Literature* (1997) which focuses on modernism and related areas of interest, as well as Vassiliki Kolocotroni, Jane Goldman and Olga Taxidou (eds) *Modernism: An Anthology of Sources and Documents* (1998). Bonnie Kime Scott's *The Gender of Modernism* (1990) presents excerpts from Lawrence's writing on men and women, as well as indicating useful contexts for his work.

General theory

Again, vast numbers of books, from 'Introductions to' to 'Readers', offer ways into contemporary literary theory, of which those listed below and in the Bibliography are representative. Anne Jefferson and David Robey (eds) *Modern Literary Theory: A Comparative Introduction* (1988), Peter Barry, *Beginning Theory: An introduction to literary and cultural theory* (1995) and Jonathan Culler, *Literary Theory: A Very Short Introduction* (1997) provide good inductions to literary and critical theory. Elizabeth Wright's *Psychoanalytic Criticism: Theory in Practice* (1989) is an excellent introduction to psychoanalytic literary theory which makes reference to Lawrence but also ranges more broadly. It can be read alongside Anthony Elliot's *Psychoanalytic Theory: An Introduction* (1994). Toril Moi, *Sexual/Textual Politics* (1985), Mary Eagleton, *Feminist Literary Theory: A Reader* (1996), and *Feminisms: an anthology of literary theory and criticism* (1997) edited by Robyn R. Warhol and Diane Price Herndl, are among many accessible introductions to feminist literary theory. For an introduction to literature, history and social criticism see Raymond Williams, *Marxism and Literature* (1977), Terry Eagleton, *Marxism and Literary Criticism* (1976) and John Brannigan, *New Historicism and Cultural Materialism* (1998). It is hoped that these texts will usefully supplement the reading suggested in this *Guide*, although the list is far from exhaustive.

CHRONOLOGY

1885	David Herbert Lawrence born, Eastwood, Nottinghamshire.
1891–8	Beauvale Board School.
1898–1901	Scholarship to Nottingham High School
1901	Clerk, Haywood's medical supplies factory, Nottingham. Friendship with the Chambers family, and Jessie Chambers. Death of Ernest Lawrence.
1902–5	Pupil-teacher at the British School, Eastwood.
1905–6	Uncertificated teacher at the British School, Eastwood.
1906–8	Nottingham University College.
1907	Wins *Nottinghamshire Guardian* short story competition with 'A Prelude'.
1908–11	School-teacher at Davidson Road School, Croydon, Surrey.
1909	Poems and short stories in the *English Review*. Support of Ford Madox Hueffer and Ezra Pound. Friendship with Helen Corke (to 1912).
1910	Ends betrothal to Jessie Chambers. Death of Lydia Lawrence. Engagement to Louisa Burrows (ends 1912).
1911	*The White Peacock*. Relationship with Alice Dax (ends 1912). Resigns post as school-teacher due to illness. Friendship with Edward Garnett.
1912	Meets Frieda Weekley. *The Trespasser*. Germany. Italy.
1913	*Love Poems and Others*. *Sons and Lovers*. England. Friendships with John Middleton Murry and Katherine Mansfield.
1914	Marries Frieda Weekley. Friendships with Richard Aldington, Catherine Carswell, Hilda Doolittle, E.M. Forster, Amy Lowell, S.S. Koteliansky, Ottoline Morrell, Bertrand Russell. *The Widowing of Mrs Holroyd*. *The Prussian Officer and Other Stories*.
1915	Quarrel with Russell. *Signature* with Murry and Mansfield. *The Rainbow* suppressed. Friendships with Dorothy Brett, Mark Gertler, Aldous Huxley. Cornwall.
1916	*Twilight in Italy*. *Amores*. Medically examined twice and declared unfit for military service. Relations strained with Murry and Mansfield.
1917	Friendship with William Henry Hocking. Expulsion from Cornwall. *Look! We Have Come Through!*.

1918	Third medical examination. *New Poems*.
1919	*Bay*. Italy. Friendships with Norman Douglas, Reggie Turner and Maurice Magnus.
1920	Sicily. Italy. Friendship with Rosalind Baynes. *The Lost Girl* (wins James Tait Black Memorial prize). *Women in Love*.
1921	Sardinia. *Movements in European History*. *Psychoanalysis and the Unconscious*. *Tortoises*. *Sea and Sardinia*.
1922	Ceylon, Australia, New Zealand, South Seas, America (New Mexico). *Aaron's Rod*. *England, My England and Other Stories*. *Fantasia of the Unconscious*. Friendships with M.L. Skinner (Australia), Witter Bynner, Willard Johnson, Knud Merrild (America). With Mabel Dodge Sterne. Taos.
1923	America and Mexico. England. *The Ladybird, The Fox, The Captain's Doll*. *Studies in Classic American Literature*. *Kangaroo*. *Birds, Beasts and Flowers*.
1924	Mexico (with Brett). Kiowa Ranch. *The Boy in the Bush* (with M.L. Skinner). Death of Arthur Lawrence.
1925	Lawrence nearly dies: tuberculosis. England. Italy. *The Princess*. *St Mawr*. *Reflections on the Death of a Porcupine and Other Essays*.
1926	Relationship with Brett. England. Italy. *The Plumed Serpent*. *David*.
1927	*Mornings in Mexico*. Lawrence tours Etruscan sites.
1928	*The Escaped Cock (The Man Who Died)* [first part] *The Woman Who Rode Away and Other Stories*. *Lady Chatterley's Lover*. *Collected Poems*. Switzerland. France.
1929	*Pansies* seized by police. Thirteen paintings by Lawrence seized from Warren Gallery, London. *The Escaped Cock (The Man Who Died)* [second part]. Spain. Germany. France.
1930	*Nettles*. Lawrence dies, Vence (France).

Posthumous publications include:

1930	*Assorted Articles*. *The Virgin and the Gipsy*. *A Propos of 'Lady Chatterley's Lover'*. *Love Among the Haystacks and Other Pieces*. *Apocalypse*.
1932	*Sketches of Etruscan Places*. *Last Poems*.
1933	*The Fight for Barbara*.
1934	*A Collier's Friday Night, A Modern Lover* [inc. *Mr Noon*, (part 1)].
1936	*Phoenix: The Posthumous Papers of D.H. Lawrence*.
1964	*The Complete Poems of D.H. Lawrence*.

1968   *Phoenix II: Uncollected, Unpublished and Other Prose Works by D.H. Lawrence.*
1984   *Mr Noon* [part 2].

SELECTED BIBLIOGRAPHY
(WORKS CITED AND ADDITIONAL READING)

GENERAL WORKS

Bakhtin, M. (1981) *The Dialogic Imagination*, Austin: University of Texas Press.

Barry, P. (1995) *Beginning Theory: An Introduction to Literary and Cultural Theory*, Manchester: Manchester University Press.

Brannigan, J. (1998) *New Historicism and Cultural Materialism*, Basingstoke: Macmillan.

Brooks, C. (1947) *The Well Wrought Urn: Studies in the Structure of Poetry*, New York: Reynal and Hitchcock.

Collier, P. and J. Davies (eds) (1990) *Modernism and the European Unconscious*, Cambridge: Polity Press; Oxford: Basil Blackwell.

Culler, J (1997) *Literary Theory: A Very Short Introduction*, Oxford: Oxford University Press.

Deleuze, G. and F. Guattari (1984; rpt. 1990) *Anti-Oedipus: Capitalism and Schizophrenia*, trans. R. Hurley, M. Seem and H.R. Lane, London: The Athlone Press.

Eagleton, M. (1996) *Feminist Literary Theory: A Reader*, Oxford and Cambridge MA: Blackwell.

Eagleton, T. (1976) *Marxism and Literary Criticism*, London: Methuen.

—— (1976) *Criticism and Ideology: A Study in Marxist Literary Theory*, London: Humanities Press.

—— (1983) *Literary Theory: An Introduction*, Oxford: Blackwell.

Eliot, T.S. (1975) *'Ulysses*, Order and Myth' in F. Kermode (ed.) *Selected Prose of T. S. Eliot*, New York: Harcourt Brace.

Elliot, A. (1994) *Psychoanalytic Theory: An Introduction*, Oxford: Basil Blackwell.

Empson, W. (1947; 2nd edn, rev.) *Seven Types of Ambiguity*. London: Chatto and Windus.

Freud, S. (1983) *The Interpretation of Dreams*, Pelican Freud Library, vol. 4, trans. James Strachey, Harmondsworth: Penguin Books.

Jefferson, A. and D. Robey (eds) (1988; 2nd edn) *Modern Literary Theory: A Comparative Introduction*, London: B.T. Batsford Ltd.

Kolocotroni, V., J. Goldman and O. Taxidou (eds) (1998) *Modernism: An Anthology of Sources and Documents*, Edinburgh: Edinburgh University Press.

Levenson, M. (1984) *A Genealogy of Modernism: A Study of English Literary Doctrine 1908–1922*, Cambridge: Cambridge University Press, 1984.

— (ed.) (1999) *The Cambridge Companion to Modernism*, Cambridge: Cambridge University Press.

MacFarlane, J. and Bradbury, M. (eds) (1976). *Modernism 1890–1930*, Harmondsworth: Penguin Books.

Merleau-Ponty, M. (1962) *Phenomenology of Perception*, trans. C. Smith, New York: Humanities Press.

Moi, T. (1985) *Sexual/Textual Politics: Feminist Literary Theory*, London: Methuen.

Ransom, J.C. (1941) *The New Criticism*, Norfolk, CT: New Directions.

Richards, I.A. (1929) *Practical Criticism: A Study of Literary Judgment*, London: Routledge & Kegan Paul.

Roberts, P. (1986) *The Royal Court Theatre 1965–1972*, London: Routledge & Kegan Paul.

Scott, B.K. (ed.) (1990) *The Gender of Modernism*, Bloomington: Indiana University Press.

Waugh, P. (1997) *Revolutions of the Word: Intellectual Contexts for the Study of Modern Literature*, London: Edward Arnold.

Warhol, R.R. and D.P. Herndl (eds) (1997) *Feminisms: An Anthology of Literary Theory and Criticism*, Basingstoke: Macmillan.

Williams, R. (1958) *Culture and Society 1780–1950*, New York: Columbia University Press.

—— (1976) *Keywords*, London: Fontana.

—— (1977) *Marxism and Literature*, Oxford: Oxford University Press.

Woolf, V. (1984) *The Common Reader 1*, ed. A. McNeillie, London: Hogarth Press.

Wright, E. (1989) *Psychoanalytic Criticism: Theory in Practice*, London and New York: Routledge.

BIOGRAPHICAL WORKS

Aldington, R. (1927) *D.H. Lawrence: An Indiscretion*, Seattle: University of Seattle Book Store.

—— (1950) *Portrait of a Genius But …* , London: Heinemann.

Boulton, J.T. (ed.) (1997) *The Selected Letters of D.H. Lawrence*, Cambridge: Cambridge University Press.

Brett, D. (1933) *Lawrence and Brett: A Friendship*, Philadelphia: J. B. Lippincott Co.

Brewster E. and A. Brewster (eds) (1934) *D.H. Lawrence: reminiscences and correspondence*, London: Secker.

Bynner, W. (1951) *Journey with Genius*, New York: J. Day Co.

Byrne, J. (1995) *A Genius for Living: A Biography of Frieda Lawrence*, London: Bloomsbury.

Carswell, C. (1932) *The Savage Pilgrimage: A Narrative of D.H. Lawrence*, New York: Harcourt, Brace and Company.

Corke, H. (1965) *D.H. Lawrence: The Croydon Years*, Austin: University of Texas Press.
—— (1975) *In Our Infancy: An Autobiography Part I: 1882–1912*, Cambridge: Cambridge University Press.
Delany, P. (1979) *D.H. Lawrence's Nightmare: The Writer and his Circle in the Years of the Great War*, Hassocks: Harvester.
Delavenay, E. (1972) *D.H. Lawrence: The Man and his Work. The Formative Years, 1885–1919*, trans. K.M. Delavenay, London: Heinemann.
Dodge Luhan, M. (1932) *Lorenzo in Taos*, New York: Knopf.
Ellis, D. (1998) *D.H. Lawrence: Dying Game 1922–1930, The Cambridge Biography of D.H. Lawrence 1885–1930*, vol. 3, Cambridge: Cambridge University Press.
E.T. [Jessie Chambers] (1935) *D.H. Lawrence: A Personal Record*, London: Cape.
Feinstein, E. (1993) *Lawrence's Women: The Intimate Life of D.H. Lawrence*, London: Harper Collins.
H.D. [Hilda Doolittle] (1960) *Bid Me To Live*, New York: Grove Press.
Huxley, A. (ed.) (1932) *The Letters of D.H. Lawrence*, London: Heinemann.
Jackson, R. (1994) *Frieda Lawrence, Including 'Not I, But the Wind' and other Autobiographical Writings*, London: Pandora.
Kinkead-Weekes, M. (1996) *D.H. Lawrence: Triumph to Exile: 1912–1922, The Cambridge Biography of D.H. Lawrence 1885–1930*, vol. 2, Cambridge: Cambridge University Press.
Lawrence, A. (1931) *Young Lorenzo: Early Life of D.H. Lawrence, Containing Hitherto Unpublished Letters, Articles and Reproductions of Pictures*, Florence: G. Orioli.
Lawrence, A. and S.G. Gelder, (1932) *Early Life of D.H. Lawrence: Together with Hitherto Unpublished Letters and Articles*, London: Martin Secker.
Lawrence F. (1934) *Not I, But the Wind*, New York: The Viking Press.
Maddox, B. (1994) *The Married Man: A life of D.H. Lawrence*, London: Sinclair Stevenson.
Merrild, K. (1938) *A Poet and Two Painters*, London: Routledge.
Moore, H.T. (1951) *The Life and Works of D.H. Lawrence*, London: Unwin Books.
—— (1961) *A D.H. Lawrence Miscellany*, London: Heinemann.
—— (ed.) (1962) *The Collected Letters of D.H. Lawrence*, London: Heinemann.
—— (1974) *The Priest of Love*, Harmondsworth: Penguin Books.
Murry, J.M. (1931) *Son of Woman*, London: Jonathan Cape.
—— (1933) *Reminiscences of D.H. Lawrence*, London: Jonathan Cape.
—— (1935) *Between Two Worlds, An Autobiography*, London: Jonathan Cape.
Nehls, E. (ed.) (1957) *D.H. Lawrence: A Composite Biography*, 3 vols. Madison: University of Wisconsin Press.
Neville, G. (1981) *A Memoir of D.H. Lawrence: (The Betrayal)*, ed. C. Baron, Cambridge: Cambridge University Press.
Tedlock, Jr. E.W. (ed.) (1961) *Frieda Lawrence: The Memoirs and Correspondence*, London: Heinemann.

West, R. (1930), *D.H. Lawrence*, London: Martin Secker.

Worthen, J. (1991a) *D.H. Lawrence: The Early Years 1885–1912, The Cambridge Biography of D.H. Lawrence 1885–1930*, vol. 1, Cambridge: Cambridge University Press.

CRITICISM OF D.H. LAWRENCE IN BOOKS

Albright, D. (1978) *Personality and Impersonality: Lawrence, Woolf and Mann*, Chicago and London: Chicago University Press.

Alldritt, K. (1971) *The Visual Imagination of D.H. Lawrence*, London: Edward Arnold.

Apter, T.E. (1978) 'Lets Hear What the Male Chauvinist is Saying: *The Plumed Serpent*' in A. Smith (ed.) *Lawrence and Women*, London: Vision

Baker, P.G. (1983) *A Reassessment of D.H. Lawrence's 'Aaron's Rod'*, Ann Arbor, MI: UMI Research Press.

Balbert, P. (1989) *D.H. Lawrence and the Phallic Imagination: Essays on Sexual Identity and Feminist Misreading*, Basingstoke: Macmillan.

Balbert, P. and P.L. Marcus (eds) (1985) *D.H. Lawrence: A Centenary Consideration*, Ithaca and London: Cornell University Press.

Bannerjee, A. (1990) *D.H. Lawrence's Poetry: Demon Liberated. A Collection of Primary and Secondary Source Material*, Basingstoke: Macmillan.

Beal, A. (1961) *D.H. Lawrence*, Edinburgh and London: Oliver and Boyd.

Becket, F. (1997) *D.H. Lawrence: The Thinker as Poet*, Basingstoke: Macmillan; New York: St Martin's Press.

Bell, M. (1992) *D.H. Lawrence: Language and Being*, Cambridge: Cambridge University Press.

—— (ed.) (1980) *The Context of English Literature 1900–1930*, London: Methuen.

Berthoud, J. (1978) '*The Rainbow* as Experimental Novel', in A. H. Gomme (ed.) *D.H. Lawrence: A Critical Study of the Major Novels and Other Writings*, Hassocks: Harvester Press; New York: Barnes and Noble.

Beynon, R. (1997) *D.H. Lawrence. 'The Rainbow' and 'Women in Love'*, Cambridge: Icon Books.

Black, M. (1986) *D.H. Lawrence: The Early Fiction. A Commentary*, Cambridge: Cambridge University Press.

—— (1991) *D.H. Lawrence: The Early Philosophical Works. A Commentary*, Basingstoke: Macmillan.

—— (1992) *D.H. Lawrence: 'Sons and Lovers'*, Cambridge: Cambridge University Press.

—— (1995) 'Leavis on Lawrence', in Ian MacKillop and Richard Storer (eds) *F.R. Leavis: Essays and Documents*, Sheffield: Sheffield Academic Press.

Blackmur, R.P. (1954) *Language as Gesture: Essays in Poetry*, London: Allen & Unwin.

Blanchard, L. (1978) 'Mothers and Daughters in D.H. Lawrence: *The Rainbow* and Selected Shorter Works' in A. Smith (ed.) *Lawrence and Women*, London: Vision.

—— (1988) '"Reading Out" a "New Novel": Lawrence's Experiments with Story and Discourse in *Mr Noon*' in D. Jackson and F. Brown Jackson (eds) *Critical Essays on D.H. Lawrence*, Boston, MA: G.K. Hall & Co.

Bloom, H. (ed.) (1988), *D.H. Lawrence's 'Women in Love'. Modern Critical Interpretations*, New York: Chelsea House Publishers.

Bonds, D. (1987) *Language and the Self in D.H. Lawrence*, Ann Arbor, MI: UMI Research Press.

Brown, K. (ed.) (1990), *Rethinking Lawrence*, Milton Keynes and Philadelphia: Open University Press.

Bridgewater, P. (1972) *Nietzsche in Anglosaxony*, London: Leicester University Press.

Britton, D. (1988) *'Lady Chatterley's Lover': The Making of the Novel*, London: Unwin Hyman.

Burgess, A. (1985) *Flame into Being: The Life and Work of D.H. Lawrence*, London: William Heinemann Ltd.

Burns, A. (1980) *Nature and Culture in D.H. Lawrence*, Basingstoke: Macmillan.

Carter, A. (1982; rev. edn, 1993) *Nothing Sacred: Selected Writings*, London: Virago.

Carter, F. (1932) *D.H. Lawrence and the Body Mystical*, London: Denis Archer.

Cavitch, D. (1969) *D.H. Lawrence and the New World*, New York: Oxford University Press.

Chong-wha, C. (1989) 'In Search of the Dark God: Lawrence's Dualism', in P. Preston and P. Hoare (eds) *D.H. Lawrence in the Modern World*, Basingstoke: Macmillan.

Clark, L.D. (1964) *Dark Night of the Body: D.H. Lawrence's 'The Plumed Serpent'*, Austin: University of Texas Press.

—— (1980) *The Minoan Distance: The Symbolism of Travel in D.H. Lawrence*, Tucson: University of Arizona Press.

—— (1989) 'Making the Classic Contemporary: Lawrence's Pilgrimage Novels and American Romance' in P. Preston and P. Hoare (eds) *D.H. Lawrence in the Modern World*, Basingstoke: Macmillan.

Clarke, C. (1969) *River of Dissolution: D.H. Lawrence and English Romanticism*, London: Routledge and Kegan Paul; New York: Barnes and Noble.

—— (ed.) (1969) *D.H. Lawrence: 'The Rainbow' and 'Women in Love': A Casebook*, Basingstoke: Macmillan.

Clarke, I. (1989) *'The Fight for Barbara*: Lawrence's Society Drama' in P. Preston and P. Hoare (eds) *D.H. Lawrence in the Modern World*, Basingstoke: Macmillan.

Cowan, J.C. (1970) *D.H. Lawrence's American Journey: A Study in Literature and Myth*, Cleveland: Case Western Reserve University Press.

—— (1988) 'Allusions and Symbols in D.H. Lawrence's *The Escaped Cock*' in D. Jackson and F. Brown Jackson (eds) *Critical Essays on D.H. Lawrence*, Boston, MA: G.K. Hall & Co.

—— (1990) *D.H. Lawrence and the Trembling Balance*, University Park and London: Pennsylvania State University Press.

Cushman, K. (1978) *D.H. Lawrence at Work. The Emergence of 'The Prussian Officer' Stories*. Charlottesville: University Press of Virginia.

Daleski, H.M. (1965) *The Forked Flame: A Study of D.H. Lawrence*, London: Faber and Faber.

Darroch, R. (1981) *D.H. Lawrence in Australia*, South Melbourne: Macmillan Co. of Australia.

Delavenay, E. (1971) *D.H. Lawrence and Edward Carpenter: A Study in Edwardian Transition*, London: Heinemann.

—— (1987) 'Lawrence, Otto Weininger and "Rather Raw Philosophy"' in C. Heywood (ed.) *D.H. Lawrence: New Studies*, Basingstoke: Macmillan.

De Beauvoir, S. (1988), *The Second Sex*, trans. J.M. Parshley, London: Picador.

De Filippis, S. (1989), 'Lawrence of Etruria' in P. Preston and P. Hoare (eds) *D.H. Lawrence in the Modern World*, Basingstoke: Macmillan.

—— (1992) 'Is There A Great Secret? D.H. Lawrence and the Etruscans' in D. Ellis and O. De Zordo (eds) *D.H. Lawrence: Critical Assessments* 4 vols, Mountfield: Helm Information.

Devlin, A.J. (1988), 'The "Strange and Fiery" Course of *The Fox*: D.H. Lawrence's Aesthetic of Composition and Revision' in G. Salgādo and G.K. Das (eds) *The Spirit of D.H. Lawrence: Centenary Studies*, Basingstoke: Macmillan.

Dix, C. (1980) *D.H. Lawrence and Women*, Basingstoke: Macmillan.

Dollimore, J. (1998) *Death, Desire and Loss in Western Culture*, Harmondsworth: Penguin.

Draper, R.P. (1986) *'Sons and Lovers' by D.H. Lawrence*, Macmillan Master Guides Series. Basingstoke: Macmillan.

—— (1987) 'The Poetry of D.H. Lawrence' in C. Heywood (ed.) *D.H. Lawrence: New Studies*, Basingstoke: Macmillan.

—— ([1966]1988) 'The Defeat of Feminism: D.H. Lawrence's *The Fox* and "The Woman Who Rode Away"' in D. Jackson and F. Brown Jackson (eds) *Critical Essays on D.H. Lawrence*, Boston, MA: G.K. Hall & Co.

—— (ed.) (1970; rpt 1972; rpt with corrections, 1979) *D.H. Lawrence: The Critical Heritage*, London: Routledge & Kegan Paul.

Eagleton, T. (1970) *Exiles and Emigrés: Studies in Modern Literature*, London: Chatto and Windus.

Ebbatson, R. (1982) *The Evolutionary Self: Hardy, Forster, Lawrence*, Hemel Hempstead: Harvester Press.

—— (1987) 'A Spark Beneath the Wheel: Lawrence and Evolutionary Thought' in C. Heywood (ed.) *D.H. Lawrence: New Studies*, Basingstoke: Macmillan.

Edwards, D. (1990) *'The Rainbow': A Search for New Life*, Boston: Twayne.

SELECTED BIBLIOGRAPHY

SELECTED BIBLIOGRAPHY

Eliot, T.S. (1934) *After Strange Gods: A Primer of Modern Heresy*, London: Faber and Faber.

Ellis, D. (1986) 'Lawrence and the Biological Psyche' in Mara Kalnins (ed.) *D.H. Lawrence: Centenary Essays*, Bristol: Bristol University Press.

—— (1998) *D.H. Lawrence: Dying Game 1922–1930, The Cambridge Biography of D.H. Lawrence 1885–1930*, vol. 3, Cambridge: Cambridge University Press.

Ellis, D. and H. Mills (1988) *D.H. Lawrence's Non-fiction: Art, Thought and Genre*, Cambridge: Cambridge University Press.

Ellis, D. and O. De Zordo (eds) (1992) *D.H. Lawrence: Critical Assessments*, 4 vols, Mountfield: Helm Information.

Feinstein, E. (1993) *Lawrence's Women: The Intimate Life of D.H. Lawrence*, London: HarperCollins Publishers.

Fernihough, A. (1990) 'The Tyranny of the Text: Lawrence, Freud and the Modernist Aesthetic' in P. Collier and J. Davies (eds) *Modernism and the European Unconscious*, Cambridge: Polity Press; Oxford: Basil Blackwell.

—— (1993) *D.H. Lawrence: Aesthetics and Ideology*, Oxford: Clarendon Press.

—— (ed.) (2001) *The Cambridge Companion to D.H. Lawrence*, Cambridge: Cambridge University Press.

Finney, B. (1990) *D.H. Lawrence: Sons and Lovers*, Harmondsworth: Penguin.

Fleishman, A. (1985) 'He Do the Polis in Different Voices: Lawrence's Later Style' in P. Balbert and P.L. Marcus (eds) *D.H. Lawrence: A Centenary Consideration*, Ithaca and London: Cornell University Press.

—— (1990) 'Lawrence and Bakhtin: Where Pluralism Ends and Dialogism Begins' in K. Brown (ed.) *Rethinking Lawrence*, Milton Keynes: Open University Press.

Ford, G. (1965) *Double-Measure: A Study of the Novels and Stories of D.H. Lawrence*, New York: Holt, Rinehart and Winston.

Freeman, M. (1955) *D.H. Lawrence: A Basic Study of His Ideas*, New York: Grossett & Dunlap.

—— (1969) 'Lawrence and Futurism', in C. Clarke (ed.) *D.H. Lawrence: 'The Rainbow' and 'Women in Love': A Casebook*, Basingstoke: Macmillan.

Furbank, P.N. (1988), 'The Philosophy of D.H. Lawrence', in G. Salgādo and G.K. Das (eds) *The Spirit of D.H. Lawrence: Centenary Essays*, Basingstoke: Macmillan.

Gilbert, S.M. (1972) *Acts of Attention: The Poems of D.H. Lawrence*, Ithaca and London: Cornell University Press.

—— (1985) 'Potent Griselda: "The Ladybird" and the Great Mother' in P. Balbert and P.L. Marcus (eds) *D.H. Lawrence: A Centenary Consideration*, Ithaca and London: Cornell University Press.

Gomme, A. H. (ed.) (1978) *D.H. Lawrence: A Critical Study of the Major Novels and Other Writings*, Sussex: Harvester.

Goodheart, E. (1963) *The Utopian Vision of D.H. Lawrence*, Chicago and London: University of Chicago Press.

Gordon, D.J. (1966) *D.H. Lawrence as a Literary Critic*, New Haven and London: Yale University Press.

Gregory, H. (1933) *D.H. Lawrence Pilgrim of the Apocalypse: A Critical Study*, New York: The Viking Press.

Guttenberg, B. (1988) 'Realism and Romance in Lawrence's *The Virgin and the Gipsy*' in D. Jackson and F. Brown Jackson (eds) *Critical Essays on D.H. Lawrence*, Boston, MA: G.K. Hall & Co.

Hamalian, L. (1973) *D.H. Lawrence: A Collection of Criticism*, New York: McGraw-Hill Book Company.

Harris, J.H. (1984) *The Short Fiction of D.H. Lawrence*, New Jersey: Rutgers University Press.

Harvey, G. (1987) *Sons and Lovers – The Critics' Debate*, Basingstoke: Macmillan.

Hayles, K.N. (1984) 'Evasion: The Field of the Unconscious in D.H. Lawrence', *The Cosmic Web: Scientific Field Models and Literary Strategies in the Twentieth Century*, Ithaca: Cornell University Press.

Heywood, C. (1987) '"Blood-Consciousness" and the Pioneers of the Reflex and Ganglionic Systems' in C. Heywood (ed.) *D.H. Lawrence: New Studies*, Basingstoke: Macmillan.

—— (ed.) (1987) *D.H. Lawrence: New Studies*, Basingstoke: Macmillan.

Hochman, B. (1970) *Another Ego: The Changing View of Self and Society in the Work of D.H. Lawrence*, Columbia: University of South Carolina Press.

Hoffman, F.J. (1945; rev. edn, 1957) *Freudianism and the Literary Mind* Louisiana: Louisiana State University Press.

Holderness, G. (1982) *D.H. Lawrence: History, Ideology and Fiction*, London: Gill and Macmillan.

Hostettler, M. (1985) *D.H. Lawrence: Travel Books and Fiction*, Berne: Peter Lang.

Hough, G. (1956) *The Dark Sun: A Study of D.H. Lawrence*, London: Duckworth.

Howe, M.B. (1977) *The Art of the Self in D.H. Lawrence*, Athens: Ohio University Press.

Humma, J.B. (1990) *Metaphor and Meaning in D.H. Lawrence's Later Novels*, Columbia: University of Missouri Press.

Hyde, G.M. (1981) *D.H. Lawrence and the Art of Translation*, Basingstoke: Macmillan.

—— (1990) *D.H. Lawrence*, Basingstoke: Macmillan.

Iida, T. (ed.) (1999) *The Reception of D.H. Lawrence Around the World*, Fukuoka: Kyushu University Press.

Ingram, A. (1990) *The Language of D.H. Lawrence*, Basingstoke: Macmillan.

Jackson, D. and Brown Jackson, F. (eds) (1988) *Critical Essays on D.H. Lawrence*, Boston, MA: G.K. Hall & Co.

Janik, D.I. (1981) *The Curve of Return: D.H. Lawrence's Travel Books*, Victoria, BC: University of Victoria Press.

Kalnins, M. (ed.) (1986) *D.H. Lawrence: Centenary Essays*, Bristol: Bristol Classical Press.

—— (1988) 'D.H. Lawrence's "Odour of Chrysanthemums": The Three Endings' in D. Jackson and F. Brown Jackson (eds) *Critical Essays on D.H. Lawrence*, Boston, MA: G.K. Hall & Co.

Kalnins, M. and G. Donaldson (eds) (1999) *D.H. Lawrence in Italy and England*, Basingstoke: Macmillan; New York: St Martins Press.

Kearney, M.F. (1997) *The Major Short Stories of D.H. Lawrence. A Handbook*, New York: Garland.

Kermode, F. (1973) *Lawrence*, London: Fontana Press.

Kinkead-Weekes, M. (1968), 'The Marble and the Statue: The Exploratory Imagination of D.H. Lawrence' in M. Mack and I. Gregor (eds) *Imagined Worlds: Essays on Some English Novels and Novelists*, London: Methuen.

—— ([1969] 1978) 'Eros and Metaphor: Sexual Relationship in the Fiction of Lawrence' in A. Smith (ed.) *Lawrence and Women*, London: Vision.

—— (1989) 'The Sense of History in *The Rainbow*' in P. Preston and P. Hoare (eds) *D.H. Lawrence in the Modern World*, Basingstoke: Macmillan.

—— (2001) 'Decolonising Imagination: Lawrence in the 1920s' in A. Fernihough (ed.) *The Cambridge Companion to D.H. Lawrence*, Cambridge: Cambridge University Press.

Laird, H.A. (1988) *Self and Sequence: The Poetry of D.H. Lawrence*, Charlottesville: University Press of Virginia.

Leavis, F.R. (1932) *D.H. Lawrence*, Gordon Fraser, Cambridge: The Minority Press.

—— (1948) *The Great Tradition: George Eliot, Henry James, Joseph Conrad*, London: Chatto and Windus.

—— (1955) *D.H. Lawrence: Novelist*, London: Chatto and Windus.

—— (1976) *Thought, Words and Creativity: Art and Thought in Lawrence*, London: Chatto and Windus.

Lerner, L. (1986) 'Lawrence and the Feminists' in Mara Kalnins (ed.) *D.H. Lawrence: Centenary Essays*, Bristol: Bristol Classical Press.

Levy, M. (1964) *The Paintings of D.H. Lawrence*, New York: Viking.

Lockwood, M.J. (1987) *A Study of the Poems of D.H. Lawrence: Thinking in Poetry*, Basingstoke: Macmillan.

Mace, H.R. (1988) 'The Genesis of D.H. Lawrence's Poetic Form' in D. Jackson and F. Brown Jackson (1988) *Critical Essays on D.H. Lawrence*, Boston, MA: G.K. Hall & Co.

Mack, M. and I. Gregor (eds) (1968) *Imagined Worlds: Essays on Some English Novels and Novelists*, London: Methuen.

MacLeod, S. (1985) *Lawrence's Men and Women*, London: Paladin.

McDonald, E.D. (1925) *A Bibliography of the Writings of D.H. Lawrence*, Philadelphia: Centaur Book Shop.

—— (1936; repr. 1961) *Phoenix: The Posthumous Papers of D.H. Lawrence*, London: William Heinemann.

McDowell, F.P.W. (1988) 'Pioneering into the Wilderness of Unopened Life: Lou Witt in America' in G. Salgādo and G.K. Das (eds) *The Spirit of D.H. Lawrence: Centenary Studies*, Basingstoke: Macmillan.

Mandell, G.P. (1984) *The Phoenix Paradox: A Study of Renewal Through Change in the Collected Poems and Last Poems of D.H. Lawrence*, Carbondale: South Illinois Press.

Marshall, T. (1970) *The Psychic Mariner: A Reading of the Poems of D.H. Lawrence*, New York: Viking.

Martz, L.L. (1968) 'Portrait of Miriam: A Study in the Design of *Sons and Lovers*' in M. Mack and I. Gregor (eds) *Imagined Worlds: Essays on Some English Novels and Novelists*, London: Methuen.

Meyers, J. (1982) *D.H. Lawrence and the Experience of Italy*, Philadelphia: University of Pennsylvania Press.

Miko, S.J. (1971) *Toward 'Women in Love': The Emergence of a Lawrentian Aesthetic*, New Haven and London: Yale University Press.

—— (ed.) (1969) *Twentieth-Century Interpretations of 'Women in Love': A Collection of Critical Essays*, Englewood Cliffs, NJ: Prentice-Hall.

Millett, K. (1969 [1977; repr. 1985]) *Sexual Politics*, London: Virago.

Milne, D. (2001) 'Lawrence and the politics of sexual politics' in A. Fernihough (ed.) *The Cambridge Companion to D.H. Lawrence*, Cambridge: Cambridge University Press.

Milton, C. (1987) *Lawrence and Nietzsche: A Study in Influence*, Aberdeen: Aberdeen University Press.

Montgomery, R.E. (1994) *The Visionary D.H. Lawrence: Beyond Philosophy and Art*, Cambridge: Cambridge University Press.

Moore, H.T. (1978) 'Bert Lawrence and Lady Jane' in A. Smith (ed.) *Lawrence and Women*, London: Vision.

Moynahan, J. (1963) *The Deed of Life: The Novels and Tales of D.H. Lawrence*, Princeton NJ: Princeton University Press; London: Oxford University Press.

Murfin, R.C. (1983) *The Poetry of D.H. Lawrence: Texts and Contexts*, Lincoln: University of Nebraska Press.

—— (1987) *Sons and Lovers: A Student's Companion to the Novels*, Boston: Twayne.

Nash, C. (1980) 'Myth and Modern Literature' in M. Bell (ed.) *The Context of English Literature 1900–1930*, London: Methuen.

Nixon, C. (1986) *Lawrence's Leadership Politics and the Turn Against Women*, Berkeley: University of California Press.

Oates, J.C. (1988) 'Lawrence's Götterdämmerung: The Apocalyptic Vision of *Women in Love*' in D. Jackson and F. Brown Jackson (eds) *Critical Essays on D.H. Lawrence*, Boston, MA: G.K. Hall & Co.

Partlow Jr., R.B. and H.T. Moore (1980) *D.H. Lawrence: The Man Who Lived*, Carbondale: Southern Illinois University Press.

Paulin, T. (1989) '"Hibiscus and Salvia Flowers": the Puritan Imagination', in P. Preston and P. Hoare (eds) *D.H. Lawrence in the Modern World*, Basingstoke: Macmillan.

Peek, A. (1987) 'The Sydney *Bulletin*, *Moby Dick* and the Allusiveness of *Kangaroo*' in C. Heywood (ed.) *D.H. Lawrence: New Studies*, Basingstoke: Macmillan.

Perloff, M. (1985) 'Lawrence's Lyric Theater: *Birds, Beasts and Flowers*' in P. Balbert and P.L. Marcus (eds) *D.H. Lawrence: A Centenary Consideration*, Ithaca and London: Cornell University Press.

Pinkney, T. (1990) *D.H. Lawrence*, Hemel Hempstead: Harvester Wheatsheaf.

Pollnitz, C. (1986) '"Raptus Virginis": The Dark God in the Poetry of D.H. Lawrence' in Mara Kalnins (ed.) *D.H. Lawrence: Centenary Essays*, Bristol: Bristol Classical Press.

Poplawski, P. (1995), foreword by J. Worthen, *The Works of D.H. Lawrence: A Chronological Checklist*, Nottingham: D.H. Lawrence Society.

—— (1996) *D.H. Lawrence: A Reference Companion*, biography by John Worthen, Westport, CT and London: Greenwood Press.

Potter, S. (1930) *D.H. Lawrence: A First Study*, London: Jonathan Cape.

Preston, P. and P. Hoare (eds) (1989) *D.H. Lawrence in the Modern World*, Basingstoke: Macmillan.

Pullin, F. (1978) 'Lawrence's Treatment of Women in *Sons and Lovers*' in A. Smith (ed.) *Lawrence and Women*, London: Vision.

Ragussis, M. (1978) *The Subterfuge of Art: Language and the Romantic Tradition*, Baltimore and London: Johns Hopkins University Press.

Roberts, W. (1982) *A Bibliography of D.H. Lawrence*, 2nd edn, Cambridge: Cambridge University Press.

Roberts, W. and H.T. Moore (1968) *Phoenix II: Uncollected, Unpublished and Other Prose Works by D.H. Lawrence*, London: Heinemann.

Rolph, C. H. (1961; 1990) *The Trial of Lady Chatterley*, London: Penguin Books.

Ross, C. L. (1991) *'Women in Love': A Novel of Mythic Realism*, Boston: Twayne.

Rossman, C. (1980) 'The Boy in the Bush in the Lawrence Canon' in R.B. Partlow Jr. and H.T. Moore *D.H. Lawrence: The Man Who Lived*, Carbondale: Southern Illinois University Press.

—— (1985) 'D.H. Lawrence and Mexico' in P. Balbert and P.L. Marcus (eds) *D.H. Lawrence: A Centenary Consideration*, Ithaca and London: Cornell University Press.

Ruderman, J. (1984) *D.H. Lawrence and the Devouring Mother*, Durham NC: Duke University Press.

Ryals, C. de L., ([1962]1988) 'D.H. Lawrence's "The Horse-Dealer's Daughter": An Interpretation' in D. Jackson and F. Brown Jackson (eds) *Critical Essays on D.H. Lawrence*, Boston, MA: G.K. Hall & Co.

Rylance, R. (ed.) (1996) *'Sons and Lovers': Contemporary Critical Essays*, New Casebook Series, Basingstoke: Macmillan.

—— (2001) 'Ideas, histories, generations and beliefs: the early novels *to Sons and Lovers*' in A. Fernihough (ed.) *The Cambridge Companion to D.H. Lawrence*, Cambridge: Cambridge University Press.

Sagar, K. (1966) *The Art of D.H. Lawrence*, Cambridge: Cambridge University Press.

—— (1979) *D.H. Lawrence: A Calendar of his Works*, Manchester: Manchester University Press.

—— (1980) *The Life of D.H. Lawrence: An Illustrated Biography*, London: Eyre Methuen.

—— (1985) *D.H. Lawrence: Life into Art*, Harmondsworth: Penguin Books.

—— (ed.) (1982) *A D.H. Lawrence Handbook*, Manchester: Manchester University Press.

Salgãdo, G. (ed.) (1969) *D.H. Lawrence: 'Sons and Lovers'*, Basingstoke: Macmillan.

—— (1982) *A Preface to D.H. Lawrence*, Harlow: Longman.

—— and G.K. Das (eds) (1988) *The Spirit of D.H. Lawrence: Centenary Studies*, Basingstoke: Macmillan.

Sanders, S. (1974) *D.H. Lawrence: The World of the Five Major Novels*, New York: Viking.

Seligmann, H. (1924) *D.H. Lawrence: An American Interpretation*. New York: Seltzer.

Scheckner, P. (1985) *Class, Politics and the Individual: A Study of the Major Works of D.H. Lawrence*, Rutherford, NJ: Fairleigh Dickinson University Press.

Schneider, D. (1984) *D.H. Lawrence: The Artist as Psychologist*, Kansas: University of Kansas Press.

Schvey, H. (1987) 'Lawrence and Expressionism' in C. Heywood (ed.) *D.H. Lawrence: New Studies*, Basingstoke: Macmillan.

Siegel, C. (1991). 'Lawrence among the Women: Wavering Boundaries in Women's Literary Traditions' in K.M. Balutansky and A. Booth (eds) *Feminist Issues: Practice, Politics, and Theory*, Charlottesville and London: University Press of Virginia.

Simpson, H. (1982) *D.H. Lawrence and Feminism*, London and Canberra: Croom Helm.

Sinzelle, C. (1989) 'Skinning the Fox: a Masochist's Delight' in P. Preston and P. Hoare (eds) *D.H. Lawrence in the Modern World*, Basingstoke: Macmillan.

Sklar, S. (1975) *The Plays of D.H. Lawrence: A Biographical and Critical Study*, London: Vision.

Sklenicka, C. (1991) *D.H. Lawrence and the Child*, Missouri: University of Missouri Press.

Smith, A. (ed.) (1978) *Lawrence and Women*, London: Vision.

Spilka, M. (1955) *The Love Ethic of D.H. Lawrence*, Bloomington: Indiana University Press.

—— (ed.) (1963) *D.H. Lawrence: A Collection of Critical Essays*, Englewood Cliffs, NJ: Prentice Hall.

—— (1978) 'On Lawrence's Hostility to Wilful Women: The Chatterley Solution' in A. Smith (ed.) *Lawrence and Women*, London: Vision.

Spender, S. (1953) *The Creative Element*, London: Hamilton.

Squires, M. (1983) *The Creation of 'Lady Chatterley's Lover'*, Baltimore: Johns Hopkins Press.

Squires, M. and Jackson, D. (eds) (1985) *D.H. Lawrence's "Lady": A New Look at Lady Chatterley's Lover*, Athens: University of Georgia Press.

Stewart, J.F. (1988) 'Expressionism in *The Rainbow*' in D. Jackson and F. Brown Jackson (eds) *Critical Essays on D.H. Lawrence*, Boston, MA: G.K. Hall & Co.

Stoll, J. (1968) *D.H. Lawrence's 'Sons and Lovers': Self-Encounter and the Unknown Self*, Muncie IN: Ball State University.

Sword, H. (2001) 'Lawrence's poetry' in A. Fernihough (ed.) *The Cambridge Companion to D.H. Lawrence*, Cambridge: Cambridge University Press.

Tedlock, Jr E.W. (1963) *D.H. Lawrence: Artist and Rebel. A Study of Lawrence's Fiction*, Albuquerque: University of New Mexico Press.

—— (ed.) (1965) *D.H. Lawrence and 'Sons and Lovers'*, New York: New York University Press.

Thornton, W. (1993) *D.H. Lawrence: A Study of the Short Fiction*, New York: Twayne.

Tindall, W.Y. (1939) *D.H. Lawrence and Susan His Cow*, New York: Columbia University Press.

Tiverton, Fr. W. (1951) *D.H. Lawrence and Human Existence*, London: Rockliff.

Torgovnick, M. (1990) *Gone Primitive: Savage Intellects, Modern Lives*, Chicago and London: University of Chicago Press.

Tracy, B.T. (1983) *D.H. Lawrence and the Literature of Travel*, Ann Arbor, MI: UMI Research Press.

Tristram, P. (1978) 'Eros and Death (Lawrence, Freud and Women)' in A. Smith (ed.) *Lawrence and Women*, London: Vision

Turner, J. (1986) 'Purity and Danger in D.H. Lawrence's *The Virgin and the Gipsy*' in M. Kalnins (ed.) *D.H. Lawrence: Centenary Essays*, Bristol: Bristol Classical Press.

Van Ghent, D. (1953) *The English Novel, Form and Function*, New York: Rinehart.

Vickery, J.B. (1988) 'D.H. Lawrence and the Fantasias of Consciousness' in G. Salgādo and G.K. Das (eds) *The Spirit of D.H. Lawrence: Centenary Studies*, Basingstoke: Macmillan.

Vivas, E. (1960) *D.H. Lawrence: The Failure and the Triumph of Art*, Evanston, IL: Northwestern University Press.

Weiss, D.A. (1962) *Oedipus in Nottingham: D.H. Lawrence*, Seattle: University of Washington Press.

Walton-Litz, A. (1985) 'Lawrence, Pound and Early Modernism' in P. Balbert and P.L. Marcus (eds) *D.H. Lawrence: A Centenary Consideration*, Ithaca and London: Cornell University Press.

Waterman, A.E. (1963) 'The Plays of D.H. Lawrence' in M. Spilka (ed.) *D.H. Lawrence: A Collection of Critical Essays*, Englewood Cliffs, NJ: Prentice Hall.

Whelan, P.T. (1988) *D.H. Lawrence: Myth and Metaphysic in 'The Rainbow' and 'Women in Love'*, Ann Arbor, MI and London: UMI Research Press.

Widdowson, P. (ed.) (1992) *D.H. Lawrence*, Longman Critical Readers, London: Longman.

Widmer, K. (1962) *The Art of Perversity: D.H. Lawrence's Shorter Fictions*, Seattle: University of Washington Press.

Williams, L.R. (1993) *Sex in the Head: Visions of Femininity and Film in D.H. Lawrence*, Hemel Hempstead: Harvester Wheatsheaf.

—— (1997) *D.H. Lawrence*, Plymouth: Northcote House.

Williams, R. (1970; 1987) *The English Novel from Dickens to Lawrence*, London: Hogarth Press.

Worthen, J. (1979) *D.H. Lawrence and the Idea of the Novel*, London: Macmillan.

—— (1991b) *D.H. Lawrence*, London: Edward Arnold.

—— (2001) 'Lawrence as dramatist' in A. Fernihough (ed.) *The Cambridge Companion to D.H. Lawrence*, Cambridge: Cambridge University Press.

Wright, A. (1984) *Literature of Crisis 1910–22: 'Howards End', 'Heartbreak House', 'Women in Love' and 'The Waste Land'*, Basingstoke: Macmillan.

Zytaruk, G.J. (1985) 'The Doctrine of Individuality: D.H. Lawrence's "Metaphysic"' in P. Balbert and P.L. Marcus (eds) *D.H. Lawrence: A Centenary Consideration*, Ithaca and London: Cornell University Press.

CRITICISM OF D.H. LAWRENCE IN ARTICLES

Included below is a small sample of material on Lawrence in periodicals. The main journals based in America and Europe dedicated to Lawrence studies are *The D.H. Lawrence Review* and *Études Lawrenciennes*.

Arcana, J. (1989) 'I Remember Mama: Mother-blaming in *Sons and Lovers'* Criticism', *D.H. Lawrence Review* 21, 2: 137–51.

Baldanza, F. (1961) 'D.H. Lawrence's *Song of Songs*', *Modern Fiction Studies* 7, 2: 106–14.

Cohn, D. (1966) 'Narrated Monologue: Definition of a Fictional Style', *Comparative Literature*, 18, 2: 97–112.

Contreras, S. (1993/4) '"These Were Just Natives to Her": Chilchui Indians and "The Woman Who Rode Away"', *D.H. Lawrence Review* 25, 1–3: 91–103.

Doherty, G. (1987) 'White Mythologies: D.H. Lawrence and the Deconstructive Turn', *Criticism* 29, 4: 477–96.

—— (1989) 'The Metaphorical Imperative: From Trope to Narrative in *The Rainbow*', *South Central Review* 6, 1: 46–61.

Goldberg, S.L. (1961) '*The Rainbow*: Fiddle-bow and Sand', *Essays in Criticism* 11, 4: 418–34.

Gordon, D.J. (1981) 'Sex and Language in D.H. Lawrence', *Twentieth-Century Literature* 27, 4: 362–75.

Hagen, P.L. (1987) 'The Metaphoric Foundations of Lawrence's "Dark Knowledge"', *Texas Studies in Language and Literature* 29: 365–76.

Hayles, K.N. (1982) 'The Ambivalent Approach: D.H. Lawrence and the New Physics', *Mosaic* 15, 3: 89–108.

Hinz, E.J. (1972) 'The Beginning and the End: D.H. Lawrence's *Psycho-analysis* and *Fantasia*', *The Dalhousie Review* 52: 251–65.

Katz-Roy, G. (1992), 'The Process of "Rotary Image-thought" in D.H. Lawrence's Last Poems', *Études Lawrenciennes* 7: 129–38.

Lodge, D. (1985) 'Lawrence, Dostoyevsky, Bakhtin: D.H. Lawrence and Dialogic Fiction', *Renaissance and Modern Studies* 29: 16–32.

Ruderman, J. (1977) '*The Fox* and the Devouring Mother', *The D.H. Lawrence Review* 10, 3: 251–69.

Sale, R. (1959) 'The Narrative Technique of *The Rainbow*', *Modern Fiction Studies* 5, 1: 29–38.

Squires, M. (1975) 'Recurrence as a Narrative Technique in The Rainbow', *Modern Fiction Studies* 21, 2: 230–6.

—— (1995) 'D.H. Lawrence's Narrators, Sources of Knowledge and the Problems of Coherence' *Criticism* 37, 3: 469–91.

Stearns, C. (1987) 'Gender, Voice, and Myth: The Relation of the Language to the Female in D.H. Lawrence's Poetry', *D.H. Lawrence Review* 17, 3: 233–42.

Stewart, G. (1975–6) 'Lawrence, "Being," and the Allotropic Style', *Novel* 9: 217–42.

Stewart, J.F. (1991) 'Dialectics of Knowing in Women in Love', *Twentieth-Century Literature* 37, 1: 59–75.

Occasional special issues of periodicals are dedicated to particular aspects of Lawrence studies. These include:

The D.H. Lawrence Review (1975) 8, 3 'D.H. Lawrence and Women'.

The D.H. Lawrence Review (1977) 10, 3 'Psychoanalytic Criticism of the Short Stories'.

The D.H. Lawrence Review (1993–4) 25, 1–3 'Lawrence in the Southwest'.

The D.H. Lawrence Review (1997–8) 27, 2–3 'D.H. Lawrence and the Psychoanalytic'.

Études Lawrenciennes (1993) 'D.H. Lawrence, his Contemporaries and Europe'.

Études Lawrenciennes (1998) 'Lawrence and Language'.

SELECTED BIBLIOGRAPHY

INDEX

Dax, A. 12, 13, 45
de Beauvoir, S. 145; *Le Deuxième Sexe* (*The Second Sex*) 144
de Filippis, S. 114
DeKoven, M. 49
Delaney, P. 30
Delavenay, E. 30, 111
Deleuze, G. 137
Derrida, J. 152
de Saussure, F. 150
Descartes, R. 103
de Sola Pinto, V. 80, 131, 132
Devlin, A.J. 91
de Zordo, O. 111, 156
The D.H. Lawrence Review 157
Dix, C. 147
Dodge Sterne, M. [Mabel Dodge Luhan] 23, 24, 25, 26, 27, 30, 121
Doherty, G. 152
Donaldson, G. 115
Dostoyevsky, F. 152
Douglas, J. 120
Douglas, N. 22
Draper, R.P. 22, 44, 48, 86, 91, 92, 102, 120, 123, 146, 156
Duckworth 15

Eagleton, M. 158
Eagleton, T. 158
Ebbatson, R. 69, 111
Eder, D. 102
Edwards, D. 69
The Egoist 16
Eliot, G. 38, 43, 78, 138; *Middlemarch* 38; *The Mill on the Floss* 38
Eliot, T.S. 16, 29, 51, 119, 122, 123, 125; *After Strange Gods* 49, 124, 126; 'Tradition and the Individual Talent' 15; 'Ulysses, Order, and Myth' 50; *The Waste Land* 14, 22, 50, 84, 88
Elliot, A. 158
Ellis, D. 31, 111, 114, 123, 136, 156
Emerson, R.W. 108
Empson, W. 125
English Review 11, 15, 22, 80
Études Lawrenciennes 157

Fascism 70, 125, 128, 155
Feinstein, E. 12
Fernihough, A. 15, 48, 79, 87, 137, 155, 157
Finney, B. 48
Fleishman, A. 61, 151, 152
Flint, F. S. 15
Ford, G. 68, 69, 98
Forster, E.M. 15, 17, 29, 119, 122, 131
Franklin, B. 105
Frazer, Sir J. *The Golden Bough* 14
Freeman, A. 69
Freeman, M. 128
Freud, S. 14, 21, 44, 48, 49, 102, 103, 104, 105, 111, 133, 134, 135, 136, 137, 138, 149; *Die Traumdeutung* (*The Interpretation of Dreams*) 102
Fry, R. 17
Futurism 15, 92, 128; *The Rainbow* 'a bit futuristic' 49

Galsworthy, J. 65, 108
Gardner, H. 131
Garnett, D. 29
Garnett, E.15, 29, 54–5, 92, 124, 126, 144
Garrett Fawcett, M. 12
Gaskell, Mrs. 78
Gelder, S. 7
Gertler, M. 26
Gilbert, S.M. 84, 86, 91
Goldman, J. 158
Gomme, A.H. 91
Goodheart, E. 133
Gordon, D.J. 111, 155
Götzsche, K. 25
Grant, D. 18
Gregory, H. 125, 133
Grey, Z. 108
Guattari, F. 137
Guttenberg, B. 91

Hagen, P. 136, 155
Hall, R. *The Well of Loneliness* 28
Hardy, T. 11, 17, 38 100; *The Hand of Ethelberta* 99; *Jude the Obscure* 99
Harris, J.H. 98